THE EVERYTHING.
One-Pot Cookbook
2ND Edition

Dear Reader,

Like you, one of my everyday realities is that I have to get meals on the table—somehow. Special occasions involve making a list, getting special ingredients, and planning my time so that I can get everything done. On the other hand, most everyday occasions require that I fix something using what I have on hand. Ideally, each meal involves as little prep and standing-over-the-stove time as possible and is planned so that I make as little mess as possible. (A meal isn't nearly as enjoyable if I know it's going to take longer to clean up the pots, pans, and dishes than it took to eat the food I prepared.)

There are a number of ways I can achieve my simplified cooking objectives. Some involve using traditional cooking methods, and others involve using gadgets and gizmos to aid in the process.

This is my third *Everything®* cookbook for Adams Media. I truly enjoy finding innovative methods for fixing and adapting traditional methods to create tasty food. I'm fortunate that I get to pass that information along through the recipes in my cookbooks. My sincere wish is that by doing so, I help make your time in the kitchen a little easier and the delicious food that comes out of that kitchen more enjoyable and easier to prepare.

Pamela Rice Hahn

Welcome to the EVERYTHING® Series!

These handy, accessible books give you all you need to tackle a difficult project, gain a new hobby, comprehend a fascinating topic, prepare for an exam, or even brush up on something you learned back in school but have since forgotten.

You can choose to read an *Everything*® book from cover to cover or just pick out the information you want from our four useful boxes: e-questions, e-facts, e-alerts, e-ssentials. We give you everything you need to know on the subject, but throw in a lot of fun stuff along the way, too.

We now have more than 400 *Everything*® books in print, spanning such wide-ranging categories as weddings, pregnancy, cooking, music instruction, foreign language, crafts, pets, New Age, and so much more. When you're done reading them all, you can finally say you know *Everything*®!

QUESTION?
Answers to common questions

FACTS
Important snippets of information

ALERTS!
Urgent warnings

ESSENTIALS
Quick handy tips

PUBLISHER Karen Cooper

DIRECTOR OF INNOVATION Paula Munier

MANAGING EDITOR, EVERYTHING SERIES Lisa Laing

COPY CHIEF Casey Ebert

ACQUISITIONS EDITOR Katie McDonough

ASSOCIATE DEVELOPMENT EDITOR Elizabeth Kassab

EDITORIAL ASSISTANT Hillary Thompson

Visit the entire Everything® series at *www.everything.com*

THE
EVERYTHING®
ONE-POT
COOKBOOK
2ND EDITION

Delicious and simple meals that
you can prepare in just one dish

Pamela Rice Hahn

Avon, Massachusetts

To all my visitors at CookingWithPam.com!

An Everything® Series Book.
Everything® and everything.com® are registered trademarks of F+W Media, Inc.

Published by Adams Media, a division of F+W Media, Inc.
57 Littlefield Street, Avon, MA 02322. U.S.A.
www.adamsmedia.com

ISBN 10: 1-59869-836-2
ISBN 13: 978-1-59869-836-7

Printed in the United States of America.

J   I   H   G   F   E   D   C   B   A

Library of Congress Cataloging-in-Publication Data
is available from the publisher.

This publication is designed to provide accurate and authoritative information with regard to the subject matter covered. It is sold with the understanding that the publisher is not engaged in rendering legal, accounting, or other professional advice. If legal advice or other expert assistance is required, the services of a competent professional person should be sought.

—From a *Declaration of Principles* jointly adopted by a Committee of the American Bar Association and a Committee of Publishers and Associations

Many of the designations used by manufacturers and sellers to distinguish their products are claimed as trademarks. Where those designations appear in this book and Adams Media was aware of a trademark claim, the designations have been printed with initial capital letters.

This book is available at quantity discounts for bulk purchases.
For information, please call 1-800-289-0963.

Contents

Acknowledgments

For their help and support, I would like to thank everyone at Adams Media. For all of their hard work and perseverance, I would like to thank my agents Sheree Bykofsky and Janet Rosen. Special thanks also go to my daughter Lara Sutton, her husband Randy, and the other joys in my life: Taylor, Charles, and Courtney; Ann, Andrew, Dennis, and Tony Rice; my mother and my sister Tam; and Eric J. Ehlers, David Hebert, everybody at ProudPatriots.org, and my other online friends.

Introduction

In an ideal world where time and money aren't issues, to plan a meal you'd step outside and choose the freshest ingredients from your organic garden, grab a few eggs courtesy of your free-range chickens, and maybe step into the smokehouse to select a ham to go with it all. Then you'd hand all of the ingredients to your chef and he would cook it for you while the rest of your staff set the dining room table.

In a world where time isn't an issue, you'd visit your local farmer's market daily to pick up the freshest produce and eggs; stop by the butcher shop or fishmonger's for your meat entrées; swing by the organic dairy for the day's butter, cream, cheese, and milk; and run into the artisan bakery for your bread and pastries.

In today's world, cooking according to season more than likely refers to using the ingredients you have on hand and cooking them based on the amount of time you have available to prepare them. Making sure that you have ingredients on hand to use usually includes having cans of food in the pantry, frozen vegetables in the freezer, and other food staples in the refrigerator. In other words, if it's in your pantry, freezer, or refrigerator, it's in season.

The recipes in this book were created for use in today's world, with an emphasis on making the main entrée in one pot—if not the entire meal. The One-Pot Meal Philosophy is meant to show you ways to serve great-tasting food in ways that save you time and effort.

While every effort was made to create foolproof recipes for this book, it's impossible to anticipate every factor that can affect cooking times. For example, a slow cooker sitting on a kitchen counter next to a drafty window on a windy, sub-zero winter's day is going to take longer to come to temperature than one sitting in direct sunlight in the summer. Regardless of the cooking method, ingredients at room temperature will cook faster than those just out of the refrigerator or freezer.

Convenience isn't a constant either. A slow cooker isn't conducive to making a meal in a hurry, the oven isn't always practical in the summer, and, when there are other chores to be done around the house, the stovetop isn't always convenient for even the most masterful multitasker. That's why the one-pot meals in this book are made using a number of methods. Different methods will suit your needs at different times.

That doesn't mean that there is only one correct way to fix each dish. For that reason, this book also includes sidebars that have bonus recipes, tips, and suggestions on how to alter some of the recipes.

Also worth noting is that exact measurements for salt are seldom given in this book. These recipes use as little salt as possible during the cooking process, giving you the freedom to add as much or as little seasoning as you like at the table. Unless otherwise indicated, when a recipe calls for salt, sea salt was used to test the recipe.

Chapter 1
The One-Pot Meal Philosophy

There is a whole world of one-pot meals for you to explore! They range from stir-fries to casseroles to spaghetti. Simplifying the cooking methods expedites your cooking and cleaning process and leaves you more time to savor your meals and enjoy the company of the people you eat them with. Most of the meals in this cookbook are meant to be enjoyed by a family, but you can adjust them to accommodate your menu. Whatever you do, this book aims to make your dining experience more pleasurable and easier on you.

The Cooking Methods

If you're cooking simply as a way to put a meal on the table in the quickest and easiest way possible, you'll find many recipes you can use in this book. If, on the other hand, you live to cook, you've probably amassed all sorts of gadgets and gizmos and immersed yourself in the process. There's something in this book for you, too. No matter how comfortable or uncomfortable you are in the kitchen, the recipes in this book address your needs, giving instructions on how to make great food using a variety of cooking methods, including the following:

- **Baking** involves putting the food that's in a baking pan or ovenproof casserole dish in a preheated oven; the food cooks by being surrounded by the hot, dry air of your oven. (In the case of a convection oven, it cooks by being surround by circulating hot, dry air.)
- **Braising** usually starts by browning a less expensive cut of meat in a pan on top of the stove, and then covering the meat with a small amount of liquid, adding a lid or covering to the pan, and slowly cooking it. Braising can take place on the stovetop, in the oven, or in a slow cooker. The slow-cooking process tenderizes the meat.
- **Poaching** is accomplished by gently simmering ingredients in broth, juice, water, wine, or other flavorful liquid until they're cooked through and tender.
- **Roasting**, like baking, is usually done in the oven, but generally at a higher oven temperature. Food can be roasted by putting it directly on a baking sheet or in a roasting pan; however, fattier cuts of meat are often roasted by placing the meat on a rack inside of a roasting pan so that the rendered fat drips away during roasting. Better cuts of meat that don't require becoming tender during the cooking process are best suited for roasting.
- **Sautéing** is the method of quickly cooking small or thin pieces of food in some oil or butter that has been brought to temperature in a sauté pan over medium to medium-high heat. Alternatively, you can sauté in a good-quality nonstick pan without using added fat; instead use a little broth, nonstick cooking spray, or water in place of the oil or butter.

- **Steaming** is a cooking method that uses the steam from the cooking liquid to cook the food. In this cookbook, steaming ingredients or vegetables in a covered container placed in the microwave is sometimes suggested.
- **Stewing** is similar to braising in that food is slowly cooked in a liquid; however, stewing involves a larger liquid to food ratio. In other words, you use far more liquid when you're stewing food. Not surprising, this method is most often used to make stew.
- **Stir-Frying** is a cooking process similar to sautéing that's used to cook larger, bite-sized pieces of meat or vegetables in oil; the cooking is done in a wok or deep nonstick frying pan.
- **Tempering** is the act of gradually increasing the temperature of one cooking ingredient by adding small amounts of a hotter ingredient to the first. For example, tempering beaten eggs by whisking small amounts of hot liquid into them before you add the eggs to the cooking pan allows them to be mixed into the dish; tempering prevents them from scrambling.

Slow Cooker

A slow cooker is one of the easiest options for today's busy cook. You add the ingredients, turn the cooker to the desired setting, and come back several hours later to a fully cooked meal.

The most efficient slow cookers have a removable stoneware cooking pot. The stoneware is good at holding the heat, you can remove the pot and serve the meal directly from it, and it's easier to clean because it can go into the dishwasher.

Programmable slow cookers like Cuisinart's 4-quart and 6.5-quart slow cookers let you start the cooking process at one temperature and automatically switch to a different setting according to how you've programmed it. For example, if you haven't had time to thaw the foods you're putting in the cooker, you have the option of starting it out on high for a couple of hours and then switching it to low heat for the duration of the cooking time. When the cooking time is completed, the cooker automatically switches to the "keep warm" setting, which holds the food at serving temperature until you're ready to serve it.

The option of having a "keep warm" setting is important for foods that can scorch or take on an unpleasant taste or texture if they're cooked too long. For that reason, even if you don't buy a slow cooker with all the bells and whistles, at least look for one that lets you set a cooking time and then automatically switches over to a warm setting when the cooking time is done.

Oven

Food can be baked, braised, or roasted in an oven. Fixing food in the oven can be simple if you know a few tricks. If a recipe calls for you to bake something at a higher temperature than your pan recommends, simply adjust the temperature down and increase the baking time accordingly. Assuming that meat was room temperature when it went into the oven, the general rule of thumb is to add 2 minutes of cooking time per pound for each 25 degrees you lower the temperature. The colder the food is when it goes into the oven, the longer it'll take it to bake. Also consider that a roast placed on a rack in a roasting pan will bake (roast) faster than one set directly in a pan because the rack allows more hot air from the oven to circulate around the meat. Then there's the matter of whether or not the temperature inside your oven is the same as the temperature you set it for when you turned it on. Not taking such variables into consideration can result in exceeding the desired internal temperature of the meat, or a roast that's more well done than you like.

Help ensure that you roast your meat to the desired doneness by using a thermometer with a probe that goes into the food in the oven and is attached to a programmable unit that sits outside the oven. A thermometer's display unit should show the current internal temperature, and it should be equipped with an alarm that goes off when the meat reaches the correct internal temperature.

There are other factors that can affect roasting time, such as the size and shape of the meat, the amount of fat and bone, and whether the meat was aged. The best way to ensure that meat is roasted to your liking is to use the suggested roasting time given in a recipe as a gauge to time when you can have your meal ready to serve, and set a programmable thermometer so you'll know when it's actually ready:

- 130°F to 140°F for medium rare
- 145°F to 150°F for medium
- 155°F to 165°F for well done

Casseroles are easier to bake because they're more forgiving: There's seldom any risk that you'll overbake them. But casseroles are everyday fare. Special occasions call for a small extra effort to make special entrées, like the Standing Rib Roast in Chapter 21.

The most important thing to keep in mind when you prepare foods in the oven is that each time you open the oven, it will take it some time to recover lost heat. An electric oven will take longer to recover than will a gas oven. Adding a pizza stone can help any oven retain heat when the oven door is open, or at least recover the heat you lose more quickly. A more expensive but more efficient option is to add a Hearth Kitchen Hearthkit Brick Oven Insert (see the appendix).

Stovetop

Foods cooked on top of the stove usually need a little more attention than those made using other methods. This is especially true if you're not used to using your stove. Use the heat settings suggested in the recipes, but until you become familiar with the temperatures that are required to achieve the desired affect (like maintaining a slow simmer, for example), plan on babysitting the pot on the stove. Having a pot boil dry can not only ruin a meal, it can cause a fire.

The cooking vessels you use will make a difference, too. Food will burn more easily in an inexpensive discount store nonstick skillet than it will in heavier cast-iron, multiclad stainless, or hard anodized steel cookware. How well your cooking pan conducts the heat will make a difference as to how high you set the burner temperature. But, with some practice, you'll soon learn the perfect heat settings for each of your pans. It might take a medium-high setting to sauté food in an inexpensive skillet and lots of stirring to prevent the food from burning, but you can accomplish the same task in your triple-ply nonstick stainless steel skillet when it's over medium-low heat, and with less frequent stirring.

On the flipside, a heavier pan will retain the heat longer once it's removed from the burner than will an inexpensive skillet, so food cooked to perfection in a heavier pan must be moved to a serving dish more quickly to prevent it from overcooking. This is especially true of foods like gravy that tend to thicken the longer they sit; gravy can turn from a succulent liquid to one big lump if it stays on the heat too long.

FACT

Once you've removed the meat and other ingredients you've cooked in the pan and rid the pan of any excess remaining fat, deglaze it by putting it over a medium-high heat and then adding enough cooking liquid to let you scrape up any browned bits stuck to the bottom of the pan. Doing this step before you add the other ingredients for your sauce or gravy gives more flavor and color to the result.

Stovetop cooking doesn't have to be intimidating. In fact, stovetop cooking methods like stir-frying are some of the quickest and most versatile ways to prepare meals. With the right instructions, it's easy to fix delicious meals for you and your family.

Pressure Cooker

Pressure cookers cook food up to 70 percent faster than other methods because steam trapped in the pot builds up pressure, which creates a hotter cooking temperature. The tight seal on the cooker also helps seal in vitamins and minerals and prevents the cooker from boiling dry during the cooking process. Stovetop pressure cooker models do require you to pay a bit more attention than do programmable countertop models because you need to verify that your burner setting is sufficient (and not too high) to maintain the needed pressure. Using either type of cooker is a convenient and quick way to cook. Pressure cookers are especially good for foods that need to be tenderized by the cooking process, like less expensive cuts of meat.

Today's pressure cookers have built-in safety features that prevent some of the problems (like an exploding cooker!) associated with earlier models. Locking the lid in place prevents anyone from removing it before the pressure in the cooker is released.

Rotisserie

There are several recipes in this book for preparing a rotisserie chicken at home. If you have a rotisserie accessory for your outdoor grill, in the summer you can prepare rotisserie chicken outdoors without heating up the oven. Otherwise, the rotisserie recipes suggest how you can take a rotisserie chicken that you bring home from the supermarket, enhance it, and make it your own.

Keep a few things in mind when you buy an already-prepared rotisserie chicken, including:

- Choose chicken with a large, full breast; it will have more meat and is less likely to have dried out under a heat lamp or in a hot box at the store.
- As soon as you get the chicken home, remove the skin and pull the chicken from the bone; the meat is easier to separate from the bone while the chicken is warm.
- Shred or cube any excess chicken; refrigerate or freeze it in cup-size portions so that it's already measured for future use.
- Reheat the already cooked meat slowly and on low heat to avoid cooking the meat any further.
- Always taste the chicken before you add it so you can adjust the seasonings (especially salt) called for in the recipe accordingly.
- Once you find a good place to purchase rotisserie chickens, ask the clerk for the best times to buy them so you'll know when the store has the largest selection that hasn't been standing under the heat lamps for a long time.

Once I remove the meat from a rotisserie chicken how can I use the bones to make chicken broth?
Put the chicken bones in a large pot and add a few black peppercorns and rough-chopped vegetables such as onion, garlic, carrots, and celery. Cover with water, bring to a simmer, and cook for 30 minutes. Strain and discard the bones and vegetables. Freeze leftover broth (skimmed of fat) in ice cube trays, and then transfer the cubes to a plastic freezer bag so that you always have broth ready in an instant.

Once the skin is removed, the average purchased rotisserie chicken will yield about 4 cups of shredded chicken. Typically that amounts to about 12 ounces of white meat and 8 ounces of dark meat. That's enough meat that you can reserve the white meat for another use. For recipes like the Deluxe Potato Soup recipe in Chapter 18 that call for other meat in addition to the chicken, only add the dark meat.

Chapter 2
Breakfast and Brunch

Crustless Cottage Cheese Quiche

Serves 4–6

Nonstick cooking spray
5 large eggs
½ pound cottage cheese
¼ cup all-purpose flour
⅛ teaspoon salt
½ teaspoon baking powder
¼ cup melted butter
½ pound Monterey jack
    cheese, grated
½ 10-ounce package frozen
    vegetables
3 green onions, chopped

Vary the vegetables according to your family's tastes. You can use something as simple as peas and carrots or as varied as your favorite stir-fry vegetable mix. Just be sure to thaw the frozen vegetables before you add them to the egg mixture.

1. Treat a microwave-safe, deep-dish pie plate with nonstick cooking spray. Add the eggs and whisk until fluffy. Stir in the cottage cheese. Add the flour, salt, baking powder, and butter, and mix well. Fold half of the cheese and the vegetables into the egg mixture.

2. Cover the filled pie plate with a paper towel to prevent splatters. Microwave for 6 minutes. Let rest for 1 minute, then remove the paper towel.

3. Top with the remaining cheese. Sprinkle the green onions over the cheese.

4. Microwave for an additional 5 minutes, or until the cheese is melted and the quiche is set.

"Eggsact" Measurement

A large egg typically is equal to ¼ cup or 2 ounces. Adjust the number of eggs if the ones you're using are smaller. Large eggs can be double the size of smaller ones. The egg carton will tell you whether your eggs are large or small.

Baked Cornmeal Mush
with Cheese and Eggs

This brunch dish is delicious topped with some salsa. For an Italian spin, substitute Parmigiano-Reggiano for the jack cheese and top it with some marinara sauce.

Serves 8

4 tablespoons butter
3 cups cornmeal mush
1 cup sour cream
1 cup Monterey jack cheese, grated
1 cup Cheddar cheese, grated
8 large eggs
Salt to taste
Freshly ground black pepper

1. Preheat oven to 350°F.

2. Melt the butter and add it to a 9" × 13" nonstick baking pan, turning the pan to coat the bottom.

3. Cut the cornmeal mush into cubes and mix it with the sour cream until it reaches the consistency of thick cake batter. If it's too thick, add more sour cream or some heavy cream or milk. Add the jack cheese and half of the Cheddar cheese; mix to combine. Spread the mixture across the bottom of the baking pan. Bake for 15 minutes.

4. Remove the pan from the oven. Press a small glass into the mush to make 8 equally spaced indentations across the pan. Crack an egg into each indentation. Top each egg with salt, if using, and some pepper. Sprinkle the remaining Cheddar cheese over the top.

5. Bake for an additional 15 minutes, or until the eggs are set as desired and the cheese is melted. Cut into 8 wedges. Serve hot or at room temperature.

Cornmeal Mush by Any Other Name

Cornmeal mush is simply the countrified name for polenta. Like polenta, it's typically made with yellow cornmeal. Grits are a similar dish made with white cornmeal. Regardless of what you call it, Baked Cornmeal Mush with Cheese and Eggs is also a great way to use leftover cornmeal mush, polenta, or grits.

Welsh Rarebit

Welsh Rarebit is a versatile dish. You can use more Worcestershire sauce and choose the beer based on the bread you'll serve it with; a hearty bread like pumpernickel, for example, goes better with stronger flavors than does a sweet challah or brioche.

Serves 6

1 tablespoon butter
Pinch cayenne pepper or hot sauce to taste
1 teaspoon Worcestershire sauce
⅔ cup warm beer
1 pound sharp Cheddar cheese, grated
2 teaspoons cornstarch
1 teaspoon dry mustard
6 thick slices bread, toasted
OPTIONAL: *tomato slices*
OPTIONAL: *bacon*
OPTIONAL: *6 poached or fried eggs*

1. In a nonstick saucepan, melt the butter and stir in the cayenne pepper or hot sauce and Worcestershire sauce over medium heat. Add the beer and bring to a simmer. Lower the heat to medium-low or low; melting the cheese over a low temperature prevents it from separating into a greasy mess.

2. Toss the cheese with the cornstarch and dry mustard. Add it to the beer mixture. Stir occasionally until the cheese is melted.

3. Place the toast on individual plates and top with the Welsh Rarebit.

4. To serve with the optional ingredients, place the toast on individual plates. Top each slice of toast with a tomato slice, crisscrossed bacon slices, and an egg. Top with the Welsh Rarebit.

Kicked-Up Welsh Rarebit

For an alternative recipe, substitute milk for the beer. Sauté a small chopped onion and a cup of mushroom slices in butter, and stir into the Welsh Rarebit along with a 10¾-ounce can of condensed cream of tomato soup; bring to temperature. To serve, arrange slices of hard-boiled egg over the toast and top with the Kicked-Up Welsh Rarebit.

Bacon, Broccoli, and Cheese Quiche

This quiche can easily be adapted to match whatever you happen to have in your fridge. Substitute other leftover vegetables or use American cheese slices instead of the Cheddar. Just keep in mind that the cooler the temperature of the filling, the longer it'll take the quiche to bake.

1. Preheat oven to 350°F.

2. Spread the bacon evenly over the bottom of the pie crust. Top with the cheese. Place the broccoli over the bacon and cheese.

3. Whisk the eggs together with the milk or cream and seasoning. Carefully pour the egg mixture over the ingredients in the pie crust.

4. Bake for 35 to 45 minutes, or until the center of the pie is set. Let sit for 10 minutes before slicing. Serve warm or at room temperature.

Serves 4–8

1 9-inch deep-dish frozen pie crust, thawed
8 slices cooked bacon, chopped
½ cup Cheddar cheese, grated
1 cup cooked broccoli florets
6 large eggs
¼ cup milk or heavy cream
Salt and freshly ground black pepper to taste

Quiche Lorraine

The ham will already be salty, so be careful about how much salt you add to the egg mixture. The optional Dijon mustard and mayonnaise punch up the flavor.

1. Preheat oven to 350°F.

2. Beat the eggs with the flour, then stir in the milk. Add salt, pepper, cayenne, mustard, and mayonnaise, if using. Fold in the cheese and ham. Pour into the pie shell.

3. Place the pie shell on a baking sheet or jellyroll pan and put in the oven. Bake for 40–45 minutes, or until the eggs are set. Let rest for 10 minutes before cutting into wedges. Serve warm or at room temperature.

Serves 4–8

6 large eggs
1 tablespoon all-purpose flour
1 cup milk
OPTIONAL: *salt and freshly ground pepper to taste*
OPTIONAL: *dash of cayenne pepper to taste*
OPTIONAL: *½ teaspoon Dijon mustard*
OPTIONAL: *1 tablespoon mayonnaise*
½ pound Swiss cheese, grated
½ pound cooked ham, cut into cubes
1 9-inch unbaked pie shell

Cottage Cheese Casserole

Serves 4–8

Nonstick cooking spray
6 large eggs
1 pound cottage cheese
¼ cup unbleached all-purpose flour
⅛ teaspoon salt
½ teaspoon baking powder
¼ cup melted butter
1 pound Cheddar cheese, grated
1 12-ounce package of frozen vegetables, thawed
OPTIONAL: *chopped red onion, shallots, or green onions to taste*

This recipe was tested using a Birds Eye Steamfresh vegetable mixture of asparagus, gold and white corn, and baby carrots. The vegetables were microwave "steamed" for 5 minutes. If you prefer a vegetable mixture without corn, omit the cornmeal and use ¼ cup of flour instead.

1. Preheat oven to 325°F if using a Pyrex pie pan or 350°F if using a metal pie pan.

2. Treat an ovenproof, deep-dish pie pan with nonstick cooking spray. Add the eggs and whisk until fluffy. Stir in the cottage cheese. Add the flour, salt, baking powder, and butter, and mix well. Fold the cheese and the vegetables into the egg mixture. Add the onion, shallots, or green onions, if using.

3. Bake for 40–45 minutes, or until the top is lightly browned. Let rest for 10 minutes before cutting into wedges for serving.

Serving Suggestions

The baked recipe will serve 4 as a standalone breakfast or brunch dish. To stretch it to 8 servings, serve it with some brown-and-serve sausages and toasted English muffins or bagels. The salsa or marinara sauce suggestions mentioned in the Crustless Cottage Cheese Quiche recipe work well with this dish, too.

Baked Monte Cristo Brunch Casserole

The quality of the bread you use makes a big difference in how good the end result will taste. This recipe is traditionally made with classic white bread, but for a slightly sweeter, richer taste, use challah or brioche.

1. Preheat oven to 350°F.

2. Beat the eggs, milk, and optional ingredients, if using, together in a shallow bowl.

3. Spread butter over one side of each slice of bread, and spread the mayonnaise on the other side. Dip 4 slices of the bread in the egg mixture and assemble them butter-side down in the baking pan.

4. Top each slice of bread with a slice of Swiss cheese, a slice of ham, and then another slice of Swiss cheese. Place the remaining 4 slices of bread on top, mayonnaise-side down.

5. Pour the remaining egg mixture over the top of the bread. Bake for 40–45 minutes, or until the cheese is melted and the eggs are set. Let rest for 10 minutes before cutting into serving pieces.

Serves 4–8

4 large eggs
½ cup milk or heavy cream
OPTIONAL: *salt and freshly ground black pepper to taste*
OPTIONAL: *dash of cayenne pepper*
OPTIONAL: *Dijon mustard to taste*
8 slices bread
8 teaspoons butter
8 teaspoons mayonnaise
8 slices Swiss cheese
4 thick slices cooked ham

Ham and Cheese Cornbread

Serves 4–8

2 tablespoons butter or bacon grease

1 large yellow onion, thinly sliced

1 large clove garlic, minced

¼ teaspoon chili powder

½ cup unsalted peanuts, chopped

Freshly ground black pepper to taste

1 10-ounce package cornbread mix

1 large egg, beaten

½ cup milk

½ pound cooked ham

3 slices American cheese

OPTIONAL: sliced pimiento-stuffed olives

The American cheese will satisfy younger tastes. Adults might prefer it made with Swiss or Cheddar cheese. You can either use chopped cooked ham or thinly sliced boiled ham.

1. Preheat oven to 350°F.

2. Melt the butter or bacon grease in a 12-inch cast-iron or ovenproof skillet over medium heat. Add the onion, garlic, and chili powder, and sauté until the onion slices are transparent. Remove from the heat and stir in the peanuts and freshly ground pepper. Stir to mix well.

3. Once the pan has cooled, add the cornbread mix, egg, and milk; combine with the other ingredients. Spread evenly over the bottom of the pan and top with the ham.

4. Bake for 15 minutes, or until cornbread is still moist but a toothpick comes out clean. Top with the cheese and return to the oven; bake for an additional 5 minutes, or until the cheese is melted. Garnish with olive slices, if desired.

Basic Omelet

Using milk in the batter makes an omelet runny, but if you want a richer-tasting dish, substitute an equal amount of heavy cream for the water. Heating the pan and then the oil and butter before you add the egg batter results in a lighter, fluffier omelet.

1. Whisk the eggs with the water or cream and salt and pepper. Bring a 10-inch nonstick skillet to temperature over medium-high heat, and then add the oil and the butter. Once the butter is melted and starts to foam, pour in the egg mixture. Tilt the pan to distribute the egg mixture evenly around the pan.

2. Lower the heat to medium and continue to cook until the eggs are almost set, occasionally tilting the pan to move any uncooked egg mixture evenly across the omelet. Once the eggs are almost set, distribute the fillings across the half of the omelet that's opposite from the skillet handle.

3. If necessary, use a spatula to loosen the edges of the omelet from the skillet. Give the pan a shake to ensure the omelet will slide out of the pan, then slide it onto a serving plate, using the pan to fold the omelet in half. Top with some additional freshly ground pepper, if desired, and serve hot.

Basic Frittata

Serves 4

6 large eggs, at room
 temperature
2 tablespoons water
Salt and freshly ground black
 pepper to taste
½ tablespoon peanut or
 vegetable oil
½ tablespoon butter
Cheese, cooked meat, or
 vegetables for toppings

A frittata is basically an unfolded omelet that's topped with precooked meat, vegetables, and cheese and then finished under the broiler. That finishing step allows you to add a bit more filling than you can to an omelet.

1. Whisk the eggs with the water, salt, and pepper. Bring a 10-inch oven-proof, nonstick skillet to temperature over medium-high heat, then add the oil and butter. Once the butter is melted and starts to foam, pour in the egg mixture. Tilt the pan to distribute the mixture evenly around the pan.

2. Lower the heat to medium and continue to cook until the eggs begin to set, occasionally tilting the pan to move any uncooked egg mixture evenly across it. Once the eggs start to set, distribute the toppings across the entire top of the frittata.

3. Place the pan in the oven and broil until the eggs are set and the cheese is melted and begins to bubble. Remove from the broiler and let the frittata rest for 2 minutes. Slice as a pie and serve hot or at room temperature. You can stretch the frittata to 8 servings if you serve it with a salad.

Asparagus Frittata

*This recipe shows an alternative one-pot way to make a frittata
by first sautéing the vegetable fillings in the pan and then adding
the egg mixture and topping it all with some cheese.*

Serves 6

6 large eggs
2 tablespoons whipping
    cream
½ teaspoon salt
¼ teaspoon freshly ground
    black pepper
1 tablespoon olive oil
1 tablespoon butter
1 pound asparagus, trimmed,
    cut into ¼- to ½-inch
    pieces
1 tomato, seeded, diced
3 ounces fontina cheese,
    diced

1. Whisk the eggs, cream, salt, and pepper together in a medium-sized bowl and set aside until needed.

2. Bring a 10-inch ovenproof, nonstick skillet to temperature over medium heat, then add the oil and the butter. Once the butter is melted, add the asparagus and sauté until crisp-tender, about 2 minutes. Increase the heat to medium-high. Add the tomato and an additional pinch of salt, if desired, and sauté 2 minutes longer. Pour the egg mixture over the asparagus mixture and cook until the eggs begin to set. Sprinkle with the cheese. Reduce heat to medium-low and cook for an additional 2 minutes.

3. Place the skillet under the broiler. Broil until the eggs are set and the cheese is golden brown on top, about 5 minutes. Remove from the broiler and let the frittata rest for 2 minutes. Slice as a pie and serve.

Hash Browns
with Sausage and Apples

Serves 4

2 tablespoons olive oil

2 tablespoons butter

5 cups frozen shredded hash brown potatoes

Salt and freshly ground pepper to taste

1½ teaspoons snipped fresh thyme

6 ounces cooked smoked sausage, coarsely chopped

1 medium apple, cut into thin slices

OPTIONAL: 1–2 tablespoons toasted walnuts, chopped

OPTIONAL: 1–2 tablespoons maple syrup

Depending on how the cooked sausage you're using is seasoned, you can substitute sage or fennel leaves or seeds for the thyme. Or, if you prefer, use a mixture of all of them.

1. Heat the oil and 1 tablespoon of the butter in a 10-inch seasoned cast-iron or nonstick skillet over medium heat. Add the hash brown potatoes and cook for 8 to 10 minutes, stirring occasionally, until they are thawed and beginning to brown. Stir in the salt, pepper, and thyme. Use a wide metal spatula to press the potatoes down firmly in the pan.

2. Add the sausage and apple over the top of the potatoes. Cover and cook for 10 minutes, or until the apple is tender. Top with the toasted walnuts and drizzle with the maple syrup, if using. Cook uncovered for an additional 10 minutes, or until the hash browns are lightly browned on the bottom.

3. Use a spatula to loosen the potatoes from the pan and slide the dish onto serving platter or serve from the pan.

Recipe Tweaks to Suit Your Tastes

Instead of using the sliced apple, you can toss the sausage with some apple butter before you add it atop the potatoes. Or, for an out-of-the-ordinary taste treat, use another fruit butter, such as American Spoon Foods Ginger Pear Butter (see the appendix). Then add another flavor dimension by sprinkling some cinnamon over the dish when you add the nuts.

Slow-Cooked Irish Oatmeal with Fruit

*Feel free to substitute other dried fruit according to your taste.
Add a dried fruit mixture like a tropical mix of coconut, papaya,
pineapple, and mango or strawberries, apples, and blueberries.
It's even a way you can sneak some prunes into your diet.*

Serves 8–10

2 cups steel-cut Irish oats
5 cups water
1 cup apple juice
¼ cup dried cranberries
¼ cup golden raisins
¼ cup snipped dried apricots
¼ cup maple syrup
1 teaspoon ground cinnamon
½ teaspoon salt
OPTIONAL: *brown sugar or
    maple syrup to taste*
OPTIONAL: *chopped toasted
    walnuts or pecans to
    taste*
OPTIONAL: *milk, half-and-half,
    or heavy cream to taste*

1. Add the oats, water, apple juice, cranberries, raisins, apricots, maple syrup, cinnamon, and salt to a 4-quart slow cooker and stir to mix.

2. Cover and cook on the low-heat setting for 6 to 7 hours, or on high for 3 to 3½ hours.

3. Serve the oatmeal warm topped with brown sugar or additional maple syrup, chopped nuts, and milk, half-and-half, or heavy cream.

Cooking Ahead

Once the oatmeal has cooled, divide any leftovers into single-serving, microwave-safe containers and freeze. When you're ready to start a new day, put it in the microwave to defrost. Cover the container with a paper towel to catch any splatters, then microwave on high for 1 to 2 minutes!

Sausage and Cheese Scramble

Serves 8

1 tablespoon extra-virgin olive oil

1 large yellow onion, diced

1 green bell pepper, diced

1 pound ground sausage

4 cups frozen hash brown potatoes

8 large eggs

¼ cup water or heavy cream

OPTIONAL: a few drops hot sauce

Salt and freshly ground pepper to taste

½ pound Cheddar cheese, grated

You can stretch this recipe to even more servings by increasing the amount of chopped peppers you sauté with the onion. In fact, a mixture of red, green, and yellow peppers makes for a delicious combo.

1. Preheat an electric skillet to medium-high or heat a deep 3½-quart nonstick sauté pan over medium-high heat and add the oil. Once the oil is heated, add the onion and pepper and sauté until the onion is transparent, about 5 minutes. Add the sausage and cook for 5 minutes, or until browned, breaking it apart as it cooks. Remove any excess fat, if necessary, by carefully dabbing the pan with a paper towel. Add the hash browns and cook covered for 10 minutes, or until the hash browns are tender and the sausage is cooked through. Stir to combine well.

2. Whisk together the eggs, water or heavy cream, hot sauce (if using), and salt and pepper. Remove the lid from the pan and pour the eggs over the sausage-potato mixture. Stir to combine and scramble the eggs until they begin to set. Add the cheese and continue to scramble until the eggs finish cooking and the cheese melts. If you prefer, instead of stirring the cheese into the mixture, you can top it with the cheese; then cover the skillet and continue to cook for 1 to 2 minutes or until the cheese is melted. Serve immediately.

Cooking with Your Feet Up

As long as you can position it so the cord is safely out of the way, you can fix this meal in an electric skillet at the table. Chop the vegetables the night before and mix the eggs together in a jar with a tight lid. You'll be able to sit down to cook while you savor your first cup of coffee.

Baked French Toast
with Toasted-Pecan Maple Syrup

You do most of the work for this dish the night before, so you can have it ready within an hour the next morning. Have maple or raspberry syrup available at the table for those who wish to add it.

Serves 8–10

1 16-ounce loaf challah or
  brioche
¾ cup butter
8 large eggs
1 cup heavy cream
2 cups milk
2 tablespoons granulated
  sugar
1 tablespoon vanilla extract
½ teaspoon ground
  cinnamon
½ teaspoon ground nutmeg
Dash salt

Topping
1 cup packed light brown
  sugar
1 cup chopped pecans
2 tablespoons light corn
  syrup
½ teaspoon ground
  cinnamon
½ teaspoon ground nutmeg

1. Slice the bread into 20 1"-thick slices. Generously butter a 9" × 13" flat baking dish. Arrange the bread slices in two rows, overlapping the slices.

2. Whisk the eggs, cream, milk, sugar, vanilla, cinnamon, nutmeg, and salt until blended but not too bubbly. Pour the egg mixture evenly over all of the bread slices. Cover the pan with plastic wrap or foil and refrigerate overnight.

3. The next day, preheat the oven to 350°F. While the oven is coming to temperature, remove the baking pan from the refrigerator so that the French toast mixture begins to come to room temperature.

4. Melt the butter and mix with the brown sugar, pecans, corn syrup, cinnamon, and nutmeg. Remove the foil or plastic wrap from the baking pan, and spread the pecan mixture evenly over the bread. Bake uncovered for 45 minutes, or until puffed and lightly golden. Serve warm.

Chapter 3
Chicken

Chicken Tortellini and Broccoli Casserole

Serves 8

1 9-ounce package cheese tortellini

3 tablespoons extra-virgin olive oil

2 cups broccoli florets

1 medium yellow onion, diced

1 red bell pepper, seeded and diced

3 tablespoons all-purpose flour

¾ cup chicken broth

¾ cup milk

1 teaspoon dried parsley

4 cups cooked chicken, diced

6 ounces Monterey jack cheese, grated

4 ounces Colby cheese, grated

To turn this into a southwestern casserole, substitute ground cumin and a pinch of cayenne pepper for the dried parsley and add a layer of crushed tortilla chips to the top of the casserole before you add the Colby cheese.

1. Preheat oven to 325°F.

2. In an ovenproof Dutch oven, cook the tortellini according to package directions; drain and keep warm.

3. Wipe out the Dutch oven. Add the oil and bring it to temperature over medium-high heat. Add the broccoli, onion, and bell pepper and stir-fry for about 3 minutes, or until crisp-tender. Remove the broccoli from the skillet; set it aside with the cooked tortellini and keep warm. Reduce the heat to low and whisk the flour into the oil and remaining vegetables in the pan, stirring constantly, until smooth.

4. Stir in the broth, milk, and parsley. Bring to a boil over medium heat, stirring constantly; remove from heat. Stir in the chicken, Monterey jack cheese, tortellini, and broccoli. Bake uncovered for 30 minutes, or until bubbly. Sprinkle the Colby cheese over the top of the casserole; return to the oven and bake for 10 minutes, or until the cheese topping is melted.

Grated Cheese

Each ounce of soft cheese like Cheddar or Colby equals ¼ cup of grated cheese. Keep this in mind when you go to the grocery store and pick up the bags of preshredded cheese. They'll tell you the weight but not the measurement in cups, so it's up to you to remember that part.

Chicken Chili

Serve this chili with an avocado salad and baked flour or corn tortilla chips.

1. Add the oil to a deep 3½-quart nonstick skillet and bring it to temperature over medium heat. Add the onion, jalapeño peppers, bell pepper, and cumin seeds; sauté for 5 minutes, or until the onion is transparent. Add the garlic and chicken; stir-fry until chicken is lightly browned.

2. Stir in the tomatoes, kidney beans, chili sauce, Worcestershire, and red wine. Bring to a simmer; lower the heat and simmer for 1 hour. Taste for seasoning and add salt and pepper if needed.

Serves 4

3 tablespoons extra-virgin olive oil

1 large yellow or white onion, diced

2 jalapeño peppers, seeded and diced

1 green bell pepper, seeded and diced

1 teaspoon cumin seeds

4 cloves garlic, minced

4 boneless, skinless chicken thighs, cut into bite-sized pieces

1 15-ounce can diced tomatoes

1 15-ounce can kidney beans, rinsed and drained

2 cups chili sauce

1 tablespoon Worcestershire sauce

1 cup red wine

Salt and freshly ground black pepper to taste

Stuffed Chicken Breast Florentine

8 boneless, skinless chicken
  breasts
3 tablespoons extra-virgin
  olive oil
8 ounces button mushrooms,
  cleaned and sliced
2 cloves garlic, minced
3 tablespoons chopped
  shallots
2 10-ounce packages frozen
  spinach, thawed and
  squeezed dry
4 large eggs, beaten
3 cups breadcrumbs
4 ounces Swiss or mozzarella
  cheese, shredded
2 tablespoons dried parsley
1 cup chicken broth
¼ pound deli ham, thinly
  sliced
Salt and freshly ground black
  pepper to taste
4 tablespoons butter

If your family isn't fond of spinach, you can replace it with chopped steamed broccoli florets. Also, remember to take the saltiness of the cheese into consideration when you season the dish.

1. Preheat oven to 350°F.

2. Place each chicken breast between 2 pieces of plastic wrap; pound until about ½" thick. Brush the bottom of a 9" × 13" nonstick baking pan with 1 tablespoon of the oil. Arrange half of the chicken breasts over the bottom of the pan.

3. Add the mushrooms, garlic, and shallots to a large microwave-safe bowl. Toss with the remaining 2 tablespoons oil. Cover and microwave on high for 1 minute; stir. Cover and microwave for 1 minute. Let cool and then stir in the spinach. Add the eggs, 2 cups breadcrumbs, cheese, parsley, and chicken broth; stir to combine.

4. Arrange half of the deli ham over the top of the chicken breasts in the pan. Spread the spinach mixture over the top of the ham, then top with the remaining ham. Place the remaining chicken breasts over the top of the ham. Season with salt and pepper. Tightly cover the pan with foil. Bake for 45 minutes.

5. Melt the butter and mix it with the remaining cup of breadcrumbs. Remove the foil from the pan and sprinkle the buttered breadcrumbs over the top of the chicken. Return to the oven and bake uncovered for 15 minutes, or until the breadcrumbs are golden brown and the chicken breasts are cooked through. Let set for 10 minutes, then cut into 8 equal pieces and serve.

Chicken Paprikash Medley

The chopped red bell pepper usually found in broccoli stir-fry mix gives this dish an unexpected flavor; however, if you don't like the crunch added by the water chestnuts, you can substitute a 1-pound bag of broccoli florets or broccoli and cauliflower mix.

Serves 8

4 cups cooked egg noodles or spaetzle

1 tablespoon butter

1 tablespoon extra-virgin olive oil

1 large yellow onion, diced

1½ pounds boneless, skinless chicken breasts

4 cloves garlic, minced

Salt and freshly ground pepper to taste

4 tablespoons Hungarian paprika

4 cups chicken broth

2 tablespoons all-purpose flour

1 1-pound frozen broccoli stir-fry mix, thawed

16 ounces sour cream

1. In a Dutch oven, cook the noodles or spaetzle according to the package directions; drain. Transfer to a serving platter, cover, and keep warm.

2. Wipe out the Dutch oven, then add the butter and oil; bring to temperature over medium-high heat. Add the onion and sauté for 3 minutes. Cut the chicken breasts into bite-sized pieces. Add the chicken to the Dutch oven and stir-fry for 5 minutes. Stir in the garlic, salt, pepper, 3 tablespoons of the paprika, and 3½ cups of the chicken broth; cover the pan. While the chicken broth comes to a boil, mix the remaining ½ cup of chicken broth with the flour. Strain out any lumps, and then whisk the broth mixture into the boiling broth. Boil for 3 minutes. Stir in the broccoli stir-fry mix; lower the temperature, cover, and simmer for 5 minutes.

3. Remove the pan from the burner and stir in the sour cream. Pour the chicken and vegetable mixture over the noodles or spaetzle. Sprinkle the remaining tablespoon of paprika over the top. Serve immediately.

Thickening or Thinning

The temperature at which you simmer the paprikash will affect how thick or thin the sauce gets. The sour cream added at the end of the cooking time will also thicken the sauce. If the sauce is too thin, add more sour cream. If it's too thick, slowly whisk in some additional chicken broth, milk, or water.

Chicken Simmered
with Olives

Serves 4

2 tablespoons extra-virgin olive oil

8 small chicken thighs

1 large yellow onion, diced

3 cloves garlic, minced

1 teaspoon ground ginger

½ teaspoon turmeric

½ teaspoon paprika

Salt to taste

½ teaspoon freshly ground black pepper

1 15-ounce can diced tomatoes

1 preserved lemon, rinsed and diced

1 teaspoon dried parsley

1 teaspoon dried coriander

1 7½-ounce jar pimiento-stuffed olives, drained

2 cups cooked couscous or rice

If you prefer, you can substitute a cut-up 3½-pound whole chicken for the chicken thighs. When you season the dish, keep in mind that the olives and the preserved lemon will affect the saltiness.

Add the oil to a deep 3½-quart nonstick skillet and bring to temperature over medium heat. Brown the chicken, frying it for about 5 minutes on each side. Remove the chicken from the pan and keep warm. Add the onions and sauté until transparent. Add the garlic, ginger, turmeric, paprika, salt, and pepper; stir into the onions and sauté for 1 minute. Add the chicken back to the pan; pour the tomatoes over the chicken and sprinkle the lemon over the tomatoes. Cover, reduce heat, and simmer for 30 minutes, or until the chicken is tender. Sprinkle the parsley, coriander, and olives over the top; cover and cook for an additional 5 minutes. Serve warm over cooked couscous or rice.

Preserved Lemons

To make preserved lemons, cut 5 lemons into partial quarters, leaving them attached at one end; rub kosher salt over the outside and cut sides of the lemons, and then pack them tightly in a sterilized 1-quart glass jar. Add 2 tablespoons kosher salt and enough lemon juice to cover the lemons. Seal and let set at room temperature for 14 days, inverting the jar once a day to mix. Store indefinitely in the refrigerator.

Italian Stuffed Chicken

Serve this chicken with a tossed salad dressed with Italian dressing. If you don't have anchovies or capers on hand, substitute Italian seasoning to season the potato mixture and use it instead of the rosemary to season the outside of the chicken.

1. Preheat oven to 375°F.

2. Add the potatoes to a microwave-safe bowl; cover and microwave on high for 5 minutes. Add the olives, parsley, garlic, anchovies, capers, olive oil, salt, and pepper to the potatoes and stir to combine.

3. Rinse the chicken inside and out. Dry the chicken with paper towels, then stuff the chicken with the hot potato mixture. Place the chicken on a rack in a roasting pan.

4. Brush the outside of the chicken with the melted butter. Season with salt and pepper to taste. Sprinkle the rosemary over the chicken.

5. Bake for 80 to 90 minutes. Remove from the oven and let rest for 10 minutes. Cut into quarters and serve with the potato stuffing.

Improvised Roasting Rack

If your roasting pan doesn't have a removable rack, arrange stalks of celery, curved side down, over the bottom of the pan and place the meat on top of the celery. This adds enough height to allow some of the fat to drain away from the meat.

Serves 4

4 medium russet potatoes, diced
10 pimiento-stuffed green olives, chopped
1 tablespoon dried parsley
2 cloves garlic, minced
OPTIONAL: 3 canned flat anchovies, mashed
1 tablespoon capers, rinsed and chopped
3 tablespoons olive oil
Salt and freshly ground black pepper to taste
1 3-pound chicken
1 tablespoon butter, melted
Dried rosemary to taste

Chicken Divan

This is a versatile casserole. You can stretch it to 8 servings by adding 1 to 2 cups of cooked diced potatoes. You can also substitute American, Cheddar, or Swiss cheese for the Parmigiano-Reggiano.

Preheat oven to 350°F. Melt the butter over medium heat in a 2-quart or larger ovenproof skillet or Dutch oven. Add the flour and cook, stirring constantly, for 1 minute. Gradually whisk in the broth and milk; cook for 3 minutes, or until it begins to thicken. Stir in salt, pepper, nutmeg, ¼ cup of the cheese, and sherry; cook until the cheese melts. Remove from the heat and stir in the chicken, broccoli, half of the almonds, and the cream. Sprinkle the remaining almonds and cheese over the top. Bake uncovered for 35 minutes, or until bubbly and golden brown.

Different Chicken Divan

For a lighter sauce, whip the cream until it reaches soft peaks and then fold it into the other Chicken Divan ingredients before you top the casserole with the remaining almonds and cheese. If you don't have heavy cream on hand, you can substitute sour cream or melt 4 ounces of cream cheese into the sauce before you add the chicken.

Chicken Braised
with Sweet Peppers

If you have fresh Roma tomatoes on hand, you can substitute 2 cups of diced fresh tomatoes for the canned tomatoes called for in this recipe.

1. Add the oil to a deep 3½-quart nonstick skillet and bring to temperature over medium heat. Add the chicken; fry for about 5 minutes, turning the chicken so it browns evenly. Drain and discard any excess fat. Add the broth, wine, garlic, rosemary, salt, and black pepper to the skillet. Bring to a boil; reduce heat, cover, and simmer for 20 minutes.

2. Add the tomatoes, sweet peppers, and mushrooms to the skillet. Cover and simmer for another 15 minutes, or until the chicken is tender and no longer pink. Transfer the chicken to a serving dish; cover with foil and keep warm.

3. Add the cornstarch and water to a small bowl; stir to combine. Mix in 1 or 2 tablespoons of the hot broth to thin the cornstarch mixture and then gently stir the mixture into the broth and vegetables. Continue to cook for 3 minutes, or until the sauce is thickened and has lost its raw cornstarch flavor. Taste for seasoning and add salt and pepper if needed. Spoon the vegetables and sauce around chicken. Serve with noodles or rice.

Serves 4

1 tablespoon extra-virgin olive or vegetable oil

8 small chicken thighs, skin removed

⅔ cup chicken broth

¼ cup dry white wine or chicken broth

2 cloves garlic, minced

¼ teaspoon dried rosemary, crushed

Salt to taste

¼ teaspoon freshly ground black pepper

1 15-ounce can diced tomatoes

1 small yellow sweet pepper, cut into ½" strips

1 small green sweet pepper, cut into ½" strips

1 small red sweet pepper, cut into ½" strips

8 ounces fresh button mushrooms, cleaned and sliced

2 tablespoons cornstarch

2 tablespoons cold water

2 cups hot cooked noodles or rice

Chicken Dinner Olé

Serves 6

3–3½ pounds chicken pieces, skin removed

¼ cup all-purpose flour

½ teaspoon salt

¼ teaspoon cayenne

2 tablespoons extra-virgin olive oil

1 28-ounce can diced Italian-style tomatoes

4 medium russet potatoes, peeled and diced

1 medium yellow onion, sliced

½ cup pitted ripe olives, cut in half

½ cup dry red wine

OPTIONAL: 2 tablespoons capers

1 teaspoon dried basil, crushed

½ teaspoon dried oregano, crushed

2 cloves garlic, minced

1 tablespoon cold water

2 teaspoons cornstarch

The is a quick and easy meal that's great when served with a tossed salad and some baked corn tortilla chips.

1. Rinse and dry the chicken pieces. Add the flour, salt, cayenne, and chicken pieces to a gallon-size food storage bag; seal and shake to coat. Bring the oil to temperature over medium heat in a 4-quart Dutch oven. Arrange the chicken pieces in a single layer in the pan and fry for 10 minutes, turning the pieces to brown them evenly.

2. Add the undrained tomatoes, potatoes, onion, olives, wine, capers (if using), basil, oregano, and garlic to the pan. Bring to a boil; reduce the heat, cover, and simmer for 35 to 45 minutes, or until chicken is tender and no longer pink. Remove the chicken to a serving dish; cover and keep warm.

3. Add the water and cornstarch to a small bowl; stir to combine. Stir the cornstarch mixture in the contents remaining in the pan; cook, stirring gently, for 3 minutes, or until the pan juices are thickened and the cornstarch taste is cooked out. Taste for seasoning and add additional salt if needed. Pour the thickened mixture over the chicken.

Chicken and Vegetable Stir-Fry

*Add some extra punch to this dish by topping it with
toasted sesame seeds, slivered almonds, or cashews.*

Serves 4

½ cup water
2 tablespoons soy sauce
2 tablespoons hoisin sauce
2 teaspoons cornstarch
1 teaspoon grated fresh
    ginger
1 teaspoon toasted sesame
    oil
2 tablespoons peanut oil
12 ounces skinless, boneless
    chicken, cut into bite-
    sized pieces
1 1-pound frozen broccoli stir-
    fry mix, thawed
1 yellow sweet pepper,
    seeded and cut into strips
2 cups chow mein noodles or
    hot cooked rice

1. In a small bowl, make the sauce by stirring together the water, soy sauce, hoisin sauce, cornstarch, ginger, and sesame oil. Set aside.

2. Add the peanut oil to a wok or large skillet and bring to temperature over medium-high heat. Add the chicken pieces and stir-fry for 5 minutes, or until the chicken is cooked through. Push the chicken to the edges of the pan; add the stir-fry mix and pepper strips and stir-fry for 3 minutes, or until the vegetables are crisp-tender.

3. Push the chicken and vegetables away from the center of pan. Pour the sauce mixture into the center of pan; cook and stir until thickened and bubbly. Stir the sauce into the chicken and vegetables. Serve over chow mein noodles or rice.

Slow-Cooked Chicken Cacciatore

Serves 6

8 ounces fresh button or cremini mushrooms, cleaned and sliced

3 stalks celery, sliced

3 large carrots, peeled and diced

2 medium yellow onions, peeled and sliced

1 large green bell pepper, cut into strips

4 cloves garlic, minced

12 skinless chicken thighs or drumsticks

½ cup chicken broth

¼ cup dry white wine

2 tablespoons quick-cooking tapioca

1 teaspoon granulated sugar

1 teaspoon dried oregano, crushed

2 bay leaves

½ teaspoon salt

¼ teaspoon freshly ground black pepper

1 14½-ounce can diced tomatoes

⅓ cup tomato paste

Hot cooked pasta or rice

This adaptation of an Italian classic recipe has all of the necessary goodies to become one of your family's favorite meals.

1. Add the mushrooms, celery, carrot, onions, sweet pepper, and garlic to a 5- or 6-quart slow cooker. Place chicken on top of vegetables. Mix the broth, wine, tapioca, sugar, oregano, bay leaves, salt, and pepper in a small bowl; pour over chicken. Cover and cook on low for 6 to 7 hours, or until the chicken is cooked through.

2. Remove and discard bay leaves. Remove the chicken to a serving platter; cover and keep warm. Turn the slow cooker to the high setting. Stir in the undrained tomatoes and the tomato paste. Cover and cook for 15 minutes. Pour the resulting sauce over the chicken. Serve with cooked pasta or rice.

Baked Long-Grain White Rice

In an ovenproof 8-cup saucepan or skillet, sauté 1 medium diced onion in 2 tablespoons of butter. Add 1 cup of rinsed long-grain white rice and 2 cups of chicken broth. Bring to a boil, cover, and then bake at 325°F for 20 minutes. Makes about 3½ cups cooked rice.

Slow-Cooked Chicken
with Creamy Lemon Sauce

For this meal, you simply add the ingredients to your slow cooker. Later in the day, all you have to do is finish the sauce, and you have meat, potatoes, and vegetables all ready to serve and eat.

Serves 4

1 1-pound bag frozen cut green beans, thawed

1 small yellow onion, cut into thin wedges

4 boneless, skinless chicken breast halves

4 medium russet potatoes, peeled and quartered

2 cloves garlic, minced

¼ teaspoon freshly ground black pepper

1 cup chicken broth

4 ounces cream cheese, cut into cubes

1 teaspoon freshly grated lemon peel

OPTIONAL: lemon peel strips

1. Place the green beans and onion in a 3-quart or larger slow cooker. Arrange the chicken and potatoes over the vegetables. Sprinkle with the garlic and pepper. Pour the broth over the top. Cover and cook on low for 5 or more hours, or until the chicken is cooked through and moist.

2. Transfer the chicken and vegetables to 4 serving plates or a serving platter; cover to keep warm.

3. To make the sauce, add the cream cheese cubes and grated lemon peel to the broth in the slow cooker. Stir until the cheese melts into the sauce. Pour the sauce over the chicken and vegetables. Garnish with lemon peel strips if desired.

The World's Easiest Vegetable Dish

When they're prepared correctly, you'd swear that freeze-dried green beans taste as good as fresh. About 5 to 10 minutes before you plan to serve them, pour boiling water over the freeze-dried green beans so that they're completely submerged. When you're ready to serve them, drain and toss the green beans with a little fresh lemon juice, extra-virgin olive oil, salt, and freshly ground black pepper.

Chicken Dinner Baked in Its Own Gravy

Serve this dinner with a tossed or cucumber salad.

Serves 6

12 small chicken thighs

¼ cup all-purpose flour

¼ cup butter, melted

6 medium russet potatoes, scrubbed and pierced with a fork

1 cup undiluted evaporated milk

1 10¾-ounce cream of mushroom soup

4 ounces American cheese, grated

Salt and freshly ground black pepper to taste

1 1-pound bag frozen baby peas and pearl onions, thawed

4 ounces button mushrooms, cleaned and sliced

Paprika, as needed

1. Preheat oven to 425°F.

2. Coat the chicken in the flour and arrange, skin-side down, in the melted butter in a 9" × 13" nonstick baking pan. Add the potatoes to the pan. Bake for 30 minutes. Use tongs to turn the chicken, reduce the oven temperature to 325°F, and bake for an additional 30 minutes.

3. Add the evaporated milk, soup, cheese, salt, and pepper to a bowl; stir to mix. Remove the potatoes from the baking pan, wrap in foil, and return to the oven. Drain any excess fat from the chicken and discard. Arrange the peas and onions over the chicken, then top with the mushrooms. Evenly pour the evaporated milk mixture over the mushrooms. Sprinkle with paprika. Cover the baking pan with foil, return to the oven, and bake for 20 minutes.

Serving Suggestion

If you want to avoid adding extra butter to the baked potatoes you serve with the Chicken Dinner Baked in Its Own Gravy, put each potato on a serving plate, cut it in half lengthwise, and lightly mash the pulp. Spoon the vegetable-gravy mixture over the potato and place a chicken thigh over the top of each half.

Curried Chicken
with Avocado

*Serve this dish with a Cucumber-Yogurt Salad
(see page 102) and pita, Indian, or Euphrates bread.*

Melt the butter and bring it to temperature in a nonstick skillet over medium heat. Add the chicken, onion, salt, and pepper; sauté until the chicken is cooked through. Add the apple, garlic, and curry powder; sauté for 2 minutes. Stir in the flour; whisk the cream and then the broth into the chicken mixture. Bring to a boil and boil for 2 minutes. To serve, place an avocado half on top of ½ cup of the cooked rice and spoon the hot chicken curry over the avocado.

Optional Condiments

This dish is good served with chopped hard-boiled egg, chopped peanuts, chutney, coconut, crumbled crisp bacon, preserved ginger, raisins, and sweet pickles as condiments. Try something new or just use whatever you have in your pantry.

Serves 6

¼ cup butter
1 pound boneless, skinless chicken breasts, cut into bite-sized pieces
1 small yellow onion, diced
Salt and freshly ground black pepper to taste
1 Golden Delicious apple, peeled, cored, and thinly sliced
1 clove garlic, minced
1 tablespoon curry powder
¼ cup all-purpose flour
1 cup heavy or light cream
1 cup chicken broth
3 large avocados, peeled, pitted, and halved
3 cups cooked rice

Chicken and Dressing

2 tablespoons butter

3 stalks celery, diced

1 medium yellow onion, diced

1 large carrot, peeled and
    shredded

1 cup chicken broth

1 loaf white bread, torn into
    bite-sized pieces

5 large eggs

2 small chickens, halved

Salt and freshly ground black
    pepper to taste

4 medium russet potatoes,
    scrubbed and halved

*Serving amounts will depend on the size of the chickens and
whether or not you leave the crusts on the bread. Round out
this meal with a steamed vegetable and a salad.*

1. Preheat oven to 350°F.

2. Add 1 tablespoon of the butter and the celery to a microwave-safe
    bowl; cover and microwave on high for 1 minute. Stir in the onion;
    cover and microwave for 1 minute. Stir in the carrot; cover and micro-
    wave for 1 minute, or until the onion is transparent. Stir in the chicken
    broth; set aside to cool.

3. Add the torn bread pieces to a 9" × 13" nonstick baking pan. Whisk
    the eggs into the cooled broth mixture and pour over the bread; stir, if
    necessary, to coat all of the bread pieces. Arrange the chicken halves
    side-by-side over the bread mixture. Rub the remaining tablespoon of
    butter over the outside of the chicken halves. Salt and pepper to taste.
    Arrange the potato halves around the chicken. Bake for 1 hour, or until
    chicken is cooked through and the potatoes are tender.

Dressing Down the Dressing

*While dressing is traditionally made with day-old or dried bread, the
Chicken and Dressing recipe will work with fresh bread, too; just keep in
mind that if the bread is fresh, it'll take longer for the bread to absorb the
broth-egg mixture you pour over it. It calls for a standard loaf of white
bread, but it's good when made with a rich sweet bread like challah.*

Chapter 4
Rotisserie Chicken

Rotisserie Chicken
with Balsamic Vinegar–Roasted Vegetables

Serves 6

1 3- to 4-pound chicken
1 medium yellow onion, quartered
2 cloves garlic, smashed
3 tablespoons extra-virgin olive oil
3 tablespoons butter, melted
⅓ cup balsamic vinegar
2 cloves garlic, minced
Salt and freshly ground black pepper to taste
1½ pounds fresh Brussels sprouts
1 pound fingerling potatoes, scrubbed
1½ pounds pearl onions, peeled

The directions for this recipe are based on making the chicken in a Cuisinart Brick Oven Premier. Adjust the instructions according to those recommended for the rotisserie unit you'll be using.

1. Preheat oven to 400°F. Cover a baking pan with foil. Arrange the fingerling potatoes on the baking pan. Place the pan in the bottom back position in the oven so that it will catch any juices from the chicken.

2. Rinse the inside and outside of the chicken and pat it dry. Stuff the chicken with the yellow onion and smashed garlic cloves. To truss the chicken, start by cutting a heavy cotton string or kitchen twine to five times the length of the chicken. Place the middle section of the string under the tail and wrap the tail. Next, wrap the ends of the string around the ends of each drumstick. Pull the string to draw the legs together, crossing the strings over one another to secure the legs in this position. Turn the chicken over. Tie the string across the wings to hold them in place. Cut off and discard any excess string.

3. Add the oil, butter, vinegar, minced garlic, salt, and pepper to a bowl and mix well. Rub 2 tablespoons of the mixture over the outside of the chicken. Insert the rotisserie skewer through the chicken; secure the forks with the rotisserie screws to stabilize the chicken and place the rotisserie spit into the oven's spit support and socket. Turn the oven to the rotisserie setting. Roast for 45 minutes.

4. Cut off the brown ends of the Brussels sprouts and pull off any yellow outer leaves. Put the Brussels sprouts, potatoes, peeled pearl onions, and the remaining vinegar-oil mixture in a large plastic bag; secure and shake to coat the vegetables. Pour them onto the pan under the chicken and roast for another 30 minutes. Open the oven door and roast for another 15 minutes to crisp the chicken skin.

5. To serve, drain and discard the excess fat from the potatoes and vegetables. Arrange the potatoes and vegetables on a serving platter, then place the chicken in the center of the platter. Cover with foil and let rest for 10 minutes before carving.

Peeling Pearl Onions

Cut off the root portion of each pearl onion bulb. Immerse the onions in boiling water for 3 minutes or place them in a microwave-safe bowl, cover, and microwave on high for 30 to 60 seconds or until they're heated through. Immediately submerge the onions in ice-cold water for a couple of minutes. To peel, squeeze each onion so it pops out of its skin.

Herb-Roasted Rotisserie Chicken
with Oven-Roasted Root Vegetables

Serves 4

1 3-pound chicken
2 lemons
2 cloves garlic, smashed
2 tablespoons extra-virgin olive oil
1 teaspoon dried basil
1 teaspoon dried thyme
1 teaspoon dried parsley
2 cloves garlic, minced
Salt and pepper to taste
¼ pound baby turnips, peeled and stem ends trimmed
¼ pound baby red carrots, peeled and stem ends trimmed
¼ pound orange carrots, peeled and stem ends trimmed
¼ pound baby golden beets, peeled and stem ends trimmed
¼ pound baby beets, peeled and stem ends trimmed
¼ pound fingerling potatoes, scrubbed and halved

For a simpler meal, pick up a lemon-pepper rotisserie chicken at the supermarket when you buy the vegetables. Roast the potatoes and vegetables for 45 minutes, placing the chicken in the oven with them for the last 15 minutes to heat it through.

1. Set oven temperature at 400°F.

2. Rinse the inside and outside of the chicken and pat it dry. Halve one lemon; stuff the chicken with the lemon halves and smashed garlic cloves. To truss the chicken, start by cutting a heavy cotton string or kitchen twine to five times the length of the chicken. Place the middle section of the string under the tail and wrap the tail. Next, wrap the ends of the string around the ends of each drumstick. Pull the string to draw the legs together, crossing the strings over one another to secure the legs in this position. Turn the chicken over. Tie the string across the wings to hold them in place. Cut off and discard any excess string.

3. Add the remaining lemon juice, oil, basil, thyme, parsley, minced garlic, salt, and pepper to a large bowl and mix well. Rub 2 tablespoons of the mixture over the outside of the chicken. Insert the rotisserie skewer through the chicken; secure the forks with the rotisserie screws to stabilize the chicken and place the rotisserie spit in the oven's spit support and socket. Cover the baking pan with foil. Place the pan in the bottom back position in the oven. Turn the oven to the rotisserie setting. Roast for 45 minutes.

4. Add the turnips, carrots, beets, and potatoes to the bowl and toss to coat in the herb-oil mixture. Pour them onto the pan under the chicken and roast for another 30 minutes. Open the oven door and roast for another 15 minutes to crisp the chicken skin.

5. To serve, drain and discard the excess fat from the potatoes and vegetables. Arrange the potatoes and vegetables on a serving platter, and place the chicken on the center of the platter. Cover with foil and let rest for 10 minutes before carving.

Rotisserie Chicken Salad

*You can substitute some of the melted chicken fat
from the rotisserie chicken for the oil in the dressing.*

Serves 4

1 3-pound Italian-seasoned
    rotisserie chicken
8 cups salad mix
2 tablespoons red wine
    vinegar
1 tablespoon Dijon mustard
1 clove garlic, minced
¼ teaspoon sea salt
¼ teaspoon freshly ground
    black pepper
4 tablespoons extra-virgin
    olive oil
OPTIONAL: *Parmigiano-
    Reggiano, grated to taste*

1. Cut the legs, thighs, and wings from the chicken. Remove and discard the skin from the rest of the chicken; remove the remaining meat from the chicken and shred it.

2. Divide 2 cups of salad mix between 4 plates. Divide the shredded chicken between the plates, placing it atop the salad mix. Place a leg or thigh on each plate.

3. Add the vinegar, mustard, garlic, salt, pepper, and oil to a jar; cover and shake vigorously to emulsify. Pour the dressing evenly over the chicken-topped salad mix on each plate. Top each salad with grated cheese if desired.

As Moist and Juicy as a Rotisserie Chicken

You can prepare a beer-can-style chicken instead of using a rotisserie. Place a Chicken Rocket (www.chickenrocket.com) or Chicken Roaster (www.mrbarbq.com) in a seasoned cast-iron skillet or roasting pan large enough to hold the chicken and vegetables. Fill the reservoir to the halfway mark with seasoned chicken broth or beer, season the chicken according to the recipe, place it on the roasting stand, and bake at 400°F for 1½ hours.

Fusion Stir-Fry

Serves 4

1 3-pound lemon-pepper
rotisserie chicken
½ cup water
2 tablespoons soy sauce
2 tablespoons hoisin sauce
2 teaspoons cornstarch
1 teaspoon grated fresh
ginger
2 teaspoons steak sauce
OPTIONAL: 1 teaspoon honey
1 teaspoon toasted sesame
oil
1 12-ounce package frozen
cheese tortellini
1 tablespoon peanut oil
1 1-pound frozen broccoli stir-
fry mix, thawed
1 red sweet pepper, seeded
and cut into strips

The steak sauce adds another flavor dimension to this stir-fry, and mixing in cheese tortellini replaces the need for cooked rice or chow mein noodles.

1. Remove and discard the skin from the chicken; remove the meat from the bones and shred it. In a small bowl, make the sauce by stirring together the water, soy sauce, hoisin sauce, cornstarch, ginger, steak sauce, honey (if using), and sesame oil. Set aside.

2. Cook the tortellini according to the package directions; drain and keep warm.

3. Add the peanut oil to a wok or large skillet and bring to temperature over medium-high heat. Add the stir-fry mix and red peppers and stir-fry for 3 minutes, or until the vegetables are crisp-tender. Stir in the shredded chicken; stir-fry for 2 minutes, or until the chicken is heated through.

4. Push the chicken and vegetables away from the center of pan. Pour the sauce mixture into the center of pan; cook and stir until thickened and bubbly. Stir the sauce into the chicken and vegetables. Add the tortellini and toss to combine.

Open-Face Chicken and Sautéed Pepper Sandwiches

Sweet red bell peppers are high in vitamin C, so this recipe gives you an inexpensive and healthful way to stretch a rotisserie chicken to feed a crowd. As a bonus, the sandwich topping could just as easily be tossed with pasta or used to top salad greens.

1. Remove and discard the skin from the chicken; remove the meat from the bones and shred it.

2. Bring the oil to temperature in a large nonstick skillet. Add the peppers; sauté for 3 minutes. Add the onion; sauté for 5 minutes, or until the onion is transparent. Stir in the garlic, oregano, rosemary, and parsley. Add the wine or broth and vinegar; simmer for 5 minutes. Stir in the shredded chicken and simmer for 5 more minutes, or until the chicken is heated through, the peppers are tender, and most of the wine is evaporated. Taste for seasoning and add salt and pepper if needed. To serve, evenly spoon the mixture over the top of the toast slices.

Seasoning Suggestions

The herbs used in this recipe go well with an Italian-seasoned rotisserie chicken; however, you may need to adjust the amounts according to how highly seasoned the chicken is. If you're using a lemon-pepper rotisserie chicken, you may wish to omit the herbs suggested in the recipe and replace them with some Mrs. Dash Lemon Pepper Seasoning Blend to taste.

Serves 8

1 3-pound rotisserie chicken

3 tablespoons extra-virgin olive oil

2 large red bell peppers, seeded and cut into thin strips

2 large orange or yellow bell peppers, seeded and cut into thin strips

2 large green bell peppers, seeded and cut into thin strips

1 large yellow onion, thinly sliced

3 cloves garlic, minced

1 teaspoon dried oregano, crushed

1 teaspoon dried rosemary, chopped

1 tablespoon dried parsley

½ cup dry red wine or ⅓ cup chicken broth and 2 tablespoons balsamic vinegar

Salt and freshly ground black pepper to taste

8 slices bread, toasted

Chicken Enchiladas

Serves 6–12

1 rotisserie chicken

¼ teaspoon freshly ground black pepper

1 10-ounce package frozen chopped spinach, thawed and well drained

6 green onions, thinly sliced

1 cup tomato salsa

4 ounces Cheddar or Monterey jack cheese, shredded

12 7-inch flour or corn tortillas

Nonstick cooking spray

1¼ cups sour cream

2 tablespoons all-purpose flour

Salt and freshly ground black pepper to taste

½ teaspoon ground cumin

½ cup milk

1 4-ounce can diced green chili peppers, drained

OPTIONAL: fresh tomato, diced

OPTIONAL: fresh cilantro, chopped

For 6 servings, allow 2 enchiladas per person along with a tomato salad. To stretch it to 12 servings, allow 1 enchilada per person along with a generous serving of tossed salad.

1. Preheat oven to 350°F.

2. Remove and discard the skin from the chicken; remove the meat from the bones and shred it. For the filling, mix together the shredded chicken, spinach, green onions, salsa, and half of the cheese in a bowl. Treat a 9" × 13" nonstick baking pan with nonstick spray. Soften the flour or corn tortillas by placing them on a microwave-safe plate; cover with a damp paper towel and microwave on high for 1 minute. Spoon the filling down the centers of the tortillas, roll them, and place seam-side down in the baking pan.

3. To make the sauce, add the sour cream, flour, salt, pepper, cumin, milk, and chili peppers to a small bowl; stir to mix. Spoon the sauce over the tops of the rolled tortillas in the baking pan. Cover and bake for 20 minutes. Uncover and bake for an additional 20 minutes, or until heated through. Sprinkle with cheese; bake for another 5 minutes, remove from the oven, and let stand for 5 minutes before serving. Garnish with chopped tomato, cilantro, or additional salsa if desired.

The Traditional Way to Soften Corn Tortillas

Heat an inch of corn oil or lard in a skillet over medium heat until the fat is hot enough that a drop of water splatters when dropped in the oil. Holding a tortilla with tongs, immerse it in the oil, turning it over a few times, until it becomes pliable. Drain on paper towels.

Chicken Fried Rice

How the chicken is seasoned will determine whether the stir-fry sauce will stand on its own or if you'll need to add toasted sesame oil, soy sauce, and/or honey for additional flavor.

1. Heat the rice pouch in the microwave according to package directions.

2. Remove and discard the skin and breast meat. Shred remaining meat.

3. Add the oil to a wok or large skillet and bring it to temperature over medium-high heat. Add the onion; stir-fry for 1 minute. Add the rice and stir-fry for 3 minutes. Stir in the shredded chicken, peas, and stir-fry sauce; stir-fry for 3 more minutes, or until heated through. Taste for seasoning and add toasted sesame oil, soy sauce, and honey to taste if desired. Sprinkle with the almonds and serve.

Serves 4

1 8.8-ounce microwaveable pouch brown or white rice
1 3-pound rotisserie chicken
1 tablespoon peanut or vegetable oil
2 green onions, sliced
½ cup frozen peas
¼ cup bottled stir-fry sauce
OPTIONAL: toasted sesame oil to taste
OPTIONAL: soy sauce to taste
OPTIONAL: honey to taste
¼ cup sliced almonds

Microwave Chicken and Rice

This is a microwaveable version of the Chicken Fried Rice recipe. You can enhance the flavor by adding some of the optional ingredients or by toasting the almond slices.

1. Heat the rice pouch in the microwave according to package directions.

2. Remove and discard the skin and breast meat. Shred remaining meat.

3. Add the chicken to a covered microwave-safe bowl large enough to hold all of the ingredients; microwave at 70 percent power for 1 minute. Stir. Repeat until the chicken is brought to temperature. Toss the rice, peas, stir-fry sauce, and broth or water with the chicken and microwave for 1 minute at 70 percent power. If the mixture is not sufficiently heated, repeat for 1 more minute. Top with the almonds.

Serves 4

1 8.8-ounce microwaveable pouch brown or white rice
1 3-pound rotisserie chicken
1 tablespoon chicken broth or water
2 green onions, sliced
½ cup frozen peas
¼ cup bottled stir-fry sauce
¼ teaspoon toasted sesame oil
OPTIONAL: soy sauce to taste
OPTIONAL: honey to taste
¼ cup sliced almonds

Chicken Tetrazzini

*This is an easy one-dish meal, and the leftovers
are great warmed over the next day.*

Serves 8

1 3-pound roasted chicken

8 ounces dried spaghetti or
   linguine, broken in half

12 ounces fresh asparagus,
   trimmed and cut into 1"
   pieces

2 tablespoons butter

8 ounces small whole fresh
   button or cremini
   mushrooms, cleaned and
   sliced

1 large red sweet pepper,
   seeded and cut into 1"
   pieces

1 large yellow sweet pepper,
   seeded and cut into 1"
   pieces

¼ cup all-purpose flour

⅛ teaspoon black pepper

1 14-ounce can chicken broth

¾ cup milk

2 ounces Swiss cheese, grated

1 tablespoon finely shredded
   lemon peel

1½ cups bread cubes

1 tablespoon extra-virgin
   olive oil

2 tablespoons snipped fresh
   parsley

1. Preheat oven to 350°F.

2. Remove and discard the skin from the chicken; remove the meat from the bones and shred it.

3. In an ovenproof Dutch oven, cook the spaghetti according to package directions. Add the asparagus during the last minute of the cooking. Drain; set aside and keep warm.

4. Wipe out the Dutch oven; add the butter and melt it over medium heat. Add the mushrooms and peppers; sauté for 8 minutes, or until the mushrooms are tender. Stir in the flour and black pepper until well combined. Whisk in the broth and milk; cook, stirring frequently, until thickened and bubbly. Add the cooked pasta, asparagus, chicken, Swiss cheese, and half of the lemon peel; toss gently to coat.

5. In a medium-sized bowl, toss together the bread cubes, olive oil, and remaining lemon peel; spread on top of the pasta mixture. Bake uncovered for 15 minutes, or until the bread cubes are golden brown. Let stand for 5 minutes before serving. Garnish with parsley before serving, if desired.

Bread Cubes Wisdom

One thick-cut slice of bread will make about ¾ cup of bread cubes. Keep in mind that the cubes will only be as good as the bread you use to make them. Sourdough bread works well in the Chicken Tetrazzini recipe.

Chicken and Cheese Tortellini Meal

You can substitute cauliflower or asparagus for the broccoli.
All three vegetables have lots of health benefits.

1. Remove and discard the skin from the chicken; remove the meat from the bones and shred it.

2. In 4-quart Dutch oven, cook the tortellini according to the package directions, adding the broccoli during the last 3 minutes of cooking. Drain. Return to Dutch oven. Stir in the undrained tomatoes, tomato pesto, and chicken. Cook, stirring occasionally, just until heated through. Garnish with freshly grated Parmigiano-Reggiano cheese if desired.

Serves 6

1 3-pound rotisserie chicken
2 9-ounce packages refrigerated cheese tortellini
1 12-ounce package frozen broccoli florets, thawed
1 14½-ounce can diced tomatoes with Italian herbs, undrained
½ cup dried tomato pesto
OPTIONAL: Parmigiano-Reggiano, freshly grated, to taste

Warm Chicken Salad

You can increase this recipe to 8 servings by using all of the meat from the chicken and doubling the other ingredients.

1. Peel and section the oranges; cut each section into 4 pieces. Add the orange pieces to a large salad bowl and toss them with the romaine, red pepper, onion, almonds, and chicken. Set aside.

2. Add the orange juice and vinegar to a microwave-safe bowl. Microwave on high for 1 minute, or until heated through. Whisk in the olive oil and mustard. Pour the warm dressing over the salad and toss to mix. Season to taste with coarsely ground black pepper if desired. Serve immediately.

Serves 4

2 medium oranges
6 cups torn romaine lettuce
1 medium red sweet pepper, seeded and diced
½ small red onion, halved and thinly sliced
½ cup slivered or sliced almonds, toasted
Breast meat from a rotisserie chicken, cut into thin bite-sized strips
⅓ cup orange juice
1 tablespoon red wine vinegar
1 tablespoon extra-virgin olive oil
1 teaspoon Dijon mustard
OPTIONAL: coarsely ground black pepper to taste

Chicken and Vegetables in Hoisin Sauce

1 8.8-ounce microwaveable pouch brown or white rice

1 3-pound rotisserie chicken

1 medium red sweet pepper, seeded and cut into thin strips

1 small yellow onion, cut into thin wedges

1 clove garlic, minced

Salt to taste

⅛ teaspoon freshly ground black pepper

2 tablespoons orange juice

2 tablespoons hoisin sauce

OPTIONAL: kumquats, sliced, to taste

OPTIONAL: green onion, sliced, to taste

OPTIONAL: sliced almonds, toasted, to taste

This recipe could be an alternative use for chicken breast that you've saved when making another recipe that calls for only part of the chicken.

1. Heat the rice pouch in the microwave according to package directions.

2. Remove and discard the skin from the chicken. Remove the breast meat; wrap and refrigerate it for a later use, such as for the Chicken Bundles (page 54). Remove the remaining meat from the bones and shred it.

3. Add the sweet pepper, onion, garlic, salt, pepper, orange juice, and hoisin sauce to a large microwave-safe bowl; stir to mix. Cover and microwave on high for 1 minute; stir and microwave at 70 percent power for 1 minute, or until the sweet pepper and onion are tender. Stir in the cooked rice and shredded chicken; cover and microwave at 70 percent power for 2 minutes, or until the entire mixture is heated through. Serve garnished with kumquat slices, sliced green onion, and/or toasted almonds if desired.

Hot Chicken Fajita Pasta Salad

You can easily stretch this recipe to 8 servings by serving the pasta salad over lettuce or along with baked corn tortilla chips.

1. Remove and discard the skin from the chicken; remove the meat from the bones and shred it. Set aside.

2. In a Dutch oven, cook the pasta according to the package directions; drain and keep warm. Wipe out the Dutch oven, add the oil, and bring it to temperature over medium heat. Add the onion, sweet pepper, and Anaheim pepper; sauté for 5 minutes, or until crisp-tender. Add the sour cream, marinade, lime juice, chili powder, cumin, and crushed red pepper to a bowl; stir to mix. Add the cooked noodles, chicken, and sour cream mixture to the sautéed vegetables; toss to coat. Leave on the heat long enough to reheat the noodles and warm the chicken, if necessary. Serve warm.

Heat Hints

The dried red pepper flakes and Anaheim chili pepper will add heat to Hot Chicken Fajita Pasta Salad, which will be somewhat tempered by the cooked noodles and sour cream. If you prefer a milder taste, reduce the amount you add at first, taste the salad, and then add more, if needed.

Serves 6

1 3-pound rotisserie chicken
12 ounces dried egg noodles
1 8-ounce carton sour cream
½ cup chipotle liquid meat marinade
2 tablespoons lime juice
1 teaspoon chili powder
1 teaspoon ground cumin
½ teaspoon dried red pepper flakes, crushed
2 tablespoons extra-virgin olive oil
1 medium yellow onion, halved and thinly sliced
1 medium red sweet pepper, seeded and cut into thin strips
1 fresh Anaheim chili pepper, seeded and cut into thin strips
OPTIONAL: fresh cilantro, chopped, to taste

Honey-Mustard BBQ Chicken Sandwiches

Serves 8

1 3-pound rotisserie chicken
1½ cups bottled barbecue
    sauce
¼ cup honey
2 teaspoons yellow mustard
1½ teaspoons Worcestershire
    sauce
8 hamburger buns

*Stretch a rotisserie chicken to a meal for a crowd by serving these
sandwiches with potato chips and tossed salad or coleslaw.*

Remove and discard the skin from the chicken; remove the meat from
the bones and shred it. Add the chicken to a nonstick saucepan or skillet along with the barbecue sauce, honey, mustard, and Worcestershire
sauce. Cook and stir over medium heat until heated through. Divide
between the buns.

Chicken Bundles

Serves 4

1 3-ounce package cream
    cheese, softened
3 tablespoons butter, melted
Salt and freshly ground black
    pepper to taste
1 tablespoon mayonnaise
1 tablespoon milk
2 cups cooked chicken, cubed
    or shredded
1 tablespoon fresh chives or
    green onion, chopped
OPTIONAL: 1 tablespoon
    pimiento, chopped
1 8-ounce can refrigerated
    crescent dinner rolls
½ cup breadcrumbs

*Serve these with a tossed salad for lunch or with
a salad and steamed vegetable for dinner.*

1. Preheat oven to 350°F.

2. Add the cream cheese, 2 tablespoons of the butter, salt, pepper, mayon-
    naise, and milk to a bowl; whisk to combine. Stir in the chicken, chives
    or green onion, and pimiento (if using).

3. Separate the dough into 4 rectangles; each rectangle will include 2
    connected crescent rolls. Place on an ungreased cookie sheet. Press
    the perforations holding the sections together to seal. Evenly spoon the
    chicken mixture onto the 4 rectangles. Pull the 4 corners of dough to
    the top center above the chicken mixture, twist slightly, and squeeze
    to seal each bundle. Brush the tops of each bundle with the remaining
    butter and sprinkle the breadcrumbs onto the brushed butter. Bake for
    25 minutes, or until golden brown.

Chapter 5
Turkey

Turkey-Topped English Muffins

A twist on the traditional Eggs Benedict, this English muffin is topped with lettuce, avocado slices, turkey breast, poached egg, and an easy homemade hollandaise-style sauce.

Serves 1–2

1 English muffin, split
⅔ cup water
⅛ teaspoon white vinegar
2 large eggs
¼ cup plain yogurt
2 teaspoons lemon juice
OPTIONAL: ¼ teaspoon Dijon or honey mustard
Lettuce leaves
½ avocado, peeled and sliced
4 ounces cooked turkey, heated
Salt and freshly ground pepper to taste

1. While you toast the muffin, put the water and vinegar in a microwave-safe bowl. Crack the eggs into the water. Pierce each egg yolk with a toothpick. Cover the bowl with plastic wrap. Microwave on high for 1½ minutes, or until the eggs are done as desired. Keep in mind that as long as the egg remains in the water, it will continue to cook, so be ready to assemble the dish quickly.

2. To make the mock hollandaise, in a small bowl mix the yogurt, lemon juice, and mustard (if using).

3. To assemble the open-face sandwiches, place the toasted English muffin halves on a plate. Arrange lettuce atop the muffins. Top the lettuce with the avocado slices and then the turkey. Use a slotted spoon to remove the eggs from the water and place them on top of the turkey. Salt and pepper the eggs to taste. Spoon the yogurt sauce over the eggs. Serve immediately.

Turkey Casserole

This casserole is a great to use leftover turkey. It also tastes great with cooked chicken or leftover roast beef.

1. Preheat oven to 350°F.

2. Add the oil and butter to an ovenproof Dutch oven and bring it to temperature over medium heat. Add the onion, green pepper, carrot, celery, salt, and pepper and sauté until tender.

3. Add the turkey and lightly sauté it with the vegetables to bring it to temperature. Stir in the mayonnaise, mushroom and celery soups, eggs, and milk; mix well. Add the bread pieces and half of the grated cheese; toss to combine.

4. Cover and bake for 45 minutes. Remove the lid and top with the remaining cheese. Bake for an additional 15 minutes, or until the cheese is melted and the casserole is cooked through. Serve immediately.

A Turkey Casserole Tweak

Add a turkey stuffing taste to your casserole by adding a teaspoon of poultry seasoning, dried sage, or a ½ teaspoon of dried marjoram and a ½ teaspoon of dried thyme.

Serves 8

1 tablespoon extra-virgin olive oil
1 tablespoon butter
1 large yellow onion, finely chopped
1 green pepper, finely chopped
1 large carrot, peeled and finely chopped
1½ cups celery, finely chopped
½ teaspoon salt
¼ teaspoon freshly ground black pepper
2 cups cooked turkey, chopped
½ cup mayonnaise
1 10¾-ounce can cream of mushroom soup
1 10¾-ounce can cream of celery soup
4 eggs, beaten
3 cups milk
1 loaf white bread, torn into small pieces
1 pound Cheddar cheese, grated

Mock Bratwurst in Beer

Serves 8

2 stalks celery, finely chopped
1 1-pound bag baby carrots
1 large yellow onion, sliced
2 cloves garlic, minced
2–4 slices of bacon, cut into small pieces
2 pounds turkey breast
1 2-pound bag sauerkraut, rinsed and drained
8 medium red potatoes, washed and pierced
1 12-ounce can beer
1 tablespoon Bavarian seasoning
Salt and freshly ground pepper to taste

The Spice House (www.thespicehouse.com) has a salt-free Bavarian seasoning blend that is appropriate for this recipe. It's a blend of Bavarian-style crushed brown mustard seeds, French rosemary, garlic, Dalmatian sage, French thyme, and bay leaves.

Add all the ingredients to a 4-quart slow cooker in the order given. Note that the liquid amount needed will depend on how wet the sauerkraut is when you add it. The liquid should come up halfway and cover the turkey breast, with the sauerkraut and potatoes being above the liquid line. Add more beer, if necessary. Slow cook on low for 6 to 8 hours. Taste for seasoning and adjust if necessary. Serve hot.

Bavarian-Style Turkey Sausage Skillet

Serves 6

1 tablespoon cooking oil
1 medium yellow onion, sliced
2 tablespoons all-purpose flour
1 cup apple cider or apple juice
½ cup chicken broth
2 tablespoons stone-ground mustard
1 20-ounce package refrigerated red potato wedges
1 pound cooked smoked turkey sausage, cut into bite-sized slices
1 14.5-ounce can sauerkraut, rinsed and drained
2 packed tablespoons light brown sugar
½ teaspoon caraway seeds
OPTIONAL: ¼ cup dried cranberries or raisins

Rinsed and drained sauerkraut will have a milder flavor. If you prefer more sour-packed punch in your sauerkraut, you can skip rinsing it and only drain it of the packing liquid in the can.

1. Add the oil to a deep 3½-quart nonstick skillet or electric skillet and bring it to temperature over medium-high heat. Add the onions and sauté for about 8 minutes, or until tender. Sprinkle the flour over the onions and cook for 2 minutes, stirring frequently.

2. Slowly whisk in the apple cider, broth, and mustard. Bring to a boil while you continue to stir, then add the potato wedges, sausage pieces, and sauerkraut. Reduce the heat and cover the pan; simmer for about 30 minutes, or until the sauce is thickened and the potatoes are tender. If desired, stir cranberries or raisins into the sausage mixture. Serve immediately.

Turkey, Spinach, and Artichoke Casserole

This is an adaptation of traditional hot spinach and artichoke dip. If you want to serve it as a dip or for a light lunch, simply mix all ingredients together in a food processor and bake it according to the recipe instructions.

1. Preheat oven to 375°F.

2. Evenly spread the artichoke hearts across the bottom of a 9" × 13" non-stick baking pan. Top with the spinach and the turkey.

3. Add the cream cheese, mayonnaise, butter or oil, and cream or milk to a food processor; process until smooth. Spread over the top of the turkey. Sprinkle with pepper, and then the cheese.

4. Bake uncovered for 40 minutes, or until the cheese is bubbly and the casserole is lightly browned on top. This dish can be assembled the night before and refrigerated; allow extra baking time if you move the casserole directly from the refrigerator to the oven.

Turkey, Spinach, and Artichoke Fondue

Add all ingredients to a food processor and process until smooth. Put into an electric fondue pot set at medium-high heat (setting 4½–5 on the Cuisinart Electric Fondue Pot); bring it to temperature, stirring frequently. Once it's heated through, reduce the setting to warm (setting 3 on the Cuisinart) to hold the fondue. Serve with bread, crackers, or crudités.

Serves 10–12

1 14-ounce jar artichoke hearts, drained and chopped

3 10-ounce packages frozen chopped spinach, thawed and well drained

2 cups cooked turkey, finely chopped

2 8-ounce packages cream cheese, cut into cubes

2 tablespoons mayonnaise

¼ cup butter or extra-virgin olive oil

6 tablespoons heavy cream or milk

Freshly ground black pepper to taste

½ cup freshly ground Parmigiano-Reggiano or Romano cheese

Turkey "Lasagna" Pie

Cook the lasagna noodles in the same Dutch oven in which you'll eventually assemble the lasagna. Baking in a deep Dutch oven means you don't have to worry about the lasagna boiling over, and it cooks more evenly than it would in a rectangular pan.

Serves 8

12 dried whole wheat or regular lasagna noodles
½ cup basil pesto
1 teaspoon grated lemon peel
1 large egg, beaten
1 15-ounce carton ricotta cheese
2 cups mozzarella cheese, grated
¼ teaspoon salt
¼ teaspoon ground black pepper
Nonstick cooking spray
2 cups fresh spinach, chopped
½ cup chopped walnuts, toasted if desired
2 cups cooked turkey, chopped
1 8-ounce package fresh button or cremini mushrooms, cleaned and thinly sliced
1 24-ounce bottle marinara or pasta sauce
½ cup dry red wine
OPTIONAL: fresh Italian flat-leaf parsley leaves

1. Preheat oven to 375°F.

2. Cook the lasagna noodles according to the package directions until almost tender. Drain the noodles in a colander and rinse in cold water to stop the cooking. Drain well and set aside.

3. In a small bowl, mix together the pesto and lemon peel; set aside. Add the egg, ricotta cheese, 1 cup of the mozzarella cheese, and the salt and pepper to a medium-sized bowl and mix well.

4. Lightly coat the Dutch oven with nonstick cooking spray. Arrange 4 cooked noodles in the bottom of the pan, trimming and overlapping them to cover the bottom of pan.

5. Top with the spinach. Sprinkle with half of the walnuts. Spread half of the ricotta cheese mixture evenly over walnuts. Spread half of the pesto evenly mixture over the ricotta, then sprinkle half of the turkey over the pesto. Pour half of the pasta sauce evenly over the turkey. Top with another layer of noodles. Top with the mushrooms. Spread the remaining ricotta cheese mixture over mushrooms. Spread the remaining pesto mixture over the ricotta. Sprinkle the remaining turkey over the pesto, and then pour the rest of the pasta sauce over the turkey. Top with another layer of noodles.

6. Pour the wine into the empty marinara sauce jar, screw on the lid and shake to mix with any sauce remaining in the jar. Pour over the top layer of noodles.

7. Cover the pan and bake for 45 minutes.

8. Remove the cover. Sprinkle the remaining mozzarella cheese over the top. Bake for an additional 15 to 30 minutes, or until the cheese is melted and bubbly and the lasagna is hot in the center. Let set for 10 minutes and then garnish with parsley if desired. To serve, cut the lasagna into pizza slice–style wedges.

Turkey Pilaf

Serves 4–6

2 tablespoons butter

OPTIONAL: 1 small yellow onion or large shallot, chopped

1 cup uncooked long-grain rice

2 cloves garlic, minced

1½ cups chicken broth

½ cup dry white wine

Salt to taste

1–2 cups cooked turkey, chopped

1 12-ounce steam-in-the-bag frozen mixed vegetables

Freshly grated Parmigiano-Reggiano cheese to taste

Adjust the amount of turkey you add to this recipe according to the number of people you need to serve or the amount of protein you prefer in a meal. Choose the vegetables according to your family's tastes.

1. Add the butter to a Dutch oven or 4-quart nonstick saucepan and melt over medium heat. Add the onion or shallot, if using, and sauté for 2 minutes. Add the rice and brown it in the butter. Add the garlic and sauté for 30 seconds. Pour in the broth and wine. Bring to a boil and then add the salt. Cover; simmer for 20 minutes, or until the rice is tender.

2. While the rice cooks, microwave the vegetables in the bag for 4 to 5 minutes.

3. Uncover the rice and add the turkey and microwave-steamed vegetables. Stir to combine. Cover and cook on low for 2 minutes. Remove the cover and stir. Cover and continue to cook until the turkey is warmed through, if necessary.

4. Serve warm topped with the cheese.

Veggies Fresh from the Garden Pilaf

This recipe variation will require a second pot, but you can cut up a pound of fresh zucchini, yellow summer squash, and/or sweet peppers and sauté them in butter until tender. Substitute them for the microwave-steamed vegetables in step 3.

Turkey Tortellini Stir-Fry

It's easy to vary this recipe. Simply choose a different vegetable mix and stir-fry sauce. For example, use a peanut stir-fry sauce and use chopped peanuts instead of the cashews.

Serves 4

1 9-ounce package refrigerated cheese-filled tortellini

1 tablespoon peanut oil

1 16-ounce package fresh-cut or frozen stir-fry vegetables (such as broccoli, pea pods, carrots, and water chestnuts)

1–2 cups cooked turkey, chopped

¾ cup stir-fry sauce

½ cup dry-roasted cashews, chopped

1. Cook the tortellini according to the package directions.

2. Add the oil to a wok or large, deep skillet. Bring to temperature over medium-high heat. Add the vegetables and stir-fry for 3 to 5 minutes for fresh vegetables or 7 to 8 minutes for unthawed frozen vegetables, or until crisp-tender. Stir in the turkey and cook until it is warmed through. Add the stir-fry sauce and stir it in with the turkey-vegetable mix. Cook until the sauce is heated through. Add the cooked tortellini and toss gently to combine. Sprinkle with cashews and serve immediately.

Cranberry Turkey Quesadilla

Mixing fruit with salsa adds a twist to a Southwestern dish. You can substitute tart cherry juice concentrate for the cranberry sauce or use dried cranberries or other dried fruit and a bit more salsa.

Serves 1

2 teaspoons extra-virgin olive oil

2 flour tortillas

1 tablespoon cranberry sauce

1 tablespoon salsa

½ cup Monterey jack or Cheddar cheese, grated

¼ cup chopped cooked turkey

OPTIONAL: 1 teaspoon chopped jalapeño pepper

1. Pour the oil into a small nonstick skillet. Add one of the tortillas and coat one side with oil. Remove and repeat with the second tortilla. Mix together the cranberry sauce, salsa, cheese, turkey, and jalapeño (if using). Spread the mixture over the tortilla in the pan. Top with the other tortilla, oiled side up. Press gently but firmly to keep the quesadilla together.

2. Place the pan over medium heat. Cook for about 2 minutes, or until the bottom is lightly browned. Flip the quesadilla and cook for another 2 minutes, or until that side is lightly browned and the cheese is melted.

Turkey and Biscuits

You can punch up the flavor of this dish by adding ½ teaspoon dried sage and 1 to 2 teaspoons dried parsley when you add the pepper. The style of biscuits you use is up to you; just keep in mind that the bigger the biscuits, the longer they'll take to bake.

Serves 4

1 tablespoon extra-virgin olive oil

1 tablespoon butter

1 medium yellow onion, chopped

1 stalk celery, chopped

Salt to taste

3 tablespoons all-purpose flour

1 cup chicken broth

1½ cups milk

1 12-ounce package frozen peas and carrots

2 cups cooked turkey, cubed

Freshly ground black pepper to taste

1 7.5-ounce can refrigerator biscuits

1. Preheat oven to 425°F.

2. Bring the oil and butter to temperature in an ovenproof Dutch oven over medium heat. Add the onion and celery and sauté for 5 minutes, or until the onion is transparent. Sprinkle the flour over the cooked vegetables and stir-fry for 2 minutes to cook the flour.

3. Slowly add the chicken broth to the pan, whisking to prevent lumps from forming. Stir the milk into the chicken broth. Increase the temperature to medium-high and bring to a boil. Reduce the heat and simmer for 5 minutes, or until mixture begins to thicken. Add the peas and carrots, turkey, and pepper. Mix well.

4. Arrange the biscuits over the top of the turkey mixture. Bake for 20 to 25 minutes, or until the biscuits are golden brown.

Ground Turkey and Biscuits

You can substitute a pound of ground turkey for the cooked turkey in this recipe. Simply add it when you sauté the onion and celery. Fry it until the turkey is cooked through, using a spatula to break up the turkey as it cooks. You may need to drain off a little excess oil before you add the flour, but otherwise you simply follow the recipe.

Oven-Roasted Turkey Breast
with Asparagus

The internal temperature of a baked turkey breast cutlet should be 170°F. The size and thickness of the cutlet can alter the baking time.

Serves 4

4 medium baking potatoes
2 tablespoons butter, softened
1 teaspoon Dijon mustard
1 7-ounce jar roasted red sweet peppers, drained and chopped
4 teaspoons red onion or shallot, finely chopped
¼ teaspoon dried tarragon, crushed
½ teaspoon dried parsley, crushed
⅛ teaspoon salt
⅛ teaspoon freshly ground black pepper
1 pound asparagus spears
2 tablespoons extra-virgin olive oil
Salt and freshly ground pepper to taste
4 boneless turkey breast cutlets

1. Preheat the oven to 325°F.

2. Clean and pierce the potatoes. Place on a microwave-safe plate and microwave on high for 6 to 10 minutes, or until they can be pierced easily with a knife.

3. In a small bowl, combine the butter, mustard, peppers, onion or shallot, tarragon, parsley, salt, and black pepper; set aside.

4. Clean the asparagus, and snap off and discard the woody bases. Carefully cut the potatoes into quarters. Add the potatoes, asparagus, and olive oil to a large sealable plastic bag. Close the bag and shake to coat the vegetables. Pour the potatoes and asparagus out of the bag into a 9" × 13" nonstick baking pan. Sprinkle salt and freshly ground black pepper over the top.

5. Evenly spread the butter mixture over the top of the turkey cutlets. Place the cutlets on top of the potatoes and asparagus. Bake for 15 to 20 minutes, or until the turkey is baked through and the asparagus is tender.

Pampering Picky Eaters

If you have someone in your family who doesn't want one food to touch another, you can bake this recipe in three separate baking dishes. Treat them with nonstick spray and put the turkey cutlets in one, the potatoes in another, and the asparagus in the third. It defeats the one-pot concept, but it will probably keep your life simpler.

Thai Turkey and Slaw

This is a dish that is a great way to take advantage of leftover turkey; however, it does require one pot and a bowl. You can save time by using coleslaw mix instead of shredding the cabbage.

Serves 4

2–3 tablespoons Thai green curry paste

¼ cup dry white wine

½ cup unsweetened coconut milk

2 cups cooked turkey, chopped

¼ cup rice or rice wine vinegar

½ teaspoon granulated sugar

6 green onions

2 cups savoy cabbage, napa cabbage, bok choy, or gai choi, finely shredded

3 tablespoons unsalted dry-roasted cashew halves or dry-roasted peanuts, chopped

1. In a large skillet, stir together green curry paste and wine. Stir over medium-high heat for 1 to 2 minutes or until most of the liquid is gone. Stir in the coconut milk and bring to a boil. Add the turkey. Reduce the heat and continue to cook, uncovered, for about 1 to 2 minutes or until the sauce thickens.

2. In a serving bowl, stir together the vinegar and sugar; whisk until the sugar dissolves. Using a sharp knife, cut the green onions lengthwise into thin slivers. Add the green onions, cabbage, and cashews or peanuts to the bowl and toss to mix.

3. To serve, divide the turkey and sauce between 4 individual plates and serve the slaw on the side.

Thai Turkey and Slaw Finger Food

Top baby romaine lettuce leaves with a little of the Thai slaw and a dab of the turkey-curry-nut mixture for some super-easy appetizers. If you prefer to work harder, serve the slaw and turkey-curry-nut mixture in pouches of lettuce instead.

Making a Coconut Milk Substitute

If you don't have coconut milk on hand, make a good substitute by mixing unsweetened flaked coconut with an equal amount of milk and simmering the mixture for 2 minutes, or until it begins to foam; strain and use in any recipe that calls for coconut milk.

Slow-Cooked Turkey Kielbasa Stew

If you're using reduced-sodium broth, start out with about ½ teaspoon each of salt and pepper. If the broth is not reduced-sodium, skip the salt altogether and taste for seasoning before serving.

Place the ingredients in a 4-quart slow cooker. Cover and cook on low for 8 to 10 hours or on high for 4 to 5 hours.

Serves 4–5

4 cups coarsely chopped cabbage

4 medium russet potatoes, peeled and cubed

1 1-pound bag baby carrots

1 pound fully cooked turkey kielbasa, sliced

½ teaspoon dried basil, crushed

½ teaspoon dried thyme, crushed

Salt and freshly ground black pepper to taste

2 14-ounce cans reduced-sodium chicken broth

Make Lime for Turkey Bake

Heat-and-eat rice and wild rice are available on the supermarket shelves. Some varieties are also available in the freezer case. This dish is good served with rice or even with dried chow mein noodles. Add a tossed salad or coleslaw and you have a complete meal.

1. Marinate the turkey cutlets in the lime juice for 30 minutes.

2. Preheat oven to 350°F.

3. Add the oil to a deep ovenproof skillet and bring to temperature over medium heat. Add the turkey cutlets to the oil. Sprinkle them with salt, pepper, and paprika. Brown on both sides. Add the olives, onion, green pepper, red pepper, and orange juice.

4. Cover and bake for 45 minutes. Serve with the pan juices.

Serves 4

4 turkey breast cutlets

Juice from 1 lime (about ⅓ cup)

1–2 tablespoons extra-virgin olive oil

Salt to taste

Freshly ground pepper to taste

1 teaspoon paprika

1 15-ounce can pitted black olives

1 large yellow onion, chopped

1 medium green pepper, seeded and sliced

1 medium red pepper, seeded and sliced

1½ cups orange juice

Polynesian Turkey and Noodles

Be sure to have soy sauce, toasted slivered almonds or chopped dry-roasted peanuts, and toasted sesame oil as condiments at the table. This dish also tastes great with crunchy dried chow mein noodles.

1. In a Dutch oven, cook the egg noodles according to the package directions. Drain in a colander; set aside and keep warm.

2. Add the egg to a small bowl and beat lightly. Put ¼ cup cornstarch in another bowl. Dip each chunk of turkey in the egg, and then roll it in the cornstarch. Add the oil to the Dutch oven and bring it to temperature over medium heat; brown the turkey pieces in the oil. Remove them with a slotted spoon and let them rest atop the egg noodles in the colander.

3. Add enough water to the reserved pineapple juice to make 1 cup; carefully add it to the oil in the Dutch oven along with the sugar, vinegar, and green pepper. Bring to a boil, stirring constantly. Reduce the heat and simmer for 2 minutes. Blend 2 tablespoons of cornstarch with the cold water and add it to the pineapple juice mixture. Heat, stirring constantly, until it thickens and boils; boil for 1 additional minute. Stir in the pineapple chunks, soy sauce, carrots, and turkey. Cook until all the ingredients are heated through.

4. To serve, either divide the noodles between serving plates and spoon the turkey-pineapple mixture over the noodles or add the noodles to the turkey-pineapple mixture and gently stir to combine.

Chapter 6
Beef

Yankee Pot Roast

Serves 6

⅛ pound salt pork or bacon, cut into cubes

2 stalks celery, diced

3-pound chuck or English roast

Salt and freshly ground black pepper to taste

2 large yellow onions, quartered

1 1-pound bag baby carrots

2 cups beef broth

Water, if needed

4 tablespoons butter

4 tablespoons all-purpose flour

1 turnip, diced

6 medium russet potatoes, peeled and halved

New England cooking is traditionally plain and straightforward. If your family prefers a heartier flavor, add ½ to 1 cup of red wine in place of some of the broth, ½ teaspoon dried thyme, a bay leaf, and 2 cloves of sliced garlic.

1. Add the salt pork or bacon and the celery to the bottom of a 4-quart slow cooker. Place the roast on top of the pork and celery; salt and pepper to taste. Add the onions and baby carrots. Pour in the beef broth. Add water, if necessary, to cover the roast completely, making sure that the water level is not more than ¾ of the depth of the crock for the slow cooker. Cover and cook on low for 6 hours.

2. Uncover the slow cooker and increase the heat to high. Mix together the butter and flour to make a paste. Evenly distribute the paste into the beef broth in ½-teaspoon-sized pieces. Add the turnip and the potatoes. Cover and cook for 1 additional hour, or until the potatoes are done. Taste the broth for seasoning and stir in more salt and pepper if necessary.

Mocking the Maillard Reaction

Contrary to myth, searing meat before it's braised doesn't seal in the juices, but it does—through a process known as the Maillard reaction—enhance the flavor of the meat via a caramelization process. Using beef broth (or a combination of beef base and water) mimics that flavor and lets you skip the browning step.

Slow Cooker Beef Brisket
with Apples

*This is a rich dish. Serve it with a crusty bread and
a tossed salad with honey-mustard dressing.*

Add all the ingredients to a 4-quart slow cooker. Add additional water to just cover the meat if needed. Cook on low for 6 hours or until meat is tender.

Adding a Second Step

Brisket will be more tender if you allow it to cool in the broth, so this is a good dish to make the day before you plan to serve it. To reheat it, bake it for 45 minutes at 325°F.

Serves 6–8

3- or 4-pound beef brisket
1 large yellow onion,
    quartered
2 large cloves garlic, chopped
4 large cloves garlic, left
    whole
1 10-ounce jar apple jelly
3 tablespoons Dijon mustard
Salt and freshly ground
    pepper to taste
¾ teaspoon curry powder
⅓ cup dry white wine
1 cup apple juice
1 cup water

Slow Cooker Texas Chili

*Texas chili is traditionally made without kidney beans. You can add some if you
prefer it that way. Serve this dish with cornbread and a tossed salad.*

Add all the ingredients to a 4-quart slow cooker, and stir to combine. The liquid in your slow cooker should completely cover the meat and vegetables. If additional liquid is needed, add more crushed tomatoes, broth, or water. Cook on low for 6 to 8 hours. Taste for seasoning, and add more chili powder if desired.

Serves 6–8

¼ pound bacon, diced
1 stalk celery, finely chopped
1 large carrot, peeled and
    finely chopped
2-pound chuck roast, cubed
2 large yellow onions, diced
6 cloves garlic, diced
6 jalapeño peppers, seeded
    and diced
Salt and freshly ground
    pepper to taste
4 tablespoons chili powder
1 teaspoon Mexican oregano
1 teaspoon ground cumin
OPTIONAL: 1 teaspoon light
    brown sugar
1 28-ounce can diced
    tomatoes
1 cup beef broth

Baked Apple Butter Steak
with Sweet Potatoes

Serves 4–6

Nonstick cooking spray
½ cup apple juice or water
¼ cup apple butter
2 tablespoons soy sauce
2 tablespoons dry sherry
½ teaspoon fresh ginger,
    grated
2 green onions, finely
    chopped
1½-pound sirloin steak, thick-
    cut
1 12-ounce bag frozen
    Brussels sprouts, thawed
2 large sweet potatoes,
    peeled and diced
Salt and freshly ground
    pepper to taste

*If you prefer your steak very rare, you can either add it to the pan 20 minutes
into the baking time or cook the Brussels sprouts and sweet potatoes in the
microwave and bake and broil the steak separately.*

1. Preheat the oven to 375°F. Treat a 9" × 13" nonstick baking pan with
   nonstick spray. Pour the apple juice or water into the pan.

2. In a small bowl, mix together the apple butter, soy sauce, sherry, ginger,
   and onion. Put the steak in the center of the pan and spread the apple
   butter mixture over the top of the meat. Arrange the Brussels sprouts
   and sweet potato pieces around the steak. Salt and pepper to taste.

3. Cover and bake for 45 minutes, or until steak reaches desired doneness
   and the potatoes are tender.

4. If you wish, uncover and put under the broiler for a couple minutes to
   glaze the sauce on top of the meat.

Chili Con Carne

Chili powder is available in mild, regular, and hot varieties. If the chili still isn't spicy enough to suit your tastes, you can punch up the dish by adding some chopped jalapeño peppers or hot sauce.

Bring the oil to temperature over medium heat in a Dutch oven. Add the hamburger, onion, chili power, and cumin. When the meat is cooked and the onions are transparent, drain any excess fat from the pan. Add the remaining ingredients and stir to combine. Lower the heat, cover, and simmer for 1–2 hours, stirring occasionally. Taste and adjust seasoning if necessary before serving.

Fiesta Chili Buffet

Have bowls of these condiments lined up so that family and guests can top their chili: crushed corn chips, shredded Cheddar cheese, cooked rice, shredded lettuce, chopped green pepper, sliced black olives, chopped tomatoes, diced onion or chopped green onions, toasted pecans or chopped peanuts, shredded coconut, and salsa.

Serves 4–6

2 tablespoons peanut oil
1 pound lean hamburger
1 large yellow onion, chopped
3 tablespoons chili powder
1 teaspoon ground cumin
3 cloves garlic, diced
1 tablespoon Worcestershire sauce
1 28-ounce can chopped tomatoes
1 large green pepper, seeded and chopped
1 15-ounce can kidney beans, rinsed and drained
Salt and freshly ground pepper to taste
OPTIONAL: 1 teaspoon granulated or light brown sugar

Tzimmes

This dish looks like you slaved in the kitchen all day, but aside from the labor of readying the ingredients and removing the pan from the oven a couple of times, your time is free to get yourself ready to greet your guests.

Serves 8

4-pound beef brisket
Salt and freshly ground black
  pepper to taste
1 large yellow onion,
  chopped
2 stalks celery, chopped
¼ cup fresh parsley, chopped
3 cups beef broth
3 tablespoons fresh lemon
  juice
3 whole cloves
1½" piece cinnamon stick
4 large sweet potatoes,
  peeled and quartered
1 1-pound bag baby carrots
1 12-ounce box pitted prunes
1 tablespoon honey
2 tablespoons white or white
  wine vinegar
OPTIONAL: 2 tablespoons butter

1. Preheat oven to 475°F.

2. Place the brisket fatty side up on a rack in a large roasting pan. Salt and pepper to taste. Bake for 25 minutes to brown the meat. Remove the meat, leaving it on the rack, and set aside.

3. Add the onion, celery, and parsley to the pan. Place the brisket directly on top of the vegetables. Add the broth, lemon juice, cloves, and cinnamon. Cover the pan, reduce the oven temperature to 300°F, and bake for 2½ hours.

4. Take the pan out of the oven and remove the cover. Add the sweet potatoes, carrots, and prunes to the pan. Mix together the honey and the vinegar and pour over the meat. Cover and return to the oven; bake for an additional 1½ hours.

5. Remove from the oven and let the meat rest, covered, for 15 minutes before serving. Remove the cover; adjust the salt and pepper seasoning if necessary. Carve the meat. Serve with the vegetables and the sauce that has formed in the pan. For a richer sauce, after you remove the meat and vegetables to a serving platter, whisk the butter into the pan juices 1 teaspoon at a time before spooning it over the dish.

Recipe Substitutions

Three tablespoons of lemon juice is equivalent to the juice of one lemon. Alternatively, you can use Minute Maid fresh lemon juice, available in the freezer case. If you don't have stick cinnamon on hand, substitute ½ teaspoon of ground cinnamon.

Beef with Whole Grain Spaghetti

If you don't have leftover roast beef on hand, you can cut up a pound of sirloin steak and sauté it along with the onions in the olive oil before you add the rest of the sauce ingredients.

1. In a large saucepan, cook the pasta according to the package directions. Drain the pasta in a colander; transfer to a covered oven-safe bowl, and keep warm in the oven.

2. Add the olive oil to the same saucepan, and bring to temperature over medium heat. Add the onion, garlic, and crushed red pepper flakes; sauté for 5 minutes or until the onion is tender, stirring occasionally.

3. Add the beef, undrained tomatoes, red peppers, balsamic vinegar, salt, and pepper to the pan. Heat through. Add the hot pasta to the pan along with the arugula or spinach and parsley; toss to combine. Top with the Romano cheese. Serve immediately.

Serves 4

4 ounces dried whole grain or whole wheat spaghetti

1 tablespoon extra-virgin olive oil

1 medium yellow onion, diced

4 cloves garlic, minced

¼ teaspoon dried crushed red pepper flakes

12 ounces cooked roast beef, cut into bite-sized pieces

1 14½-ounce can diced tomatoes with Italian herbs

1 cup bottled roasted red sweet peppers, drained and coarsely chopped

1 tablespoon balsamic vinegar

Salt to taste

½ teaspoon freshly ground black pepper

2 cups fresh baby arugula or spinach leaves

1 tablespoon snipped fresh Italian flat-leaf parsley

1 ounce Romano cheese, grated or shaved

Enchilada Chili

Serves 6

1½-pound boneless beef
    chuck roast, cut into bite-
    sized pieces
1 15-ounce can pinto and/or
    red kidney beans, rinsed
    and drained
1 14½-ounce can diced
    tomatoes, undrained
1 10½-ounce can condensed
    beef broth
1 10-ounce can enchilada
    sauce
1 large yellow onion, chopped
2 teaspoons bottled minced
    garlic
½ cup water
2½ tablespoons fine cornmeal
2 tablespoons fresh cilantro,
    snipped
2 ounces queso blanco or
    Monterey jack cheese,
    shredded

This chili can be served as a dip. After step 2, reduce the heat to low and stir in the cheese; continue to stir until the cheese is melted. Reduce the heat setting to warm. Serve with baked corn tortilla chips.

1. Add the beef, beans, tomatoes, broth, enchilada sauce, onion, and garlic to a 4-quart slow cooker. Cover and cook on low for 8 hours.

2. In a small bowl, whisk the water and cornmeal together; stir into the chili. Cover and cook on high for an additional 15 to 30 minutes, or until the chili is thickened.

3. Top each serving with the snipped cilantro and cheese.

Slow-Roasted Sirloin Dinner

Slow roasting is the perfect way to get a beef sirloin tip roast to a succulent rare or medium-rare. Thinly sliced leftovers are perfect for sandwiches.

1. Preheat oven to 200°F.

2. To ensure the roast cooks evenly, tie it into an even form using butcher's twine. Mix together the salt, pepper, garlic powder, onion powder, cumin, thyme, and paprika. Pat the seasoning mixture on all sides of the roast. Heat a medium-sized roasting pan over medium-high heat. Add the oil and bring to temperature; place the roast in the pan and sear it for 3 minutes on all sides, or until brown.

3. Arrange the turnips, parsnips, potatoes, carrots, and sprouts around the roast. Distribute the garlic and arrange the onion slices over the vegetables. Drizzle with olive oil. Lightly salt and pepper.

4. Roast, basting occasionally with the pan juices, for 3 hours or until an instant-read thermometer inserted in the center registers 130°F for rare. Remove to a serving platter; cover and let rest for about 15 minutes.

5. Put the pan on the stovetop over two burners on medium-high heat. Add the wine and water. Bring to a boil, stirring to scrape up any browned bits from the bottom of the pan. Cook for about 5 minutes, or until reduced by half. To serve, thinly slice the roast across the grain. Serve drizzled with some of the pan juices.

Jelly Juiced-Up Au Jus

For a different taste, only add the water and omit the wine in step 5. Bring to a boil, scraping the bottom of the pan and stirring frequently; cook until the juices and water are reduced by half. Lower the heat and whisk in a tablespoon of redcurrant jelly; taste and add more jelly if needed. Whisk in 2 tablespoons of butter, 1 teaspoon at a time.

Serves 8

4-pound beef sirloin tip roast
1 teaspoon kosher or sea salt
½ teaspoon freshly ground pepper
1 teaspoon garlic powder
1 teaspoon onion powder
1 teaspoon ground cumin
1 teaspoon dried thyme leaves, crushed
½ teaspoon sweet paprika
2 tablespoons extra-virgin olive oil
2 turnips, peeled and cut into 2" pieces
2 parsnips, peeled and cut into 2" pieces
4 large red potatoes, peeled and quartered
1 1-pound bag baby carrots
1 12-ounce package frozen Brussels sprouts
8 cloves garlic, halved lengthwise
2 large yellow onions, sliced
Extra-virgin olive oil to taste
Salt and freshly ground black pepper to taste
½ cup dry red wine
1 cup water

Pot Roast
with Fruit Sauce

Serves 8–10

2 cloves garlic, minced

1 teaspoon dried sage,
crushed

½ teaspoon salt

½ teaspoon freshly ground
black pepper

⅛ teaspoon cayenne pepper

3-pound boneless beef chuck
pot roast

2 tablespoons vegetable oil

1 cup beef broth

1 large yellow onion,
quartered

1 cup pitted prunes, halved

2 large apples, peeled, cored
and cut into thick slices

1 pound parsnips, peeled and
cut into ½" pieces

1 1-pound bag baby carrots

½ cup cold water

¼ cup all-purpose flour

1 tablespoon balsamic
vinegar

Parsnips go well with the gravy that results from this dish, but you can substitute 8 medium red potatoes, washed and halved or quartered, if you prefer.

1. In a small bowl, stir together the garlic, sage, salt, black pepper, and cayenne. Spread the garlic mixture over both sides of the meat. Add the oil to a 6-quart Dutch oven and bring it to temperature over medium heat; add the roast and brown it on all sides. Drain off the fat. Pour the broth over the roast and add the onion. Increase the heat to medium-high and bring to a boil. Tightly cover and reduce the heat; simmer for 1½ hours.

2. Add the fruit and vegetables to the pan. Add some water to the pan if needed to cover all the ingredients. Increase heat to return it to boiling, cover, and reduce the heat; simmer for 30 minutes or until the parsnips, carrots, and apples are tender. With a slotted spoon, transfer the meat, fruit, and vegetables to a serving platter.

3. Skim the fat off the juices that remain in the pan. Add water if necessary to bring the pan juices to 1½ cups. Bring to a boil over medium-high heat. In a small bowl, whisk together the cold water and flour until smooth. Slowly whisk the flour mixture into the boiling pan juices. Boil for 1 minute, then reduce the heat to medium and continue to cook and stir until thickened. Taste for seasoning and add salt and pepper if necessary. Stir in the balsamic vinegar. Serve the gravy over the roast, vegetables, and fruit.

Add Some Germanic Flair

Rather than adding the balsamic vinegar at the end, stir several finely crushed ginger snaps into the pan juices before you add the flour mixture. Once it's thickened, stir a teaspoon of red wine vinegar into the gravy.

Herbed Pot Roast

You can stretch this meal to serve more by also preparing a 12-ounce package of steam-in-the-bag frozen green beans or Brussels sprouts. Mix them with the potatoes and carrots.

1. Add the celery, roast, salt, pepper, onion, garlic, broth, vinegar, and thyme to a 4-quart slow cooker. Cover and cook on low for 6 hours.

2. Wash the potatoes and peel off a strip of the skin from around each one. Add to the slow cooker along with the baby carrots. Cover and cook for an additional 2 hours on low.

3. If you wish to thicken the pan juices to make gravy, use a slotted spoon to transfer the meat and vegetables to a serving platter; keep warm. Increase the temperature on the slow cooker to high and bring 1½ cup of the strained pan juices to a boil. In a small bowl, use a fork to blend together the butter and flour. Whisk the flour mixture into the boiling juices, 1 teaspoon at a time. Once you've added all of the mixture, boil for 1 minute and then reduce the setting to low. Stir and simmer for 2 to 3 more minutes, or until the mixture is thickened. Taste for seasoning and add salt and pepper if desired.

Iranian Beef Roast

In step 1, omit the thyme and add a small can of diced tomatoes, ⅓ cup fresh snipped cilantro, ¾ teaspoon freshly ground black pepper, ¾ teaspoon ground cumin, ½ teaspoon ground coriander, ¼ teaspoon ground cloves, and a pinch each of ground cardamom, ground nutmeg, and ground cinnamon. In step 2, substitute thawed frozen green beans for the carrots.

Serves 8

2 stalks celery, diced
3-pound boneless beef chuck roast
Salt and freshly ground black pepper to taste
2 large yellow onions, quartered
2 cloves garlic, minced
2 cups beef broth
¼ cup red wine vinegar
1 teaspoon dried thyme, crushed
8 medium red potatoes
2 pounds baby carrots
OPTIONAL: ¼ cup butter, softened
OPTIONAL: ¼ cup all-purpose flour

Roast Beef
with Horseradish Potatoes

Horseradish gives this beef dish an extra flavor dimension.

෴

Serves 6–8

⅓ cup prepared horseradish

2 tablespoons extra-virgin olive oil

1 teaspoon freshly ground black pepper

1 teaspoon dried thyme, crushed

½ teaspoon salt

1 3-pound boneless beef chuck roast

2 celery stalks, halved

¼ cup dry white wine or beef broth

1¼ cups beef broth

2 pounds small red potatoes

OPTIONAL: water as needed

1 1-pound package baby carrots

OPTIONAL: 2 tablespoons all-purpose flour

OPTIONAL: 2 tablespoons butter

1. In a small bowl, mix together the horseradish, oil, pepper, thyme, and salt. Trim the fat from the roast and cut it into 2" cubes. Rub half of the horseradish mixture into meat. Add the seasoned roast, celery, white wine, and broth to a 4-quart slow cooker. Cover and cook for 1 to 2 hours on high, or until the celery is limp.

2. Wash the potatoes and peel off a thin strip of the skin from around each one. In a small bowl or a resealable plastic bag, mix the potatoes together with the remaining horseradish sauce.

3. Discard the celery. Add more water, if necessary, to bring the liquid level up to just the top of the meat. Add the potatoes and carrots to the cooker. Cover and cook on low for 4 to 6 hours, or until the meat is tender and the vegetables are cooked through. Serve warm.

4. If you wish to thicken the pan juices, remove the meat and vegetables to a serving platter. Cover with aluminum foil and keep warm. Turn the slow cooker to the high setting and bring the juices to a boil. Mix together the flour and butter, and whisk it into the boiling pan juices, 1 teaspoon at a time.

Luck of the Leftovers: Horseradish - Hearty Beef Stew

If you have leftovers, you can make a hearty beef stew by cutting the meat into bite-sized pieces and adding them to the thickened pan juices. Add a tablespoon or two of ketchup or some hot sauce for an extra punch of flavor, if desired. Reheat and serve with hard rolls, or serve over biscuits.

Slow-Cooked Mushroom Steak and Vegetables

*You can easily make this dish into a complete meal by serving it with
ready-made mashed potatoes. Heat the potatoes in the microwave.
Add your choice of microwave steam-in-bag vegetables or a salad.*

Trim the fat from the steak; cut the meat into 8 serving-size pieces. Add the oil to a 4-quart slow cooker and bring to temperature on the high setting. Add the meat and brown it while you ready the remaining ingredients. Combine the beef gravy and mushroom gravy mix. Remove the meat from the cooker and spread the onions over the bottom of the crock. Place the meat on top of the onions, and arrange the mushrooms over the top of the meat. Pour the gravy mixture over the top. Lower the temperature to the low setting and cook for 8 to 10 hours.

Serves 8

2 pounds boneless beef round
    steak, cut ¾" thick
1 tablespoon vegetable oil
1 12-ounce jar beef gravy
1 1-ounce package dry
    mushroom gravy mix
2 medium yellow onions,
    sliced
3 cups cleaned and sliced
    fresh button or cremini
    mushrooms

Slow-Cooked Beef Stew
with Parsnip and Raisins

*With this recipe, you have a choice: You can either stir the olives and raisins in
just before serving or you can have them at the table as condiments.*

1. Add the oil to a 4-quart slow cooker and bring to temperature over high heat. Toss meat in flour. Add half of the meat to the slow cooker and sauté until brown; push the meat to the side and add remaining meat, stirring to coat all the meat in the hot oil. Wipe out any excess fat.

2. Add the carrots, parsnips, onion, tomatoes, broth, garlic, bay leaf, thyme, and pepper to the cooker; stir to combine. Reduce the heat setting to low; cover and cook for 8 to 10 hours.

3. Remove and discard the bay leaf. Stir in the olives and raisins. Serve warm.

Serves 4–6

2 tablespoons vegetable oil
2 tablespoons all-purpose
    flour
1½-pound beef chuck roast,
    cut into 1" cubes
1 1-pound bag baby carrots
2 large parsnips, peeled and
    sliced into ½" pieces
1 large yellow onion, roughly
    chopped
1 14½-ounce can diced
    tomatoes, undrained
1 14-ounce can beef broth
2 cloves garlic, minced
1 bay leaf
1 teaspoon dried thyme,
    crushed
¼ teaspoon freshly ground
    black pepper
½ cup almond- or pimiento-
    stuffed green olives
⅓ cup golden raisins

Grilled Herbed Tenderloin
with Vegetables

Serves 4

2 cloves garlic, minced

1 tablespoon dried basil

2 teaspoons dried thyme

1 teaspoon dried rosemary

1 teaspoon dried mint leaves

2 tablespoons extra-virgin
olive oil

½ teaspoon salt

½ teaspoon freshly ground
black pepper

4 4-ounce beef tenderloin
steaks, cut 1" thick

2 large yellow tomatoes, cut
in half crosswise

1 pound asparagus spears,
cleaned and trimmed

You can "grill" this meal indoors. Grill the steaks on high for 3 to 5 minutes; remove to a serving platter and keep warm. Lower the grill temperature to medium and grill the vegetables until the tomatoes are heated through and the asparagus is crisp-tender, about 2 to 4 minutes.

1. In a small bowl, mix together the garlic, basil, thyme, rosemary, mint, and oil. Coat both sides of the steaks and the cut half of the tomatoes with the mixture.

2. Evenly coat the asparagus with the remaining garlic-herb mixture. Divide the mixture among four pieces of aluminum foil and fold the foil over to make a packet.

3. Bring the grill to temperature. Add the asparagus packets to the back of the grill. Grill the steaks over direct medium heat for 5 minutes. Turn the steaks and asparagus packet; add the tomatoes to the grill, cut-side down. Grill until the steaks reach the desired doneness: another 2 minutes for medium-rare or 3 to 4 minutes for medium.

Recipe Alternative: Fresh Herbs Marinade

Add 2 peeled garlic cloves, ¼ cup fresh basil, 2 tablespoons fresh thyme leaves, 1 tablespoon fresh rosemary, and 1 tablespoon fresh mint leaves to a food processor. Cover and process until the herbs are chopped. With the food processor running, add 2 tablespoons extra-virgin olive oil in a thin, steady stream. Scrape the sides of the bowl, and stir in salt and freshly ground black pepper to taste.

Chapter 7
Pork

Cranberry Roast Pork
with Sweet Potatoes

Serves 6–8

3-pound pork butt roast
Salt and freshly ground
  pepper to taste
1 16-ounce can sweetened
  whole cranberries
1 medium yellow onion,
  chopped
¾ cup orange juice
¼ teaspoon ground
  cinnamon
¼ teaspoon ground cloves
3 large sweet potatoes,
  peeled and quartered
OPTIONAL: 1 tablespoon
  cornstarch
OPTIONAL: 2 tablespoons cold
  water

This recipe calls for a slow cooker, but if you prefer, you can braise the dish, covered, in the oven at 325°F for 3 hours, or until the internal temperature of the meat registers 175°F. Either way, the meat will be pull-apart tender.

1. Place the pork, fat-side up, in a 4-quart slow cooker. Salt and pepper to taste. Combine the cranberries, onion, orange juice, cinnamon, and cloves in a bowl or large measuring cup; stir to mix and then pour over the pork roast. Arrange the sweet potatoes around the meat. Cover and cook on low for 5½ to 6 hours.

2. To serve with a thickened sauce, transfer the meat and sweet potatoes to a serving platter. Cover and keep warm. Skim the fat off of the pan juices, leaving about 2 cups of juice in the cooker. Bring to a boil on the high setting. Combine the cornstarch with the water. Whisk into the boiling juices. Reduce the temperature setting to low and continue to cook and stir for an additional 2 minutes, or until the sauce is thickened and bubbly.

Pamper the Pork

Many slow cooker recipes can be changed from cooking on low to cooking on high simply by dividing the cooking time in half. It's trickier with pork, especially when cooking with a sugar-based or fruit sauce. If the dish scorches, the whole taste will change; if you cook on high, monitor it carefully during the last hour of cooking.

Pork and Vegetables Sautéed
with Apples

Serves 4–6

2 pounds pork steak,
    deboned and cut into
    thin strips
2 tablespoons soy sauce
2 tablespoons dry sherry
¼ teaspoon freshly grated
    ginger
3 tablespoons peanut oil
1 large yellow onion, diced
3 Golden Delicious apples,
    peeled and thinly sliced
4 cloves garlic, thinly sliced
1 12-ounce package steam-
    in-the-bag stir-fry mixed
    vegetables
OPTIONAL: 1 teaspoon toasted
    sesame oil
Freshly ground black pepper
    to taste
4 green onions, chopped

*Some people love the taste of ginger; others find it tastes medicinal. If
you fall within the "love it" category, feel free to increase the amount
of ginger according to your personal taste.*

1. Place the pork steak, soy sauce, sherry, and ginger in a resealable plastic bag. Shake to evenly coat the meat. Let marinate in the bag for 15 minutes.

2. Add the oil to a wok or large, deep nonstick skillet and bring it to temperature over medium-high heat. Drain the marinade from the meat; add the meat to the skillet and sauté for 3 minutes. Add the onion and continue to sauté for another 3 minutes, or until the meat is done and onion is transparent. Add the apple slices and sauté until the apples begin to turn brown. Push the contents of the pan to the side and add the garlic; sauté the garlic for 30 seconds before stirring it into the meat mixture.

3. While the meat and apples are cooking, microwave the stir-fry vegetables according to the package directions for crisp-tender. Drain off any liquid from the vegetables. Add the vegetables, toasted sesame oil (if using), and pepper to the pan and toss with the meat mixture. Garnish with the chopped green onion.

Milk-Baked Pork Tenderloin Meal

*The meat juices and milk in this dish magically combine to create a
succulent gravy, so all that's left to do is carry the food to the table.*

1. Preheat the oven to 350°F. Treat an 8" square Pyrex baking dish with
   nonstick spray.

2. Mix together the brown sugar, ginger, and ground mustard. Spread it
   over the meat. Lay the meat flat in the baking dish. Season with salt and
   pepper to taste. Pour the milk over the meat.

3. Wash the potatoes. Prick each with a fork. Rub each potato with 1 teaspoon of the butter or oil, and wrap in individual pieces of aluminum
   foil. Place the potatoes in the dish with the meat. Bake for 1½ hours, or
   until all the milk liquids evaporate.

Stuffed Acorn Squash

*The hash browns, peas, and sausage will be easier to mix together if the hash
browns and peas are still frozen (broken apart) and the sausage is at room
temperature.*

1. Preheat the oven to 350°F.

2. Halve a squash lengthwise, remove seeds, and lay skin-side down in a roasting pan. Cut the squash in half lengthwise and scrape out the seeds.

3. In a bowl, mix together the hash browns, peas, and sausage. Divide
   the mixture between the halves. Drizzle 1½ teaspoons of the oil over
   each of the squash halves. Season with salt and pepper to taste. Tightly
   cover the pan with heavy-duty foil. Bake for 1 hour. Remove the foil.
   Return the pan to the oven and bake for another 15 minutes, or until
   the squash is tender and the sausage is cooked through.

Baked Bratwurst in Beer

This makes a great football night supper for those times when you're watching the game at home. It's an easy recipe to double or triple. Simply increase the size of the pan. The baking times won't change. Serve with a salad or coleslaw.

Serves 4

4 bratwurst

4 medium red potatoes, peeled and quartered

1 2-pound bag sauerkraut, rinsed and drained

1 large yellow onion, roughly chopped

1 12-ounce can of beer, room temperature

4 hot dog buns

Stone-ground or Bavarian-style mustard to taste

1. Preheat oven to 425°F. Treat an ovenproof Dutch oven with nonstick spray and lay the bratwurst in the pan. Bake uncovered for 15 minutes.

2. Remove the pan from the oven and arrange the potato wedges around the meat. Add the sauerkraut and onion over the potatoes and meat. Pour the beer into the pan, being careful that it doesn't foam up. Cover and bake for 45 minutes. Remove the cover and bake for an additional 15 minutes, or until the potatoes are tender and much of the beer has evaporated.

3. Serve the bratwurst on buns generously spread with mustard; add some drained sauerkraut and onions to each sandwich. Serve the potatoes and additional sauerkraut on the side.

Baked Bratwurst in Beer for a Crowd

If you'll be serving the bratwurst for a casual meal with potato chips on the side, omit the potatoes. There will be enough sauerkraut for 8 to 12 sandwiches. Add the desired amount of bratwurst and otherwise follow the baking instructions.

Swedish Pork Loin

Serves 8

15 pitted prunes
12 pitted dried apricots
½ cup boiling water
1 cup chicken broth
1 cup dry white wine or apple
    juice
3½-pound pork loin, trimmed
    of fat and silver skin
4 large sweet potatoes,
    peeled and quartered
Salt and freshly ground
    pepper to taste
1 tablespoon cornstarch
2 tablespoons cold water

*Leaner cuts of meat can get dry in a slow cooker. A pork sirloin roast is a
good compromise; it's low in fat, yet it cooks up tender and moist. For gravy
instead of sauce, mix the reduced pan juices with heavy cream.*

1. Add the prunes and apricots to a 4-quart slow cooker. Pour the boiling water over the dried fruit; cover and let set for 15 minutes.

2. Add the chicken broth, wine, pork loin, and sweet potatoes. Cover and cook on low for 5 to 6 hours, or until the internal temperature of the roast is 155°F.

3. Remove the meat and sweet potatoes from the cooker; cover and keep warm.

4. Turn the cooker to high. Use an immersion blender to purée the fruit. In a small bowl, mix the cornstarch into the cold water. Once the liquid in the slow cooker comes to a boil, slowly whisk in the cornstarch liquid. Reduce the heat to low and simmer the sauce for several minutes, stirring occasionally, until thickened. Place the pork roast on a serving platter and carve into 8 slices. Arrange the sweet potatoes around the pork. Ladle the sauce over the meat. Serve immediately.

Roast Pork Loin
with Apples

Herbes de Provence is a mixture of equal amounts of thyme, savory, marjoram, and oregano. It sometimes also includes some sage, rosemary, dried lavender flowers, and/or fennel seeds.

1. Preheat oven to 375°F.

2. Mix the salt, pepper, and herbes de Provence together and rub it into the meat. Add the butter and oil to a 9-quart Dutch oven, and bring to temperature over medium-high heat. Add the roast and brown it for 2 minutes on all sides, or for about 8 minutes. Remove the meat from the pan and arrange the apple slices over the bottom of the pan. Sprinkle the apples with the sugar. Nestle the meat on top of the apples. Arrange the potato wedges around the meat. Season the potatoes with salt and pepper to taste.

3. Cover and bake for 30 minutes. Remove the cover and baste the meat with the pan juices. Continue to bake uncovered for 45 minutes, or until the internal temperature of the roast is 150°F. Remove the roast to a serving platter and tent with aluminum foil; let rest for 10 minutes.

4. Slice the pork crosswise into 8 slices. Arrange the apples and potatoes around the roast. Ladle the pan juices over the roast. Serve immediately, along with microwave steam-in-the bag Brussels sprouts or baby peas tossed with butter, a tossed salad with your choice of dressing, and dinner rolls.

Pan Size

The amount of air space between the food and the lid may add to the cooking time, but when in doubt, go bigger. It saves you the aggravation of having to move the ingredients to a bigger pot if the one you picked doesn't have enough room to hold all of the ingredients, and it prevents boil-overs in the oven.

Serves 8

1 teaspoon kosher or sea salt

¼ teaspoon freshly ground black pepper

2 teaspoons herbes de Provence

4-pound pork loin, trimmed of fat and silver skin

2 tablespoons butter

1 tablespoon vegetable oil

3 large Golden Delicious apples, cored and cut into wedges

¼ teaspoon granulated sugar

4 large Yukon gold potatoes, peeled and quartered

Pork Steaks in Plum Sauce

Serves 4

12 pitted prunes
2 cups boiling water
OPTIONAL: ½ cup port
3 tablespoons vegetable oil
2 tablespoons all-purpose
    flour
½ teaspoon salt
¼ teaspoon freshly ground
    pepper to taste
4 4-ounce or larger pork
    steaks
2 large shallots, minced
3 tablespoons red wine
    vinegar
⅔ cup beef broth
1 tablespoon plum jam
1 tablespoon ketchup

The first part of the meal does take a little work, so go easy on yourself for the rest of it and serve the pork steak with baked potatoes, a microwave steam-in-the-bag vegetable, a tossed salad, and some dinner rolls.

1. At least 2 hours before you plan to cook the pork, put the prunes in a bowl and pour in the boiling water. Tightly cover with plastic wrap right away and set aside.

2. Before you begin cooking, drain the water from the prunes and mix them with the port (if using). Cover and allow the prunes to macerate.

3. Add the oil to a large nonstick skillet, and bring to temperature over medium heat. Put the flour, salt, and pepper in a resealable plastic bag; shake to mix. Add the pork steaks to the bag; shake to coat the steaks in the flour. When the oil is hot, lay the steaks flat in the pan. Cook until the meat is almost cooked through and the floured-surface touching the pan forms a crust, about 15 to 20 minutes; turn the steaks and cook until done, about another 10 to 15 minutes. Place crust-side up on a serving platter; set in a warm oven to keep warm.

4. Add the shallots to the pan and sauté for 30 seconds. Deglaze the pan with vinegar. Add the broth and bring to a gentle boil; cook for about 5 minutes or until the liquid is reduced by half. Whisk in the jam and ketchup. Stir until the jam is melted. Arrange the prunes and pour the sauce over the meat. Serve immediately.

Sensible Substitutions

Not a big fan of prunes? That's okay! Sugar Plum Jam is available from American Spoon Foods (www.spoon.com). Or, if you prefer, you can use blackcurrant jam or seedless blackberry jam instead. These alternate ingredients can also be used on your favorite sandwiches and snacks, unlike regular prunes.

Slow-Cooked Pork Roast

*This recipe makes enough for 12 sandwiches. You can also serve
it with mashed potatoes or along with steamed cabbage.*

Serves 12

1 tablespoon vegetable oil
1 3-pound pork roast
1 10½-ounce can French
　onion soup
1 cup ketchup
¼ cup cider vinegar
3 packed tablespoons light
　brown sugar
OPTIONAL: 12 sandwich rolls

1. Add the vegetable oil to a 4-quart slow cooker. Bring to temperature on the high setting. Add the pork roast, fat-side down. Cover and cook for 30 minutes. Turn the roast; cover and cook for another 30 minutes.

2. Mix together the soup, ketchup, vinegar, and brown sugar. Pour over the meat. Reduce the slow cooker setting to low, and cook covered for 8 hours, or until the meat pulls apart and registers 175°F in the center of the roast. Within the slow cooker, shred the meat using 2 forks, and mix it with the sauce. Remove the meat with a slotted spoon, and divide it between the sandwich rolls (if using).

Mexican Pork Steak

*Spicy Mexican tortilla filling doesn't always have to have a
tomato salsa base. If tortillas aren't to your taste, serve the meat
with country-fried potatoes and a salad.*

Serves 4

1–2 tablespoons peanut oil
1-pound boneless pork steak,
　cut into thin strips
2 cloves garlic, thinly sliced
1 small yellow onion, sliced
1 green pepper, seeded and
　diced
¼ teaspoon ground cumin
¼ teaspoon dried Mexican
　oregano
Salt and freshly ground black
　pepper to taste
OPTIONAL: cayenne pepper or
　dried red pepper flakes
　to taste
2 tablespoons beer
4 flour or corn tortillas, heated
OPTIONAL: refried beans, heated
OPTIONAL: shredded lettuce
OPTIONAL: sour cream
OPTIONAL: 2 green onions,
　chopped

1. Add the oil to a nonstick skillet and bring to temperature over medium-high heat. Sauté the pork for 2 to 3 minutes, and then add the garlic, onion, and green pepper. Continue to sauté until the onion is transparent and the pork is cooked through. Stir in the cumin, oregano, salt, black pepper, and cayenne or dried red pepper flakes (if using). Add the beer and cook until most of the moisture evaporates.

2. To fill the tortillas, spread refried beans on each tortilla. Top with the meat, shredded lettuce, sour cream, and green onion. Roll and eat like a burrito.

Pork and Vegetable Stir-Fry

3 boneless pork steaks, cut into thin strips

4 tablespoons soy sauce

3 tablespoons dry sherry or beer

2 teaspoons fresh ginger, grated

2 tablespoons peanut oil

2 cloves garlic, minced

2 medium yellow onions, diced

6 stalks celery, chopped

8 ounces fresh button mushrooms, cleaned and sliced

3 cups coleslaw mix

2 cups bean sprouts

½ cup chicken broth

½ teaspoon granulated sugar

1 tablespoon cornstarch

½ tablespoon toasted sesame oil

If you like to keep things simple, use the coleslaw mix. If you prefer to remain traditional, you can substitute a cup of chopped Chinese or napa cabbage and 2 cups of chopped bok choy for the coleslaw mix.

1. Put the pork steak strips in a resealable plastic bag along with 3 tablespoons of the soy sauce, the sherry or beer, and the ginger; seal and shake to mix. Marinate for 15 minutes.

2. Add 1 tablespoon of the peanut oil to a wok and bring to temperature over medium-high heat. Sauté the pork for 5 minutes, or until cooked through. Remove the pork from the pan and keep warm.

3. Add the remaining tablespoon of peanut oil to the wok. Add the garlic, onion, and celery; sauté for 3 minutes. Stir in the mushrooms, coleslaw mix, and bean sprouts. Sauté until the vegetables are crisp-tender. Stir the pork back into the vegetables.

4. In a small bowl, whisk together the remaining tablespoon of soy sauce, the chicken broth, sugar, and cornstarch. Add to the wok and stir until the mixture thickens and the cornstarch taste is cooked out of the liquids in the pan. Stir in the toasted sesame oil. Serve immediately.

Slow-Cooked Pork
with Apple and Prune Sauce

Serve this dish with some mashed potatoes and some steam-in-the-bag green beans.

Serves 6–8

12 pitted prunes
3 pounds boneless pork
    steaks, trimmed of fat
2 Granny Smith apples,
    peeled, cored, and sliced
¾ cup dry white wine or
    apple juice
¾ cup heavy cream
Salt and freshly ground
    pepper to taste
1 tablespoon red currant jelly
OPTIONAL: 1 tablespoon butter

1. Add the prunes, pork steaks, apple slices, wine or apple juice, and cream to a 4-quart slow cooker. Salt and pepper to taste. Cover and cook on low for 6 to 8 hours. Remove the meat and fruit to a serving platter and keep warm.

2. Bring the liquid in the cooker to a boil over the high setting. Reduce the setting to low and simmer until the mixture is reduced by half and thickened. Whisk in the redcurrant jelly. Taste for seasoning and add more salt and pepper if desired. Whisk in the butter 1 teaspoon at a time for a richer, glossier sauce. Ladle the sauce over the meat or pour it into a heated gravy boat.

Microwave Baked Potatoes

To serve 8, wash 8 medium baking potatoes and pierce each one twice with a knife. Arrange on a microwave-safe plate; microwave on high for 10 minutes. Test for doneness; microwave longer if necessary. Wrap each potato in foil until it's time to serve them. Have butter and sour cream available at the table.

Three-Cheese Polenta Gratin

12 ounces sweet or hot bulk Italian sausage

8 ounces fresh button or cremini mushrooms, cleaned and sliced

1 medium yellow onion, diced

2 cloves garlic, minced

2 cups purchased tomato-basil pasta sauce

1 tablespoon extra-virgin olive oil

1 24-ounce package prepared cornmeal mush

1 cup ricotta cheese

1 cup shredded mozzarella or provolone cheese

½ cup finely shredded Asiago cheese

OPTIONAL: fresh chopped basil to taste

Think of this dish as an improvisation of a deep-dish pizza, only with a polenta crust. Serve with a tossed salad dressed with Italian dressing.

1. Preheat oven to 400°F.

2. Add the sausage to a 3- or 4-quart ovenproof nonstick skillet; brown over medium-high heat, breaking apart the sausage as it cooks. When the sausage is cooked through, add the mushrooms, onion, and garlic. Lower the heat to medium and sauté until the onion is transparent. Drain off any excess oil and transfer to a bowl; mix with the pasta sauce.

3. Wipe out the pan and add the olive oil, turning the pan to evenly coat the bottom of the pan. Set the pan over low heat. Drain the liquid off of cornmeal mush; cut it into 1-inch-thick slices and arrange around the bottom of the pan. As the mush softens from the heat, spread it out evenly over the bottom of the pan to form a crust.

4. Spread the ricotta cheese over the crust. Top the ricotta cheese with the sausage sauce mixture. Spread the remaining cheeses over the top. Bake uncovered for 30 minutes, or until the cheese is melted, bubbling, and lightly golden brown. Remove from the oven and let stand for 10 minutes before cutting into 4 wedges to serve. Garnish with fresh basil, if desired.

Slow-Cooked Pork Lo Mein

You can steam the noodles by adding them along with the other ingredients in your slow cooker. If you prefer, you can prepare the noodles according to the package directions and add them already cooked to the dish.

1. Trim the fat from the pork and cut the meat into ¾-inch pieces. Add the pork, onions, carrots, teriyaki glaze, celery, water chestnuts, bamboo shoots, and ginger to a 4-quart slow cooker. Cover and cook on low for 7 hours.

2. Turn the cooker setting to high; add the sugar snap peas and broccoli. Cover and cook for 10 to 15 minutes, or until the snap peas are crisp-tender. Add the egg noodles and stir to mix. Reduce the setting to warm and cover; let steam for 30 minutes or until the pasta is done. Serve immediately. Sprinkle cashews over each serving.

Serves 6–8

1½ pounds boneless pork shoulder

2 medium yellow onions, sliced

2 cups frozen sliced carrots

1 12-ounce jar teriyaki glaze

1 cup thinly bias-sliced celery

1 8-ounce can sliced water chestnuts, drained

1 5-ounce can sliced bamboo shoots, drained

1 teaspoon grated fresh ginger

1 6-ounce package frozen sugar snap peas

1 cup broccoli florets

8 ounces dried egg noodles

½ cup cashew halves

Slow-Cooked Pork Stew

Serves 6–8

2 pounds boneless pork
    shoulder
1 tablespoon vegetable oil
1 pound tiny new potatoes,
    washed and quartered
1 cup chopped yellow onions
OPTIONAL: 2 fresh poblano
    peppers, seeded and cut
    into 1" pieces
OPTIONAL: 1 fresh jalapeño
    pepper, seeded and
    chopped
4 cloves garlic, minced
1 2-inch cinnamon stick
2 cups chicken broth
1 14½-ounce can diced
    tomatoes
1 tablespoon chili powder
1 teaspoon dried oregano,
    crushed
¼ teaspoon black pepper
OPTIONAL: ¼ cup snipped fresh
    cilantro or parsley

This stew is good served over cooked rice and garnished with strips of green onion. Only add the poblano and jalapeño peppers if you want a hot, spicy stew; otherwise, omit them entirely or substitute chopped green pepper.

1. Trim the fat from the pork and cut the meat into 1" cubes. Add the oil to a 4-quart or larger slow cooker and bring it to temperature over high. Add the pork; cover and let brown for 15 minutes. Stir the pork and brown for another 15 minutes. Drain off fat. Add the remaining ingredients except the cilantro or parsley; stir to combine. Reduce the heat to low; cover and cook on low for 8 hours.

2. Discard the cinnamon stick. Stir in additional chicken broth if the stew is too thick and bring it to temperature. Stir in the cilantro or parsley, if desired. Serve warm.

Hot Pepper Precautions

Wear gloves or sandwich bags over your hands when you clean and dice hot peppers. It's important to avoid having the peppers come into contact with your skin or your eyes. As an added precaution, wash your hands (don't forget underneath your fingernails) thoroughly with hot soapy water after your remove the gloves or sandwich bags.

Chapter 8
Ground Meat

Ground Pork and Eggplant Casserole

If you prefer, this dish will fit in a 2-quart baking dish, but using a 4-quart Dutch oven will give you plenty of room to mix the meat and vegetables together and let you do the stovetop cooking and baking in one pot.

Serves 8

2 pounds lean ground pork

2 tablespoons peanut or extra-virgin olive oil

2 large yellow onions, chopped

3 celery stalks, chopped

1 green pepper, seeded and chopped

4 medium eggplants, cut into ½" dice

6 cloves garlic, chopped

⅛ teaspoon dried thyme, crushed

1 tablespoon freeze-dried parsley

3 tablespoons tomato paste

OPTIONAL: 1 teaspoon hot sauce

2 teaspoons Worcestershire sauce

Salt and freshly ground pepper to taste

1 large egg, beaten

½ cup breadcrumbs

1 tablespoon melted butter

1. Preheat the oven to 350°F.

2. Bring the Dutch oven to temperature over medium-high heat. Add the ground pork and fry until done, breaking it apart as it cooks. Remove from the pan and keep warm.

3. Drain off and discard any pork fat from the pan; add the oil to the pan and bring to temperature over medium heat. Add the onion, celery, and green pepper; sauté until the onion is transparent. Add the garlic, eggplant, thyme, parsley, and tomato sauce. Stir to combine. Cover and sauté, stirring often, for 20 minutes, or until the vegetables are tender. Return the ground pork to the pan. Add the hot sauce (if using), Worcestershire sauce, salt, pepper, and egg; stir to combine. Sprinkle the breadcrumbs over the top and drizzle with the melted butter or oil. Bake for 40 minutes, or until the crumb topping is lightly browned and the casserole is hot in the center.

Why Freshly Ground Black Pepper?

Bottled ground black pepper contains anti-caking agents that can cause stomach upset for some people and can also change the flavor. That last reason is why dishes always taste more peppery when you grind the pepper yourself.

Lamb Chili

Serve this chili with a tossed salad that includes avocado slices, papaya pieces, and goat cheese. A little drizzle of extra-virgin olive oil is the only dressing it needs.

Add the lamb, oil, onion, garlic, chili powder, and cumin seeds to a large Dutch oven over medium heat. Sauté until the meat is brown and the onion is transparent, and then add the remaining ingredients. Add water, if needed, so that all the ingredients are covered by liquid. Continue to cook on medium for about 15 minutes to bring all the ingredients to temperature, then lower the heat, cover, and simmer for 1½ hours. Check the pot periodically to stir the chili and to make sure that it doesn't boil dry. Add more water, if necessary.

Make Your Own Chili Powder

Add 5 dried poblano peppers, 1 dried ancho chili pepper, ⅜ teaspoon ground cumin, ¾ teaspoon dried oregano, and 1 teaspoon garlic powder to a spice grinder, food processor, or blender. Process until fine. Add cayenne pepper to taste if you wish to make it hotter. Store in the freezer in a tightly covered container and it'll keep indefinitely.

Serves 6–8

2 pounds ground lamb
3 tablespoons extra-virgin olive oil
1 large yellow onion, diced
4 cloves garlic, crushed
2 tablespoons chili powder
1 tablespoon whole cumin seeds
¼ teaspoon dried oregano, crushed
2 jalapeño or red peppers, seeded and diced
2 green bell peppers, seeded and diced
1 28-ounce can diced tomatoes
1 8-ounce can tomato sauce
1 tablespoon Worcestershire sauce
2 15-ounce cans red kidney beans, rinsed and drained
Salt and freshly ground black pepper to taste
Water, if necessary

Country Meatloaf

Serves 6–8

1 pound lean ground beef
½ pound lean ground pork
1¼ teaspoons salt
¼ teaspoon ground black pepper
1 medium yellow onion, finely chopped
1 stalk celery, very finely chopped
½ cup carrot, peeled and grated
1 small green pepper, seeded and finely chopped
1 large egg
½ cup plus ⅓ cup ketchup
½ cup tomato sauce
½ cup quick-cooking oatmeal
½ cup butter-style crackers, crumbled
2 tablespoons light brown sugar
1 tablespoon prepared mustard

The grated carrots and butter-style crackers make this a sweeter-tasting meatloaf. It's good served with green beans or carrots and country-style hash browns or mashed potatoes and gravy made from the pan juices.

1. Preheat oven to 375°F.

2. Add the ground beef and pork, salt, pepper, onion, celery, carrot, green pepper, egg, ½ cup ketchup, tomato sauce, oatmeal, and cracker crumbs into a large bowl and mix well; shape into a loaf and place in a nonstick 2-pound loaf bread pan or in the center of a 9" × 13" nonstick baking pan. In a small bowl, mix together ⅓ cup ketchup, the brown sugar, and mustard; spread it over the top of the meatloaf. Bake for 1 hour.

Meatloaf
with Creamy Mushroom Gravy

Once you've removed the meatloaf from the oven and are letting it rest, you can heat ready-made mashed potatoes, your choice of steam-in-the-bag microwave vegetables, and the mushroom gravy in the microwave.

Serves 8

1 tablespoon extra-virgin olive oil
1 teaspoon butter
3 cloves garlic, minced
1 medium yellow onion, finely chopped
2 stalks celery, finely chopped
½ cup carrots, peeled and grated
8 ounces fresh button or cremini mushrooms, cleaned and chopped
¼ cup dry red wine
½ cup fine breadcrumbs
½ cup milk
¾ pound lean ground beef
½ pound lean ground pork
¼ pound mild Italian sausage
1 large egg
1 tablespoon freeze-dried parsley
1 teaspoon sweet paprika
Salt and freshly ground pepper to taste
OPTIONAL: Worcestershire sauce
1 10-ounce jar beef-mushroom gravy

1. Preheat oven to 350°F.

2. Put the oil, butter, garlic, onion, celery, carrot, and mushrooms in a microwave-safe bowl; cover with plastic wrap and microwave on high for 30 seconds. Uncover and stir; repeat at 30-second intervals until the onions are transparent. Add the red wine, breadcrumbs, and milk; cover and wait for 10 minutes or until the crumbs absorb the moisture in the bowl. Mix in the beef, pork, sausage, egg, parsley, paprika, salt, and pepper. Pack the mixture into a loaf pan. Brush the top of the meatloaf with Worcestershire sauce, if desired.

3. Cover the loaf pan with foil and bake for 30 minutes. Remove the foil and bake for an additional 30 minutes, or until a meat thermometer inserted in the center of the meatloaf registers at least 165°F. Remove from the oven and let stand for 10 minutes.

4. While the meatloaf is resting, warm the gravy in a saucepan or in the microwave. Serve with the gravy spooned over the top of the meatloaf or serve on the side in a warmed gravy boat.

Crumb Wisdom

The amount of moisture that remains in the bowl after you microwave the vegetables and mushrooms can affect the amount of breadcrumbs needed. If, after mixing, the mixture is too wet to form some of it in a ball that will hold its shape, add more breadcrumbs.

Stuffed Grape Leaves

*This dish is often used as an appetizer, but it's also good
as a light supper. Serve it with a cucumber yogurt-salad.*

Serves 4–6

1 pound lean ground lamb
1 cup uncooked long-grain
   rice
¼ teaspoon ground
   cinnamon
¼ teaspoon ground allspice
Salt and freshly ground
   pepper to taste
1 1-pound jar of grape leaves
Nonstick cooking spray
Water or chicken broth as
   needed
Juice of 2 lemons

1. In a bowl, mix together the lamb, rice, cinnamon, allspice, salt, and pepper.

2. Drain the grape leaves. Use any small leaves to line the bottom of a heavy saucepan or Dutch oven treated with nonstick spray. Lay each larger leaf on a flat surface, vein-side up; trim off any stem. Spoon some of the lamb mixture onto the center of each grape leaf. To form each roll, fold the stem end over the filling, then fold the sides over each other, and fold down the tip. Carefully place each roll, seam-side down, in the saucepan. Place the rolls close together in the pan to prevent them from unrolling while they cook. You may end up with several layers of rolls, depending on the size of the pan.

3. Place a plate over the rolls and then add enough water or broth to cover the plate. Bring to a boil over medium-high heat, then reduce the heat, cover, and simmer for 30 minutes. Add the lemon juice; cover and continue to simmer for an additional 30 minutes. The stuffed grape leaves (*dolmas* or *dolmades*) are done when they're tender when pierced with a fork. You can serve them warm, at room temperature, or cool.

Cucumber-Yogurt Salad

In a serving bowl, mix together 3 cups of drained plain yogurt and 2 or 3 peeled, seeded, and thinly sliced cucumbers. Add 12 fresh chopped mint leaves, 2 minced garlic cloves, and some salt to a small bowl, and crush them together. Stir the mint mixture into the salad. Add more salt, if needed. Chill until ready to serve.

Unstuffed Green Peppers Casserole

You can use a can of whole tomatoes instead of diced, if you prefer. Just crush or cut up the tomatoes when you add them (and their juices) to the casserole.

1. Preheat oven to 400°F.

2. Add the beef and onion to a 4-quart ovenproof Dutch oven; brown the hamburger over medium-high heat. Pour off any excess fat. Add the tomatoes, corn, 2 cups of the breadcrumbs, and green pepper pieces. Mix well.

3. Cover and bake for 25 minutes, or until the green peppers are tender. In a small bowl, mix the remaining breadcrumbs with the melted butter. Remove the cover from the casserole and sprinkle the breadcrumbs over the top. Bake for an additional 5 minutes, or until the breadcrumbs are golden brown.

Serves 4–6

1 pound ground beef
1 medium yellow onion, chopped
1 14½-ounce can chopped tomatoes
1 8-ounce can whole kernel corn, drained
2½ cups herb-seasoned breadcrumbs
2 large green bell peppers, seeded and cut into large dice
1 tablespoon butter, melted

Slow-Cooked Meatballs

This is an adaptation of a youvarlakia (Greek-style meatball) recipe. You can serve the meatballs and sauce over pasta, beans, or a combination of both.

1. Make the meatballs by mixing the ground beef with the rice, onion, garlic, parsley, dill, and egg; shape into small meatballs and roll each one in flour.

2. Add the tomato or tomato-vegetable juice to a 4-quart slow cooker. Carefully add the meatballs. Pour in enough water to completely cover the meatballs. Add the butter. Cover and cook on low for 6 to 8 hours, checking periodically to make sure the cooker doesn't boil dry. Taste for seasoning and add salt and pepper if needed.

Serves 8

1½ pounds lean ground beef
1 cup uncooked long-grain white rice
1 small yellow onion, finely chopped
3 cloves garlic, minced
2 teaspoons dried parsley
½ tablespoon dried dill
1 egg
¼ cup all-purpose flour
2 cups tomato juice or tomato-vegetable juice
2–4 cups water
2 tablespoons butter
Salt and freshly ground black pepper to taste

Greek Meatball, Egg, and Lemon Soup

This recipe is adapted from a Greek soup (youvarlakia avgolemono). The traditional version doesn't have the vegetables added to the broth, but it's those vegetables that make this soup a one-pot meal. Serve it with some feta cheese sprinkled over the top and crusty bread on the side.

Serves 6

1 pound lean ground beef
¼ pound ground pork
1 small yellow onion, minced
1 clove garlic, minced
6 tablespoons uncooked long-grain white rice
1 tablespoon dried parsley
2 teaspoons dried dill or mint
1 teaspoon dried oregano
Salt and freshly ground black pepper to taste
3 large eggs
4–6 cups chicken or vegetable broth
1 medium yellow onion, chopped
1 cup baby carrots, each sliced into thirds
2 large russet potatoes, peeled and cut into cubes
1 stalk celery, finely chopped
2 tablespoons corn flour
⅓ cup fresh lemon juice

1. In a large bowl, mix together the meat, minced onion, garlic, rice, parsley, dill or mint, oregano, salt, pepper, and 1 of the eggs. Shape into small meatballs and set aside.

2. Add 2 cups of the broth or water to a 4-quart slow cooker. Add the meatballs, chopped onion, carrots, and celery, then pour in enough of the remaining broth or water to cover the meatballs and vegetables. Cook on low for 6 hours.

3. In a small bowl or measuring cup, beat the 2 remaining eggs and then whisk in the corn flour. Gradually whisk in the lemon juice, and then ladle in about 1 cup of the hot broth from the slow cooker, doing so in a slow, steady stream, beating continuously until all of the hot liquid has been incorporated into the egg mixture. Stir this mixture into the slow cooker, being careful not to break the meatballs. Continue to cook on low for 1 hour, or until mixture is thickened.

Stuffed Onions

At the end of a long day, few things are better than sweet stuffed onions served with a salad.

1. Halve the onions by cutting through the center, not from top to bottom. Scoop out the onion cores. Chop the onion cores and add to the ground beef or lamb, allspice, dill, 2 tablespoons of the lemon juice, parsley, salt, pepper, and egg; mix well. Fill the onion halves to overflowing with the meat mixture. Sprinkle the flour over the top of the meat.

2. Add the oil to a deep 3½-quart nonstick skillet or electric skillet and bring to temperature. Add the onions to the pan, meat-side down, and sauté until browned. Turn the onions so that the meat side is up. Add the remaining tablespoon of lemon juice and enough water to come up to just to the top of the onion. Lower the heat, cover, and simmer for 1 hour, or until the onion is soft and the meat is cooked through.

Serves 4–6

4 large Vidalia onions, peeled
½ pound ground beef or lamb
¼ teaspoon ground allspice
¼ teaspoon dried dill
3 tablespoons fresh lemon juice
2 teaspoons dried parsley
Salt and freshly ground black pepper to taste
1 large egg
1–2 tablespoons all-purpose flour
2 tablespoons extra-virgin olive oil
Water or chicken broth

Frito and Chili Casserole

Corn chips are salty, so consider using a reduced- or low-sodium chili in this recipe.

1. Preheat the oven to 350°F.
2. Treat a deep-dish pie pan with nonstick cooking spray. Spread 2 cups of the corn chips over the bottom of the pan. Distribute the onion and ½ cup of the cheese over the top of the corn chips, and then top them with the chili. Add the remaining corn chips and cheese over the top of the chili. Bake for 15 to 20 minutes, or until the casserole is heated through and the cheese is melted.

Serves 4–8

Nonstick cooking spray
3 cups corn chips
1 large yellow onion, chopped
1 cup grated American cheese
1 19-ounce can chili con carne

Salisbury Steak in Onion Gravy

1 10¾-ounce condensed
    onion soup
1½ pounds lean ground beef
½ cup dry breadcrumbs
1 large egg
Salt and freshly ground
    pepper to taste
1 tablespoon all-purpose
    flour
¼ cup ketchup
¼ cup water
1 teaspoon Worcestershire
    sauce
½ teaspoon prepared
    mustard

Serve as an open-faced sandwich or with mashed potatoes.
Add a salad and steam-in-the-bag peas.

1. In a bowl, mix together half of the soup with the beef, breadcrumbs, egg, salt, and pepper. Shape into 6 or 8 patties.

2. Add the patties to a deep 3½-quart nonstick skillet or electric skillet; brown on both sides over medium-high heat, then pour off any excess fat.

3. Mix the remaining soup together with the remaining ingredients. Pour over the patties. Cover and simmer on low heat, stirring occasionally, for 20 minutes, or until the meat is cooked through and the gravy is thickened.

All-in-One Salisbury Steak Dinner

After you brown the meat patties, remove them from the pan and add a thawed 12-ounce package of frozen hash brown potatoes to the skillet. Place the meat on top of the potatoes and cook according to the directions in step 3. Add a thawed 12-ounce package of frozen baby peas, cover, and cook for an additional 5 minutes, or until the peas are heated through.

Layered Casserole

You can substitute 2 tablespoons bacon bits for the cooked bacon if you prefer.

Serves 4

Nonstick cooking spray
1 cup uncooked long-grain white rice
1 16-ounce can whole kernel corn, undrained
½ teaspoon seasoned salt
¼ teaspoon freshly ground black pepper
¾ cup beef broth, boiling
1 15-ounce tomato sauce
1 teaspoon Worcestershire sauce
1 teaspoon Italian herb seasoning
1 large yellow onion, diced
1 green pepper, seeded and chopped
2 stalks celery, finely chopped
1 pound lean ground beef
1 cup Cheddar cheese, grated
2 slices cooked bacon, crumbled

1. Preheat the oven to 375°F.

2. Treat a 2-quart casserole dish with nonstick cooking spray. Add the rice, corn, half of the salt and pepper, and the broth to the casserole dish and mix together. Mix together the tomato sauce, Worcestershire sauce, and Italian herb seasoning; pour half of it over the rice mixture in the casserole dish. Layer the onion, green pepper, and celery over the top. Mix the other half of the salt and pepper into the ground beef; break the beef apart over the top of the celery. Top with the remaining tomato sauce mixture. Cover and bake for 45 minutes.

3. Remove the cover and sprinkle the cheese over the casserole. Bake, uncovered, for an additional 15 minutes, or until the cheese is melted. Sprinkle the crumbled bacon over the cheese before serving.

Bacon Bits

If you don't want to cook the bacon separately, cut it into small pieces and mix it with the ground beef layer of the casserole. This will save you time, and it will also save you the hassle of cleaning up another cooking vessel.

Everything Sloppy Sandwiches

1 teaspoon coriander seeds

1 tablespoon extra-virgin olive or vegetable oil

1 medium yellow onion, chopped

2 cloves garlic, minced

1 pound ground beef or turkey

1 teaspoon ground cumin

Salt and freshly ground black pepper to taste

3 carrots, peeled and sliced in ¼" rounds

1 zucchini, halved and cut into ¼" rounds

½ cup chicken broth

1 8-ounce can whole kernel corn, drained

8 ounces Cheddar cheese, grated

8 onion or Kaiser rolls or hamburger buns

OPTIONAL: ketchup to taste

OPTIONAL: choice of pickles to taste

To serve this sloppy dish as open-faced sandwiches, toast the rolls before topping them with the meat. Instead of stirring the cheese into the meat mixture, top the sandwiches with it and place them under the broiler until the cheese melts.

1. Add the coriander seeds to a deep 3½-quart nonstick skillet and toast for 1 to 2 minutes over medium heat, tossing or stirring so that the seeds don't burn. Remove from the pan, cool, and coarsely chop in a coffee mill or crush under the flat side of a knife. Add the oil to the skillet and bring to temperature over medium heat; add the onions and sauté until golden. Add the garlic and sauté for 1 minute. Stir in the ground beef or turkey and fry until browned, breaking it apart as it cooks.

2. Stir in the cumin, salt, and pepper. Add the carrots and sauté for 1 minute. Stir in the zucchini, broth, and corn; cover and simmer for 2 minutes. Uncover and simmer until most of the broth has evaporated. Top with the cheese; turn off the heat and cover for 1 minute, or until the cheese is melted. Divide the mixture between the rolls or buns to serve as sandwiches.

Ground Round in Mushroom Cream Sauce
with Spinach

*The heat from the meat and mushroom sauce will wilt the spinach slightly,
which makes this meal a salad and main course rolled all into one.*

Serves 4

1 pound ground round
*Salt and freshly ground
    pepper to taste*
*2 tablespoons chopped
    roasted red pepper*
*OPTIONAL: 1 jalapeño pepper,
    seeded and diced*
*OPTIONAL: butter or extra-
    virgin olive oil as needed*
*8 ounces button or cremini
    mushrooms, cleaned and
    sliced*
1 cup heavy cream
1 large egg, beaten
4 big handfuls baby spinach
*Freshly grated Parmigiano-
    Reggiano cheese to taste*

1. Add the ground round to a nonstick skillet and cook over medium heat until no longer pink, breaking it apart while it cooks. Season with salt and pepper to taste. Stir in the red pepper and the jalapeño (if using). If additional fat is needed to sauté the mushrooms, add some butter or oil to the skillet. Sauté the mushrooms until tender.

2. Mix the cream and egg together, then stir into the meat mixture in the skillet. Bring to a boil, then lower the heat; simmer until heated through and slightly thickened.

3. To serve, put a handful of spinach on each of 4 plates. Spoon the meat and mushroom sauce over the spinach. Top each serving with freshly grated Parmigiano-Reggiano to taste.

Marzetti Casserole

Serves 8

8 ounces dried medium egg
   noodles
1 pound lean ground beef
1 medium yellow onion,
   chopped
2 stalks celery, diced
Salt to taste
1 16-ounce jar spaghetti
   sauce with mushrooms
1 green pepper, seeded and
   cut into thin strips
1 cup frozen peas
1 cup tomato juice
1 tablespoon Worcestershire
   sauce
½ teaspoon dried oregano,
   crushed
Freshly ground pepper to
   taste
8 ounces Cheddar cheese,
   grated
Freshly ground Parmigiano-
   Reggiano cheese to taste

You can make this casserole the night before. Cover and refrigerate it overnight. To prepare the casserole, preheat the oven to 350ºF. Bake uncovered for 45 minutes, or until the casserole is heated through.

1. In a 4-quart Dutch oven, prepare the egg noodles according to package directions. Drain in a colander and keep warm.

2. Brown the beef, onion, and celery in the Dutch oven over medium heat, breaking the beef apart as it cooks. Once the beef has lost its pink color and the onion is transparent, drain off any excess fat. Add the remaining ingredients except for the cheeses. Lower the heat and simmer, covered, for 10 minutes. Stir in the noodles and Cheddar cheese. Serve immediately, adding grated Parmigiano-Reggiano to the top of each serving.

Day Two

If you're baking the Marzetti Casserole the next day, you can add another flavor dimension by mixing 1 cup of dried breadcrumbs with 1 tablespoon of melted butter or extra-virgin olive oil. Sprinkle the crumb mixture and some Parmigiano-Reggiano over the top of the casserole; bake until the casserole is heated through and the breadcrumbs are golden brown.

Chapter 9
International Flavors

Cuban Black Beans

Serves 4–6

1 pound dried black beans

4 cups water, or more, as needed

3 cloves garlic, minced

1 green pepper, seeded and chopped

1 large yellow onion, chopped

½ pound salt pork or bacon, chopped

1 pound smoked ham hocks

2 teaspoons paprika

1 tablespoon ground cumin

2 bay leaves

4 cups chicken broth

¼ teaspoon chili powder

1 tablespoon red wine vinegar

Salt and freshly ground black pepper to taste

As with almost any bean dish, you can add chopped celery and carrots if you like.

1. Rinse the beans and put them in a 6-quart Dutch oven with the 4 cups water. Bring to a boil over medium-high heat; cover and boil for 2 minutes. Turn off the heat and let set for 1 hour.

2. Add the garlic, green pepper, onion, salt pork or bacon, ham hocks, paprika, cumin, bay leaves, chicken broth, and chili powder. Add enough additional water so that the beans are completely covered. Cover and simmer for 2 hours over low heat, or until the beans are tender. Remove the ham hocks and take the meat off of the bones; return the meat the to the pot. Remove and discard the bay leaves. Add the vinegar, salt, and pepper, and stir to mix.

Using Leftovers

It's easy to turn Cuban Black Beans into a satisfying soup. Once the beans are tender, simply add more chicken broth and bring to temperature. After you've added the vinegar, salt, and pepper, taste for seasoning and adjust by adding more vinegar and other seasonings if needed.

Filipino Pork
with Rice Noodles

Annatto seeds are available at Asian markets or specialty spice shops. If the seeds aren't available, you can substitute toasted sesame oil for the annatto oil.

1. Put the rice noodles in a bowl and pour tepid (105°F) water over them. Allow to soak while you prepare the rest of the dish.

2. Heat a wok over medium-high heat; and add the oil, garlic, and pork. Stir-fry until the pork is done. Add the sausage, onion, and cabbage. Stir-fry for several minutes, and then add the soy sauce, broth, fish sauce, leeks, and annatto oil. Stir-fry until the cabbage is tender. Add the drained rice noodles; reduce the heat to medium and stir-fry until the noodles are tender. Serve garnished with the chopped cilantro.

Annatto Oil

Put ½ cup of peanut, sesame, or vegetable oil in a small heavy saucepan and heat until the oil smokes, or reaches about 350°F. Remove the pan from the heat and stir ¼ cup of annatto seeds into the oil. Cool and strain the seeds from the oil. Store in a covered jar in the refrigerator.

Serves 6–8

1 8-ounce package rice noodles
¼ cup peanut oil
2 cloves garlic, minced
½ pound pork tenderloin, cut into thin strips
½ pound sweet Chinese sausage, cut into thin slices
1 large yellow onion, diced
1 cup napa cabbage, chopped
2 tablespoons soy sauce
1½ cups chicken broth
2 tablespoons fish sauce
¼ cup chopped leeks, well rinsed
1 tablespoon annatto oil (recipe follows)
Fresh chopped cilantro to taste

Hungarian Goulash

2 strips bacon

1 large yellow onion, diced

1 tablespoon extra-virgin olive oil

2½ pounds stewing beef, cut into ½" cubes

1 clove garlic, minced

Pinch caraway seeds, chopped

2 tablespoons sweet paprika

2 cups beef broth

Water as needed

1 15-ounce can diced tomatoes

1 green bell pepper, seeded and diced

4 large russet potatoes, diced

2 tablespoons sour cream, plus more for serving

Hungarian Goulash is often served with prepared spaetzle (German dumplings) and Cucumber Salad. Make the cucumber salad before you prepare the goulash so the cucumbers marinate in the dressing while you make the stew.

1. Add the bacon to a 6-to 8-quart stewing pot; fry over medium heat until the fat is rendered, then discard the bacon slices. Sauté the onion in the bacon fat and olive oil until the onion is transparent. Add the beef; sauté with the onions about 10 minutes, or until the meat is browned. Stir in the garlic and caraway seeds and sauté for 1 more minute.

2. Remove the pot from the heat and quickly stir in the paprika. Add the beef broth; if needed, add enough water to cover the meat. Cover and simmer over low heat for 1½ hours. Add the can of tomatoes with juice and green pepper. Add more water, if needed to cover the beef. Cover and simmer for 1 more hour, or until the meat is tender. Add the potatoes; cover and cook for an additional 30 minutes, or until the potatoes are fork tender. Stir the 2 tablespoons of sour cream into the goulash. Serve with additional sour cream on the side if desired.

Cucumber Salad

Thinly slice 2 cucumbers; put the slices in a bowl and sprinkle with salt. Let rest for 30 minutes. Drain off the excess moisture and add a small, thinly sliced yellow onion, 1 or 2 tablespoons dry white wine or cider vinegar, ¼ cup heavy or sour cream, 2 teaspoons granulated sugar, ⅛ teaspoon sweet paprika, a pinch of dried or fresh dill, and freshly ground black pepper to taste. Mix well, cover, and refrigerate until ready to serve.

Indian Chicken Vindaloo

If some members of your family like white meat and others like dark, you can substitute a quartered and skinned 3½-pound chicken for the thighs. This makes a rich, spicy stew you can serve over cooked rice or cook diced potatoes.

1. Bring the ghee to temperature over medium heat in a 6-quart Dutch oven. Fry the chicken pieces until browned, about 5 minutes on each side. Remove the chicken from the pan and keep warm.

2. Add the garlic and onion to the pan and sauté until golden brown. Stir in the ginger, cumin, mustard seeds, cinnamon, cloves, turmeric, cayenne, and paprika; sauté for a few minutes. Stir in the tamarind paste, lemon juice, vinegar, brown sugar, salt, and water. Add the chicken pieces. Bring to a boil; cover, lower the heat, and simmer for 45 minutes, or until chicken is tender. Remove the cover and continue to simmer for another 15 minutes, or until sauce thickens.

Cucumber Salad with Yogurt

Chicken Vindaloo is good with a simple cucumber salad. Thinly slice 2 cucumbers; dress the slices with 2 tablespoons of fresh lemon juice, ¼ cup extra-virgin olive oil, and salt and freshly ground black pepper to taste. Add a dollop of plain yogurt to each serving of the salad.

Serves 4–8

¼ cup ghee
8 chicken thighs, skin removed
3 cloves garlic, minced
2 large yellow onions, diced
2 tablespoons fresh ginger, grated
2 teaspoons ground cumin
2 teaspoons yellow mustard seeds, crushed
1 teaspoon ground cinnamon
½ teaspoon ground cloves
1 tablespoon turmeric
1½ teaspoons cayenne pepper, or to taste
1 tablespoon paprika
1 tablespoon tamarind paste
2 teaspoons fresh lemon juice
2 tablespoons white vinegar
1 teaspoon light brown sugar
1–2 teaspoons salt
2 cups water

Irish Boiled Dinner

Serves 8–10

2 tablespoons extra-virgin
    olive oil or butter
3 cloves garlic, minced
2 cups leeks, white part only,
    chopped and rinsed
1 large yellow onion, sliced
3½-pound beef brisket
2 12-ounce bottles lager-style
    beer
2 cups water, or more as
    needed
2 bay leaves
10 black peppercorns
½ cup fresh parsley, chopped
2 teaspoons salt
1 1-pound bag baby carrots
1 pound small red potatoes
1 pound turnips, peeled and
    quartered
2 small heads cabbage, cored
    and sliced
Salt and freshly ground black
    pepper to taste

You can substitute beef broth for the lager if you'd prefer to cook without alcohol.

1. Add the oil or butter to an 8- or 10-quart Dutch oven and bring to temperature over medium heat. Add the garlic, leeks, and onion; sauté until the onions are transparent.

2. Add the brisket to the Dutch oven along with the beer, water, bay leaves, peppercorns, parsley, and salt. Add additional water if more is needed to completely cover the meat. Bring to a boil, then lower the temperature to low, cover, and simmer for 3½ hours. Add the carrots and potatoes, cover, and simmer for 30 minutes. Add the turnips and cabbage; cover and cook for an additional 15 minutes, or until all the vegetables are cooked according to desired doneness. Taste for seasoning and add additional salt and pepper, if needed.

Cooking with Cabbage

If you'd rather keep the cabbage in wedges, cut each cabbage into quarters, remove the cores, and secure the wedges with toothpicks. Remove the toothpicks before serving. Cabbage is a cruciferous vegetable that is very high in vitamin C and also has respectable levels of folate and vitamin B_6.

Lebanese Baked Kibbe

Serve with a Greek salad or cucumber and yogurt salad. If you are serving the yogurt salad, omit the dill and garnish it with chopped fresh mint.

1. In a bowl, mix the bulgur and onion flakes together; add the water and set aside to soak for 30 minutes. Drain the bulgur and mix it with 2 pounds of the ground lamb and the parsley, salt, allspice, ¼ teaspoon cinnamon, mint, and water.

2. Melt the butter in a 4-quart Dutch oven. Add the remaining ½ pound of ground lamb, pine nuts, onion, ⅛ teaspoon cinnamon, ⅛ teaspoon allspice, salt, and pepper. Sauté until the onions are transparent. Remove the meat mixture from the pan and set aside.

3. Preheat the oven to 400°F.

4. Coat the bottom of the Dutch oven with 2 tablespoons olive oil. Press half of the bulgur-lamb mixture into the pan. Evenly spread the sautéed lamb mixture over the bulgur-lamb mixture. Spoon the remaining bulgur-lamb mixture on top and use the back of a spoon or a spatula to press it down evenly over the sautéed mixture. Drizzle the remaining 3 tablespoons of olive oil over the top of the casserole. Bake for 20 minutes; reduce the oven temperature to 300°F and bake for another 30 minutes, or until golden brown. To serve, cut into 8 wedges; use a spatula to remove each wedge from the pan.

Serves 8

2 cups fine-grain bulgur
¼ cup dried onion flakes
4 cups water
2½ pounds ground lamb
2 teaspoons dried parsley
½ teaspoon salt
¼ teaspoon ground allspice
¼ teaspoon ground cinnamon
1 teaspoon dried mint
¼ cup cold water
2 tablespoons butter
¼ cup pine nuts
1 medium yellow onion, chopped
⅛ teaspoon ground cinnamon
⅛ teaspoon ground allspice
Salt and freshly ground black pepper to taste
5 tablespoons extra-virgin olive oil

Moroccan Chicken and Vegetables

Serves 4–8

3 tablespoons extra-virgin olive oil

4 chicken thighs, skin removed

2 chicken breasts, halved and skin removed

1 large yellow onion, diced

3 cloves garlic, minced

1 large eggplant

3 cups chicken broth

2 2" cinnamon sticks

1 teaspoon curry powder

1 teaspoon ground cumin

¼ teaspoon turmeric

¼ teaspoon freshly ground black pepper

2 large carrots, peeled and diced

1 large zucchini, diced

1 large white turnip, diced

1 small red pepper, seeded and diced

2 cups tomatoes, diced

½ cup golden raisins

2 tablespoons fresh cilantro, chopped

This is an adaptation of a chicken tagine recipe. It's traditionally served in deep soup bowls over the top of cooked rice, noodles, or couscous.

1. Add the oil to a 6- or 8-quart Dutch oven; bring to temperature over medium-high heat. Add the chicken pieces and brown on both sides. Remove from the pan and keep warm.

2. Reduce the heat to low and add the onion, garlic, and eggplant. Sauté for 5 to 10 minutes, or until the onion is transparent. Increase the heat to medium-high; stir in the broth, cinnamon sticks, curry powder, cumin, turmeric, and black pepper and bring to a boil. Reduce the heat and simmer for 10 minutes.

3. Add the chicken, carrots, zucchini, turnip, and red pepper. Cover and simmer for 10 minutes. Add the chicken breasts, tomato, raisins, and half of the cilantro; cover and simmer for 10 minutes, or until the chicken is cooked through. Taste for seasoning and add more salt and pepper, if necessary. Garnish with the remaining cilantro.

Eggplant Matters

Some people find the taste of eggplant to be bitter unless it's first salted and allowed to sit for 20 minutes. If you take that step, drain off any liquid after 20 minutes, then rinse the eggplant and let it drain well again.

Moroccan Lamb Stew

Preserved lemon and orange-blossom water are available at Middle Eastern markets or from specialty spice shops, like the Spice House (www.thespicehouse.com). They add the authentic flavors to this dish, which is traditionally served with couscous.

Serves 6

2 pounds boneless lamb
   shoulder, trimmed of fat
1 teaspoon salt
2 teaspoons freshly ground
   black pepper
½ teaspoon saffron
1 teaspoon ground ginger
2 cloves garlic, minced
1 large yellow onion, diced
1 tablespoon dried parsley
4 tablespoons ghee or extra-
   virgin olive oil
2½ cups water, or more as
   needed
½ preserved lemon, diced (no
   pulp)
2 teaspoons ground
   cinnamon
¼ cup honey
2 tablespoons orange-
   blossom water
OPTIONAL: 1 tablespoon
   sesame seeds
OPTIONAL: ¾ cup blanched
   slivered almonds

1. Cut the lamb into 1" cubes and add to a 6-quart Dutch oven along with the salt, pepper, saffron, ginger, garlic, onion, parsley, and 3 tablespoons of the ghee or oil. Add the water, increasing the amount if necessary to completely cover the meat. Bring to a boil over medium-high heat; lower the heat and simmer, covered, for 1½ hours, or until the meat is very tender.

2. Add the lemon and cinnamon; cover and simmer for 15 minutes. Add the honey and orange-blossom water; simmer, stirring frequently, until the sauce is reduced and thickened.

3. If desired, add the remaining tablespoon of ghee or oil to a nonstick skillet and bring to temperature over medium heat. Add the sesame seeds and almonds; stir-fry until toasted to a light brown. Garnish each serving with the seed and nut mixture.

Couscous Consciousness

Couscous is a pasta made from semolina wheat granules that are coated in finely ground wheat flour. Regular couscous requires a multi-stage process of boiling, hand rubbing, and steaming. Quick-cooking couscous is also available. Another option is to substitute orzo, a semolina flour pasta shaped like grains of rice.

Sukiyaki

This is an Americanized dish. Serve it over cooked spaghetti, rice, or thinly sliced lettuce, or a combination of cooked rice and lettuce.

1. Cut the meat across the grain in paper-thin slices. In a small bowl, combine the soy sauce, broth, beer or sherry, sugar, and pepper.

2. Add the oil to a deep 3½-quart nonstick skillet or wok and bring it to temperature over medium-high heat. Add the meat and stir-fry for 3 minutes. Stir in half of the soy sauce mixture and stir-fry for 1 more minute. Push the meat to the side of the pan, and add the onion, bamboo shoots, mushrooms, and celery; stir-fry for 3 minutes. Pour the remaining sauce into the pan; add the green onions and bean sprouts. Stir-fry for an additional 3 minutes. Taste for seasoning and add more soy sauce, if needed, and add the toasted sesame oil if desired.

Portuguese Caldo Verde

Kale provides the green in this soup. If kale isn't available, you can substitute collard greens but it will change the flavor somewhat.

Serves 6–8

1 pound kale
1 tablespoon extra-virgin olive oil
1 large yellow onion, thinly sliced
½ pound linguiça or kielbasa, sliced
4 large russet potatoes, peeled and diced
4 cups chicken broth
2 15-ounce cans cannelloni beans, rinsed and drained
Salt and freshly ground black pepper to taste

1. Trim the large ribs from the kale. Slice it into thin strips. Put the kale strips into a bowl of cold water and soak for 1 hour; drain well.

2. Add the oil to a 6-quart Dutch oven and bring to temperature over medium-high heat. Add the onions and sauté until transparent. Add the linguiça or kielbasa and potatoes; sauté for a few minutes. Add the chicken broth, drained kale, and beans. Bring to a boil. Lower the heat; cover and simmer for 1 hour. Taste for seasoning and add salt and pepper to taste.

Bubble and Squeak

Adding some ham and bacon to this traditional British dish makes it a complete meal, even if you choose to serve it without a salad. For variety, you can add some chopped celery and grated carrots, too.

Serves 4–6

4 slices bacon, cut into pieces
1 small yellow onion, diced
1 zucchini, peeled and grated
3 large russet potatoes, cut into cubes
¼ cup cooked ham, chopped
1 small head cabbage, cored and chopped
Salt and freshly ground black pepper to taste

1. Add the bacon pieces to a deep 3½-quart nonstick skillet; fry over medium-high heat until the bacon just begins to crisp. Lower the heat to medium and add the onion; sauté until the onion is transparent. Stir in the zucchini and potatoes. Reduce the heat to low, cover, and cook for 5 minutes, or until the potatoes are soft enough to mash. Spread the ham over the potato mixture, add cabbage. Cover and cook for 20 minutes.

2. Uncover the pan and test to make sure the cabbage is tender. Season to taste with salt and pepper. If necessary, leave the pan over the heat until any excess moisture from the cabbage and zucchini evaporates. To serve, invert onto a serving plate.

Puerto Rican Rice and Pigeon Peas

Serves 8

½ pound dried gandules
(pigeon peas)

3 cups water

1 tablespoon extra-virgin
olive oil

1 ounce salt pork or bacon,
chopped

2 ounces cooked ham,
chopped

2 cloves garlic, minced

1 red bell pepper, seeded and
diced

1 green pepper, seeded and
diced

1 large yellow onion, diced

1 medium tomato, finely
chopped

1 tablespoon annatto oil
(page 113)

2 cups chicken broth or water

1 cup instant white rice

Salt and freshly ground black
pepper to taste

If you want to serve this as a main dish, increase the amount of ham called for in the recipe. Otherwise, the recipe serves 8 as a side dish.

1. Add the gandules and water to a 6-quart Dutch oven; bring to a boil over medium heat. Cover and turn off the heat; allow to sit for 1 hour. Drain, reserving 1½ cups of the water.

2. Add the oil, salt pork or bacon, and ham to the Dutch oven and sauté over medium heat for 3 minutes. Add the garlic, red pepper, green pepper, and onion; sauté until the onion is transparent. Add the tomato, drained gandules, and reserved water. Bring to a boil; cover and lower the heat, and simmer 15 minutes or until the gandules are almost tender and have absorbed most of the liquid.

3. Stir in the annatto oil and broth or water. Bring to a boil over medium heat. Add the rice, cover, turn off the burner, and let set for 30 minutes, or until the liquid is absorbed and the rice is tender. Stir to fluff the rice. Taste for seasoning and add salt and pepper to taste.

Russian Borscht

If fresh tomatoes are available, you can substitute about a pound of diced vine-ripened tomatoes for the canned.

1. Add the oil, garlic, and lamb to a 6-quart Dutch oven or stockpot. Brown the lamb over medium heat, stirring frequently to keep the garlic from burning. Add the onion and sauté until transparent.

2. Peel and dice the beets. Rinse the beets well and cover them with cold water until needed.

3. Add the beets, cabbage, tomatoes, beef broth, vinegar, bay leaves, and lemon juice to the pot. Bring to a boil; cover, reduce the heat, and simmer for 2 hours.

4. Chop the reserved beet greens and add to the soup; cover and simmer for another 15 minutes. Taste for seasoning and add salt and pepper to taste. Ladle the soup into bowls and garnish each bowl with sour cream and fresh dill.

Serves 6–8

1½ tablespoons extra-virgin olive oil
1 clove of garlic, minced
½ pound lamb, cut into ½" pieces
1 small yellow onion, diced
1 pound red beets
1 small head cabbage, cored and chopped
1 15-ounce can diced tomatoes
7 cups beef broth
¼ cup red wine vinegar
2 bay leaves
1 tablespoon lemon juice
Salt and freshly ground black pepper to taste
6–8 tablespoons sour cream
6–8 teaspoons fresh dill

Unstuffed Arabian Vegetables

Rather than choosing whether you want to stuff tomatoes, zucchini, or green peppers, this option lets you stretch the meal to more servings by using all three veggies. For variety and an additional flavor boost, use 2 green and 2 red bell peppers.

Serves 6–8

2 cups chicken broth
1 cup instant white rice
½ pound ground lamb or chicken
½ pound ground beef
⅛ teaspoon ground cinnamon
¼ teaspoon freshly ground nutmeg
¼ teaspoon ground allspice
Salt and freshly ground pepper to taste
3 tablespoons butter
3 medium zucchini, diced
1 cup cherry tomatoes, halved
4 medium green bell peppers
¼ cup water
¼ cup tomato juice
3 tablespoons fresh lemon juice
6–8 tablespoons plain yogurt, drained

1. Add the chicken broth to a deep 3½-quart nonstick skillet and bring to a boil. Add the rice; cover, turn off the heat, and let sit for 30 minutes. Fluff the rice and pour into a large bowl; cover.

2. Add the ground lamb or chicken and ground beef to the skillet; brown over medium-high heat, stirring to break apart the meat and mix it together. Pour the cooked meat into the bowl with the rice and mix together with the cinnamon, nutmeg, allspice, salt, and pepper.

3. Melt the butter in the skillet and add the zucchini; stir-fry until the zucchini is crisp-tender and much of the moisture is evaporated. Add the tomatoes and stir-fry until warm. Add to the rice-meat mixture and mix well.

4. Cut the in half peppers lengthwise, and remove the stems, seeds, and white membrane. Pour the water, tomato juice, and lemon juice into the skillet. Arrange the peppers around the bottom of the skillet, cut side up. Spoon the rice-meat mixture into and around the pepper halves. Bring the juice mixture in the pan to a boil over medium heat. Reduce the heat, cover, and simmer for 20 to 30 minutes, or until the peppers are tender. Top servings with a dollop of plain yogurt.

Extra Flavor

You can make a Middle Eastern–style yogurt sauce by flavoring it with a little lemon juice and some raw, minced, or roasted garlic. The lemon will add a bit of a kick, and the garlic will impart a bit of sweetness to the dish.

Scottish Broth

This is an adaptation of a recipe sometimes referred to as Scotch Broth. The people who love it insist it's as therapeutic and comforting as chicken soup.

Serves 6–8

¼ cup butter or extra-virgin olive oil
1 large yellow onion, diced
2 stalks celery, diced
3 large carrots, peeled and finely chopped
½ cup leeks (white part only), well-rinsed and chopped
½ teaspoon salt
¼ teaspoon ground black pepper
2 pounds lamb neck bones or lamb shanks
4 cloves garlic, minced
2 bay leaves
½ cup Scotch whisky or chicken broth
½ cup pearl barley, rinsed and drained
½ small head cabbage, cored and shredded
1 cup turnip, diced
Water as needed
½ cup frozen peas
¼ cup minced fresh parsley

1. Melt the butter over medium heat in a 6-quart Dutch oven or stockpot. Add the onion, celery, carrots, leeks, salt, and pepper; sauté for 5 minutes, or until the onion is transparent and the other vegetables are soft.

2. Cut away any excess fat from the lamb. Use a cleaver to cut the bones and meat into pieces. Add several pieces of the lamb and sauté until browned on all sides. Add the garlic and bay leaves; sauté for 1 minute. Turn off the heat under the pan and remove the pan from the burner. Deglaze the pan with the Scotch or broth.

3. Add the remaining lamb, barley, cabbage, and turnip; pour in enough water to cover all the ingredients in the pan by 2 inches. Return the pan to the burner and bring to a boil over medium-high heat; lower the heat to medium-low and simmer uncovered for 2 hours, or until thickened and the meat is tender. Periodically skim off any fat from the top.

4. Use tongs or a slotted spoon to remove the meat from the pot. When it's cool enough to handle, cut the meat away from the bone; discard the bones. Stir the meat into the broth along with the peas and parsley. Bring to temperature, and taste for seasoning, adding additional salt and pepper if needed. Ladle into bowls to serve.

Scottish Broth Options

You can substitute a cup of coleslaw mix for the shredded cabbage. For a richer soup, substitute chicken broth for some of the water. Add extra flavor by putting a few tablespoons of blue cheese into the bottom of each serving bowl before you ladle in the soup. The cheese will melt into the soup and give it a rich, hearty flavor.

Chapter 10
Fish and Seafood

Shrimp and Crab Bisque

2 tablespoons plus ½ cup butter

4 stalks celery with leaves, finely chopped

1 1-pound bag baby carrots

1 large yellow onion, finely chopped

2 cloves garlic, minced

3 cups fish or shrimp stock, or chicken broth

4 large russet potatoes, peeled and diced

2 whole cloves

1 bay leaf

6 peppercorns

2 cups whole milk

½ cup all-purpose flour

1 pound raw shrimp, peeled and deveined

1 pound cooked crabmeat, broken apart

2 cups heavy cream

OPTIONAL: salt

OPTIONAL: white pepper to taste

OPTIONAL: dry sherry to taste

OPTIONAL: fresh parsley or 2 green onions (green part only), chopped

Adding carrots and potatoes to this dish turns it into a one-pot meal. It may be stretching it to continue to call it "bisque," but when you consider the cost of the ingredients, it still deserves an expensive-sounding name.

1. Melt 2 tablespoons of the butter in a 6-quart Dutch oven or stockpot over medium heat. Add the celery and stir into the butter. Finely dice 6 of the baby carrots and stir them into the butter and celery; sauté for 2 minutes. Add the onion and sauté until transparent. Stir the garlic into the sautéed mixture. Chop the remaining carrots into thirds, and then add them along with the stock or broth and the potatoes. Wrap the cloves, bay leaf, and peppercorns in cheesecloth or put them in a muslin cooking bag; add to the broth. Bring to a boil; lower the temperature, cover, and simmer for 10 minutes.

2. Add the milk. Bring to a boil over medium heat. Mix ½ cup butter and flour together to form a paste and stir it into the broth, 1 teaspoon at a time. Once all of the butter-flour mixture is added, boil for 1 minute, then lower the temperature and let simmer until the mixture begins to thicken and the raw flour taste is cooked out of the broth. Remove the cheesecloth or cooking bag.

3. Add the shrimp and cook just until they begin to turn pink; do not overcook. Stir in the crabmeat and cream. Bring to temperature. Taste for seasoning, and, if desired, season with salt, white pepper, and/or dry sherry. Remove from the heat and serve immediately. Garnish with chopped parsley or chopped green onion, if desired.

Clam Chowder

Canned clams are salty, so chances are you won't need to add any salt to the chowder. Also, be sure to read the label on the cans if anyone in your family has food sensitivities; some canned clams have monosodium glutamate.

1. Melt the butter in a 6-quart Dutch oven over medium heat. Add the garlic, celery, and carrots; sauté for 2 minutes. Add the onion and sauté until transparent. Stir in the pepper, thyme, and flour. Whisk until the butter is absorbed into the flour. Slowly add the broth or water, whisking continuously to blend it with the butter-flour roux. Add the milk, bay leaf, and potatoes. Bring to a boil; reduce heat, cover, and simmer for 10 to 15 minutes, or until the potatoes are tender. Check and stir the chowder frequently to prevent it from burning.

2. Stir in the clams and cream. Bring to temperature, remove the bay leaf, taste for seasoning, and serve immediately.

Clam Salad

Chop leftover steamed clams and add them to a macaroni salad. For a complete quick and easy lunch, serve it over lettuce and garnish the clam-macaroni salad with chopped fresh parsley or dill.

Serves 8–10

½ cup butter
2 cloves garlic, minced
1 stalk celery, finely chopped
2 baby carrots, grated
1 large yellow onion, diced
½ teaspoon white pepper
⅛ teaspoon dried thyme, crushed
½ cup all-purpose flour
3 cups chicken broth or water
3 cups whole milk
1 bay leaf
4 large russet or red potatoes, peeled or unpeeled, and diced
2 6½-ounce cans chopped or minced clams
2 cups heavy cream

Oyster Stew

Serves 4

4 tablespoons butter

1 tablespoon yellow onion or
    shallot, finely chopped

1 cup whole milk

1 cup heavy cream

Salt and white pepper to taste

2 pints fresh oysters

OPTIONAL: fresh parsley,
    chopped, to taste

*This stew rich enough for a meal. Serve it with bread or crackers and
a tossed salad. In the Midwest, it's served with butter-style crackers.*

1. Shuck the oysters. Start by folding a thick cloth several times to create a square. Use the cloth to steady each oyster firmly on a flat surface as you shuck it; the cloth will also help protect your hand. Insert the tip of an oyster knife between the shell halves and work it around from one side to the other as you pry the shell open. Use a sharp filet or paring knife to cut away the muscles from the flat shell. Bend the shell back, break it off, and discard it. Run the knife underneath the oyster to detach it completely and pour it and the oyster juices into a measuring cup. Discard the bottom shell. Repeat until you have 3 cups.

2. Melt the butter in a heavy 2-quart saucepan over medium heat. Add the onion and sauté until transparent. Reduce the heat to low, add the milk, cream, salt, and pepper; bring to a light simmer.

3. Add the oysters and juices. Heat only until the oysters are hot; do not overcook. Ladle into bowls and serve immediately. Garnish with parsley, if desired.

Roasted Black Sea Bass

You can substitute snapper or grouper for the sea bass.

1. Heat oven to 450°F.

2. Cut 4 or 5 slits in the skin of the sea bass. Place in a 9" × 13" ovenproof baking pan. Spread ½ cup of the olive purée over the surface of the bass and into the slits of the fish. Mix together the paprika, onion powder, cayenne, oregano, and thyme; sprinkle it and the pepper to taste over the fish. Sprinkle ½ cup of the capers over the fish, arrange the lemon slices over the top, and drizzle with 3 tablespoons of the olive oil. Splash with white wine.

3. Season the fennel and eggplant with salt, pepper, and the remaining 3 tablespoons olive oil. Arrange around the fish. Roast for 45 minutes.

4. Remove the fish from the oven and place on a serving tray. Add the remaining olive purée to the baking pan and mix it with the remaining 2 tablespoons capers and the chives, parsley, and fennel tops. Pour over the fish, fennel, and eggplant. Serve immediately.

Serves 4

2 whole black sea bass, about 4 pounds each
¾ cups kalamata olive purée, divided
1 tablespoon paprika
1 teaspoon onion powder
½ teaspoon cayenne pepper
1 teaspoon dried oregano
1 teaspoon dried thyme, crushed
Freshly ground black pepper to taste
½ cup plus 2 tablespoons capers
2 Meyer lemons, sliced
6 tablespoons extra-virgin olive oil
4 tablespoons dry white wine
2 fennel bulbs
2 eggplants, cut in ½" slices
1 tablespoon chives, chopped
1 tablespoon fresh parsley leaves, chopped
2 tablespoons fennel tops, chopped

Seafood Bread

Serves 8

1 10- to 12-inch round loaf of bread

Extra-virgin olive oil as needed

½ cup freshly grated Parmigiano-Reggiano cheese, plus more to taste

4 large vine-ripened tomatoes, peeled, seeded, and diced

½ teaspoon sea salt

4 cloves garlic, minced

2 teaspoons dried minced onion

1 teaspoon dried parsley

½ teaspoon dried oregano, crushed

½ teaspoon dried basil, crushed

OPTIONAL: dried red pepper flakes to taste

1–2 teaspoons granulated sugar (to taste)

2 cups cottage cheese, drained

1 large egg

3 cups mozzarella cheese, grated

2 cans 6-ounce tuna, drained

8 ounces fresh button or cremini mushrooms, cleaned and sliced

You can substitute other canned seafood for the tuna, or use a combination of seafood such as salmon, crabmeat, clams, and tuna; if the bread is deep enough, you can increase the amount of meat in the recipe.

1. Preheat the oven to 400°F.

2. Cut the top off of the loaf of bread. Starting about ½ inch from the outer crust, cut a circle around the loaf, cutting down to about ½ inch from the bottom of the crust; be careful not to pierce it. Remove the soft bread from the inside of the loaf; use a blender or food processor to make 2 to 3 cups of course breadcrumbs. Mix 1 cup of the breadcrumbs with a ½ cup of the freshly grated Parmigiano-Reggiano; set aside.

3. In a small bowl, mix together the tomatoes, salt, garlic, dried onion, parsley, basil, sugar, and red pepper flakes (if using).

4. In another bowl, mix the cottage cheese with the egg and 1 cup of the mozzarella cheese.

5. Use a pastry brush to liberally coat the inside and the outside of the bread with extra-virgin olive oil. Place the bread crust-side down on a baking sheet. Sprinkle freshly grated Parmigiano-Reggiano to taste over the bottom inside of the bread. Use a slotted spoon to spoon half of the tomato mixture over the top of the grated cheese; avoid getting too much of the tomato juice in this layer. Spread the cottage cheese mixture over the top of the tomatoes, spread the tuna over the cottage cheese mixture, and top the tuna with the mushrooms. Ladle the remaining tomato mixture and juices over the top of the mushrooms. Sprinkle the remaining mozzarella cheese over the tomato mixture. Sprinkle the breadcrumb-cheese mixture over the mozzarella, carefully pressing the mixture down over the cheese. Add more breadcrumbs, if desired. Liberally drizzle extra-virgin olive oil over the top of the breadcrumbs.

6. Bake for 1 hour, or until the breadcrumbs on top are deep brown and the mozzarella cheese underneath is melted and bubbling. Serve immediately.

Seafood Bread Baking Tips

Bread like challah lends a sweet flavor to the Seafood Bread, and because its crust is already soft, it should bake okay if it is just placed on the baking sheet. If you are using bread with an already crusty crust, you may need to wrap the outer crust in foil for the first 45 minutes of the baking time.

Lobster Paella

Serves 6

¼ cup extra-virgin olive oil

2 large yellow onions, diced

2 red bell peppers, seeded and sliced into ½" strips

4 cloves garlic, minced

2 cups uncooked white basmati rice

5 cups chicken broth

½ teaspoon saffron threads, crushed

¼ teaspoon crushed red pepper flakes

1 teaspoon sea or kosher salt

½ teaspoon freshly ground black pepper

⅓ cup licorice-flavored liqueur, such as Pernod

1½ pounds cooked lobster meat

1 pound kielbasa, cut into ¼" rounds

1 10-ounce package frozen peas

Fresh parsley, chopped, to taste

2 lemons, cut into wedges

If your budget is tight, you can substitute cooked shrimp for the lobster.

1. Preheat oven to 425°F.

2. Add the oil to a large Dutch oven and bring it to temperature over medium heat. Add the onions and sauté for 5 minutes, stirring occasionally. Add the bell peppers; sauté for 5 minutes. Lower the heat; add the garlic and sauté for 1 minute. Stir in the rice, chicken stock, saffron, red pepper flakes, salt, and pepper; bring to a boil over medium-high heat. Cover, move the pot to the oven, and bake for 15 minutes. Take the pot out of the oven and remove the lid; gently stir the rice using a wooden spoon. Return the pot to the oven and bake uncovered for 10 to 15 minutes, or until the rice is fully cooked.

3. Move the paella back to the stovetop; add the liqueur. Cook over medium heat for 1 minute, or until the liqueur is absorbed by the rice. Turn off the heat, and add the lobster, kielbasa, and peas, gently stirring to mix in the added ingredients. Cover and let it set for 10 minutes. Uncover, sprinkle with the parsley, garnish with lemon wedges, and serve hot.

Shrimp and Artichoke Fettuccine

You can prepare this entire meal in three steps using the same deep 3½-quart nonstick skillet. Cooking the pasta in less water will leave it a bit starchy, which will help thicken the sauce.

1. Peel and devein the shrimp, reserving the shells. Add the shells, water, parsley, lemon slice, and pepper to the skillet and bring to a boil over high heat; reduce the heat and simmer, uncovered, for 10 minutes. Strain; set aside and keep warm until serving time.

2. Cook the pasta according to the package directions; drain and set aside.

3. Add 2 tablespoons of the oil to the skillet and bring to temperature over medium heat; add the garlic and sauté for 30 seconds. Add the artichokes and sauté for 1 minute. Stir in the shrimp and wine; bring to temperature and cook until the shrimp turns pink, about 2 minutes. Stir in the tomatoes, broth, butter, lemon peel, salt, nutmeg, and cooked pasta; heat through.

4. To serve, place a piece of the toasted bread in each of 4 shallow soup bowls. Divide the pasta mixture among bowls, adding additional shrimp broth as desired. Garnish with the parsley and drizzle with the remaining oil. Squeeze lemon juice from 1 wedge over each serving, and garnish each with the remaining lemon wedges.

Serves 4

1 pound shrimp in shells
3 cups water
4 sprigs fresh parsley
1 slice lemon
1 teaspoon freshly ground black pepper
8 ounces dried fettuccine or spaghetti
3 tablespoons extra-virgin olive oil
4 cloves garlic, minced
1 9-ounce package frozen artichoke hearts, thawed and halved lengthwise
½ cup dry white wine
2 plum tomatoes, finely chopped
1 cup shrimp broth
1 tablespoon butter
1 teaspoon freshly grated lemon peel
½ teaspoon sea salt
½ teaspoon freshly ground nutmeg
4 slices Italian country loaf bread or other hearty bread, toasted
1 tablespoon fresh Italian parsley, finely chopped
2 lemons, quartered

Dilled Shrimp Dinner

Serves 4

1 tablespoon butter

⅔ cup leeks, well-rinsed and thinly sliced

1½ cups peeled and shredded carrots

1 cup sugar snap pea, cut in half

¼ cup chicken broth

12 ounces fully cooked, peeled, and deveined shrimp

2 cups hot cooked white rice

1 teaspoon freshly grated lemon peel

1 tablespoon fresh chopped dill

If fresh dill isn't available, you can use dried dill. The usual rule of thumb is to use one-third the amount; however, dried dill can sometimes taste a bit stronger, so start with ½ teaspoon, taste the dish, and adjust the seasoning if necessary.

1. Melt the butter in a wok or deep skillet over medium-high heat. Add the leeks, carrots, and pea pods; sauté for 2 to 3 minutes, or until the vegetables are crisp-tender.

2. Stir in the broth, shrimp, rice, and lemon peel. Cook about 5 minutes, or until heated through, stirring occasionally. Stir in the dill. Serve immediately.

Using Frozen Precooked Shrimp

The instructions for the Dilled Shrimp Dinner are meant for refrigerated or thawed frozen shrimp. If you'll be using frozen shrimp, thaw them by placing a colander in a large bowl. Rinse them under cold running water for several minutes. Pull the colander from the bowl to drain the shrimp before adding them in step 2.

Pecan-Crusted Fish
with Vegetables

Adding some oil to the egg wash helps create a crisp crust as the fish bakes.

1. Preheat the oven to 425°F.

2. Line a jellyroll pan with heavy-duty aluminum foil. Pour 1 teaspoon of the oil onto the foil and use a pastry brush to distribute it evenly over the foil; set aside. Rinse the fish and pat dry with paper towels.

3. Stir together the pecans, cornmeal, and onion salt in a shallow dish. Stir the flour and ground red pepper together in another shallow dish. Beat together the egg, 1 teaspoon of the oil, and the water together in a small bowl or shallow dish. Working with one piece of fish at a time, dip it in the flour mixture to coat lightly, shake off any excess, dip in the egg mixture, and then in the pecan mixture. Place the coated fish on the foil-lined pan.

4. Put the remaining oil in a plastic bag and add the peppers, zucchini, and squash. Add the salt, close the bag, and toss to coat. Arrange the oil-coated vegetables around the fish, overlapping them as needed to fit in pan. Bake, uncovered, for 25 minutes, or until the fish flakes easily with a fork and the vegetables are tender. Serve immediately.

Serves 4

1 tablespoon plus 2 teaspoons peanut or vegetable oil
4 skinless catfish, white fish, or orange roughy fillets, ½" thick
½ cup finely chopped pecans
⅓ cup yellow cornmeal, finely ground
½ teaspoon onion salt
¼ cup all-purpose flour
¼ teaspoon ground red pepper
1 egg
2 teaspoons water
1 small red pepper, seeded and quartered
1 small orange or yellow pepper, seeded and quartered
1 medium zucchini, cut into ½" diagonal slices
1 medium yellow summer squash, cut into ½" diagonal slices
¼ teaspoon sea or seasoned salt

Flounder Baked in Sour Cream

You can use other white fish in this recipe. Sole, haddock, and orange roughy all taste delicious.

4 tablespoons butter, melted

4 cups frozen hash browns, thawed

4 skinless flounder fillets

½ teaspoon hot sauce

1 tablespoon paprika

¼ cup freshly grated Parmigiano-Reggiano cheese

1 cup all-natural sour cream

¼ cup fine breadcrumbs

1 12-ounce bag frozen baby Brussels sprouts, thawed

Salt and freshly ground pepper to taste

OPTIONAL: 1 lemon, quartered

1. Preheat oven to 350°F.

2. Add 2 tablespoons of melted butter to a 9" × 13" nonstick baking pan. Add the hash browns; stir to coat with the butter. Bake for 15 minutes while you prepare the fish.

3. Wash the fillets and pat dry with paper towels. In a small bowl, mix together the hot sauce, paprika, cheese, and sour cream.

4. Remove the pan from the oven. Working fast, stir the hash browns and then push them to the sides of the pan. Arrange the fish fillets flat in the middle of the pan. Distribute the Brussels sprouts evenly over the hash browns. Spoon the sour cream mixture evenly over the fish. Top the fish with the breadcrumbs. Salt and pepper to taste. Drizzle the remaining 2 tablespoons of melted butter over the Brussels sprouts and breadcrumbs. Bake for 30 more minutes, or until the fish flakes easily with a fork. Garnish each serving with a lemon wedge, if desired.

Watching Your Salt Intake?

Omit the paprika, salt, and pepper in the Flounder Baked in Sour Cream recipe; instead, before you return it to the oven, liberally sprinkle the entire dish with Mrs. Dash salt-free lemon-pepper seasoning.

Tuna and Fresh Tomato Pizza

This is a quick-and-easy, totally "to taste" recipe. Feel free to use fresh herbs if you have them on hand, but the succulent taste of the fresh tomato stands up to the hearty flavor of the dried seasonings.

1. Preheat oven to 450°F.

2. Coat both sides of the tortilla with the oil. Place on a baking sheet.

3. Peel and chop the tomato. Add it to a small bowl and mix it with a pinch of sugar. Spread the tomato and juices over the tortilla. Sprinkle the garlic, onion, oregano, basil, parsley, salt, and pepper over the tomatoes, to taste. Add as much of the tuna as you wish, and top with the cheeses.

4. Bake for 5 minutes, or until the cheese is melted and bubbly. Drizzle more extra-virgin olive oil over the top of the baked pizza, if desired.

Serves 1

1 flour tortilla
Extra-virgin olive oil to taste
1 small vine-ripened tomato
Dash granulated sugar
Dash dried minced garlic or garlic powder
Dash dried minced onion or onion powder
Dash dried oregano
Dash dried basil
Dash dried parsley
Salt and freshly ground black pepper to taste
1 12-ounce can reduced-sodium tuna, drained
Mozzarella cheese, grated, to taste
Freshly grated Parmigiano-Reggiano cheese to taste

Shrimp Salad
with Louis Dressing

You can prepare the shrimp, the hardboiled eggs, and the dressing the night before so that your salad is ready to assemble for lunch the next day.

1. To make the Louis dressing, add the mayonnaise, spinach, watercress, onion, garlic, lemon juice, and sugar to a blender or food processor; pulse until smooth. Cover and chill until ready to assemble the salad.

2. For each salad serving, put 1 cup of salad mix on a serving plate and top with 1 sliced tomato, 1 sliced hardboiled egg, and ¼ of the shrimp. Season with salt and pepper to taste, and top with the Louis dressing.

Serves 4

1 cup mayonnaise
½ cup fresh spinach leaves
5 watercress sprigs
½ small yellow onion
1 clove garlic, minced
1 tablespoon fresh lemon juice
1½ teaspoons granulated sugar
4 cups lettuce or salad mix
4 small tomatoes, sliced
4 hardboiled eggs, peeled and sliced
1 pound cooked shrimp, peeled, deveined, and cooled
Salt and freshly ground pepper to taste

Crab Newburg

Crab Newburg is traditionally served over hot rice. Serve it along with a tossed salad or steamed vegetable and you have a complete meal!

Serves 4

¼ cup butter
2 tablespoons all-purpose flour
⅛ teaspoon freshly ground nutmeg
Pinch cayenne pepper
2 cups half-and-half or light cream
3 egg yolks, beaten
8 ounces cooked crabmeat
OPTIONAL: 1½ tablespoons dry sherry
Salt to taste

1. Melt the butter in a medium saucepan over medium heat. Whisk in the flour, nutmeg, and cayenne; stir until smooth. Gradually whisk in the half-and-half, and then simmer for 8 to 10 minutes, stirring constantly, or until slightly thickened.

2. Temper the egg yolks by slowly stirring ½ cup of the hot half-and-half mixture into them. Then, slowly whisk the yolk mixture into the contents of the saucepan. Add the crabmeat and any juices, and continue to cook, stirring constantly, for another 1 to 2 minutes, or until the crabmeat is heated through and the mixture is thickened. Remove from the heat and stir in the sherry, if using. Taste for seasoning and add salt, if needed.

Linguini in Red Clam Sauce

You can cook fresh pasta in less water than you'd need to cook dried pasta, which enables you to use the same pan to cook the pasta and then make the sauce.

Serves 4

8 ounces fresh linguini
2 tablespoons extra-virgin olive oil
1 medium yellow onion, diced
1 clove garlic, minced
2 6½-ounce cans minced clams, drained and juice reserved
1 6-ounce can tomato paste
1 cup water
2 tablespoons fresh lemon juice
1 tablespoon fresh parsley, chopped
1 teaspoon granulated sugar
⅛ teaspoon dried rosemary
¼ teaspoon dried thyme
Freshly grated Parmigiano-Reggiano cheese to taste

1. Cook linguini until al dente. Drain and set aside; keep warm.

2. Wipe out the pan and add linguini; bring the oil to temperature over medium heat. Sauté the onion until transparent. Add the garlic and drained clams and sauté for 30 seconds. Stir in the clam juice, tomato paste, water, lemon juice, parsley, sugar, rosemary, and thyme. Bring to a boil, then reduce the heat and simmer, uncovered, for 15 minutes. Gently stir in the cooked linguini, and cook until the pasta is brought to temperature. Serve topped with freshly grated Parmigiano-Reggiano cheese.

Salmon Quiche

Unless you use steam-in-the-bag spinach, you will have to get a pan dirty along with the bowl you use for the egg mixture. But, because the quiche is baked in the pie shell, you're essentially using one pot to fix this meal.

Serves 6–8

1 10-inch pie shell
1 15½-ounce can pink salmon
1 9-ounce package frozen chopped spinach
1½ cups Monterey jack cheese, grated
1 3-ounce package cream cheese, softened
Salt to taste
½ teaspoon dried thyme, crushed
4 eggs, lightly beaten
1 cup milk
OPTIONAL: 1 tablespoon mayonnaise

1. Preheat the oven to 375°F. While you mix the quiche filling, bake the pie shell for 10 minutes.

2. Drain the salmon and remove any skin pieces, if desired. Mash any salmon bones and mix them into the salmon. Spread the salmon in an even layer over the bottom of the partially baked pie shell.

3. Cook the spinach according to package directions; drain well. In a medium-sized bowl, mix together the spinach, jack cheese, cream cheese, salt, and thyme. Spoon the spinach-cheese mixture evenly over the salmon. Use the same bowl to mix the eggs and milk together, and then pour it over the salmon-and-spinach mixture in the pie shell. Bake for 40 to 45 minutes. Remove from the oven and let stand for 10 minutes before cutting and serving.

Salmon Specifics

Because of the cooked bones, salmon is high in calcium. It is also an easily digestible protein high in heart-healthy omega-3 fatty acids, which also help lower cholesterol. It also contains healthy amounts of vitamins A and B.

Chapter 11
Quick and Easy

Microwave Hamburger and Macaroni Casserole

Serves 4

½ pound lean ground beef
1 cup uncooked macaroni
1 small yellow onion,
    chopped
1 8-ounce can tomato sauce
1 cup water
¼ cup ketchup
⅓ cup green pepper, seeded
    and chopped
1 tablespoon light brown
    sugar
½ teaspoon salt
½ teaspoon freshly ground
    black pepper
¼ teaspoon chili powder
1 8-ounce can corn,
    undrained

Feel free to increase the amount of chili powder, according to your tastes.

Place all the ingredients in a 2-quart glass or otherwise microwave-safe casserole dish. Stir well, making sure the ground beef is broken into small pieces. Cover and microwave on high for 8 minutes. Uncover and stir well. Cover and microwave for an additional 7 minutes. Let the casserole rest for 5 minutes, covered. Stir and serve.

Meaty Alternatives

You can substitute ground turkey for the ground beef in this recipe. If you want a lower-fat dish, microwave the ground meat on high until done. Break the meat apart and drain the fat; blot the meat with a paper towel to remove any fat clinging to the meat. Add the other ingredients and make the casserole according to the recipe instructions.

Hearty Beef Stew

Serve this stew with crackers or dinner rolls and you have an easy, complete comfort-food meal.

1. Add the roast beef, soups, Worcestershire sauce, water, and vegetables to a 6-quart or larger Dutch oven. Bring to a boil over high heat. Lower the heat, cover, and simmer for 6 minutes.

2. In a small bowl, mix the butter into the flour to make a paste. Ladle about ½ cup of the soup broth into the bowl and whisk into the paste, then pour it into the stew. Increase the heat to medium-high and return the pot to a boil; boil for 2 minutes, stirring occasionally. Reduce the heat, cover, and simmer for an additional 2 minutes, or until the vegetables are tender and the stew is thickened. Taste for seasoning, and add salt and pepper, if needed.

Serves

1 pound cooked roast beef, cut into bite-sized pieces

1 10¾-ounce can condensed tomato soup

1 10½-ounce can condensed French onion soup

1 tablespoon Worcestershire sauce

2 cups water

4 cups frozen vegetables of your choice

1 tablespoon butter

1 tablespoon all-purpose flour

Salt and freshly ground black pepper to taste

Salmon Soup

Smoked salmon will add another flavor dimension to this soup, but it is usually very salty. Therefore, either use reduced-sodium chicken broth or taste before you salt the soup to be sure that it needs it.

Add the broth, salmon, onion, salt, and pepper to a 3-quart saucepan. Bring to a boil over high heat. Reduce the heat and simmer, covered, for 15 minutes. Add the spinach, cover, and cook for another 5 minutes.

Serves 4

4 cups chicken broth

1 pound fresh or smoked salmon

1 medium yellow onion, thinly sliced

Salt to taste

⅛ teaspoon freshly ground black pepper

1 bunch fresh spinach, well washed and chopped

Smoked Salmon Alternatives

If you use fresh salmon in the Salmon Soup recipe but still want to add a smoky flavor to the dish, garnish each serving with some finely chopped crisp bacon. You can find smoked salmon everywhere from Costco to Whole Foods.

Slow Cooker Tzimmes

Serves 8

3-pound beef brisket

1 large yellow onion, chopped

2 stalks celery, chopped

1 12-ounce box pitted prunes

1 tablespoon dried or freeze-dried parsley

3 cups beef broth

3 tablespoons fresh lemon juice

¼ teaspoon ground cloves

1 teaspoon ground cinnamon

1 tablespoon honey

2 tablespoons white or white wine vinegar

Salt and freshly ground black pepper to taste

4 large sweet potatoes, peeled and quartered

1 1-pound bag baby carrots

OPTIONAL: *2 tablespoons butter*

Taste the broth before you add the sweet potatoes and carrots. That's the perfect time to add more cloves and cinnamon to taste if you want to add some extra punch to the sauce.

1. Add the brisket, onion, celery, prunes, and parsley to a 6-quart slow cooker. Mix the broth, lemon juice, cloves, cinnamon, honey, and vinegar together and pour over the meat. Season with salt and pepper to taste. Cover and cook on low for 6 hours. Add the sweet potatoes and carrots. Cover and cook on low for another 2 hours, or until the brisket and vegetables are tender.

2. For a richer sauce, after you remove the meat and vegetables to a serving platter, whisk the butter into the pan juices 1 teaspoon at a time before spooning it over the dish.

Vegetable Swap

To help flavor the broth, add a few chopped baby carrots during the first 6-hour cooking stage. Omit the remaining carrots called for in the recipe when you add the sweet potatoes. Cover and cook on low for 1½ hours. Uncover and add a 12-ounce package frozen cut green beans to the cooker. Cover and cook on low for another 30 minutes to steam the vegetables.

Swedish Sauerkraut Dinner

Serve this dinner with crusty rolls or pumpernickel bread and some cheese.

Put the bacon or pork jowl in a 6-quart Dutch oven, and fry the meat over medium heat to render out most of the fat. Spoon out some of the excess fat, leaving at least 2 tablespoons of it in the pan. Add the onion and sauté until transparent. Add the potatoes and mix with the bacon and onion. Add the cabbage and cook, covered, for 5 minutes, or until the cabbage wilts. Squeeze any excess moisture out of the sauerkraut and add it to the pan, along with the remaining ingredients. Lower heat, cover, and simmer gently for 1 hour, stirring occasionally.

Serves 8

1 pound slab bacon or smoked pork jowl, diced
2 medium yellow onions, sliced
4 large russet or red potatoes, peeled or unpeeled, and diced
1 pound green cabbage, cored and shredded
1 2-pound bag sauerkraut, rinsed and well-drained
1 apple, cored and chopped
2 cups dry white wine, apple juice, or chicken broth
1 tablespoon light brown sugar
1 teaspoon caraway seeds
1 teaspoon freshly ground black pepper

Wieners and Baked Beans

You can leave the hot dogs whole or cut them into pieces, depending on how you plan to serve the dish. Or you can do a combination of the two: Leave the number you need for sandwiches whole and cut the remaining hot dogs into pieces.

Add the bacon to a deep nonstick skillet and brown it over medium heat. Leave 1 tablespoon of bacon fat in the pan and drain off any excess. Add the onion and sauté until transparent. Add the baked beans, brown sugar, molasses, Worcestershire sauce, dry mustard, and ketchup or barbecue sauce and mix well. Stir in the hot dog pieces. If you are keeping any of the hot dogs whole, lay them across the top of the beans. Cover and simmer for 15 minutes.

Serves 6–8

1 8-ounce package bacon, cut into pieces
1 medium yellow onion, chopped
3 1-pound cans baked beans
¼ cup light brown sugar, firmly packed
1 tablespoon molasses
2 teaspoons Worcestershire sauce
½ teaspoon dry mustard
½ cup ketchup or barbecue sauce
1 1-pound package hot dogs

Improvised Shepherd's Pie

Serves 8–10

4 cups leftover meat or
cooked hamburger

1 large yellow onion, diced

1 tablespoon extra-virgin
olive oil

1 12-ounce bag frozen peas
and carrots, thawed

1 12-ounce bag frozen corn,
thawed

1 12-ounce jar gravy

1 cup sour cream

4 cups mashed potatoes

8 ounces Cheddar cheese,
shredded

*Use beef gravy with shredded roast beef or hamburger and use
chicken gravy if you're using chicken or shredded pork;
mushroom gravy works with any of them.*

1. Preheat the oven to 350°F.

2. Spread the meat evenly over the bottom of a 9" × 13" nonstick baking pan. Mix the onion with the oil and sprinkle the mixture over the meat. Evenly distribute the frozen vegetables over the meat and onions, then spread the gravy over the top of the vegetables. Mix the sour cream into the mashed potatoes; spread the potatoes over the gravy. Cover the pan with foil and bake for 45 minutes.

3. Remove the foil and top with the cheese. Bake, uncovered, for 15 minutes, or until the cheese is melted.

A Kinda Crust

If you prefer a solid "crust" of sorts to the bottom of the Shepherd's Pie, mix the meat with onion, oil, 2 beaten large eggs, and a cup of cornflake or breadcrumbs. This recipe is your chance to use the vegetable and gravy leftovers you've been hiding in the freezer. Thaw and bring them to room temperature before using them.

Pork Chops
with Roasted Red Peppers

There's no need for gravy with this dish. The chicken broth and meat juices combine to make a succulent sauce.

1. Bring the oil to temperature in a deep 3½-quart nonstick skillet or electric skillet over medium heat. Add the pork chops. Season the chops with salt and pepper to taste. Brown for 5 minutes on each side. Remove from the pan and keep warm.

2. Add the potatoes and onion, and sauté for 5 minutes or until browned, stirring occasionally. Add the oregano and broth and stir to mix. Return the chops to the pan. Top with the peppers and green beans. Bring to a boil and then reduce the heat, cover, and simmer for 10 minutes, or until done.

Serves 4

1 tablespoon extra-virgin olive oil

4 boneless pork chops, ½" thick

Salt and freshly ground black pepper to taste

4 medium red potatoes, peeled and diced

1 medium yellow onion, diced

1 teaspoon dried oregano, crushed

1 cup chicken broth

1 4-ounce jar roasted red pepper, drained and chopped

1 12-ounce bag frozen cut green beans

Sausage, Bacon, and Bean Feast

The simple step of sautéing the vegetables as you fry the bacon and sausage gives this dish that simmered-all-day, comfort-food flavor.

1. Add the bacon and sausage to a 4-quart Dutch oven and fry over medium heat until some of the fat begins to render from the meat. Add the carrot and celery; sauté along with the meat, stirring occasionally. When the meat is cooked through, drain all but 1 or 2 tablespoons of the rendered oil. Add the onion and sauté until transparent. Add the garlic and sauté for 30 seconds.

2. Add the bay leaf, thyme, broth, and beans. Stir to combine. Bring to a boil and then lower the heat and simmer, covered, for 15 minutes. Discard the bay leaf and add salt and pepper, to taste, immediately before serving. Add a few drops of hot sauce to enhance the flavor, if desired.

Serves 6–8

1 8-ounce package bacon, cut into pieces

8 ounces ground pork sausage

3 large carrots, peeled and finely chopped

2 celery stalks, finely chopped

1 large yellow onion, finely chopped

2 garlic cloves, minced

1 bay leaf

½ teaspoon dried thyme, crushed

3 cups chicken broth

2 15-ounce cans cannelloni beans, rinsed and drained

Salt and freshly ground black pepper to taste

OPTIONAL: hot sauce to taste

Braised Pork Roast
with Kalamata Olives

*Think of this as a prime rib of pork meal. Have the butcher separate
the meat from the rack and tie it to the rack of bones. Serve with a
steamed vegetable, dinner rolls, and a tossed salad.*

1. Add the oil to a large Dutch oven and bring it to the smoking point over medium-high heat. Add the pork, and sear it on all sides until lightly browned, about 5 minutes on each side. Use tongs and a spatula to remove the meat. Add the onion and sauté until transparent; stir in the garlic and sauté for another 30 seconds. Add the bay leaves, and then deglaze the pan with the vinegar. Stir in the red wine and chicken stock. Season the pork with salt and pepper and return it to the pot. Peel off a strip of skin around each potato and add them to the pot.

2. Cover and cook the pork and potatoes over low heat for about 45 minutes, basting occasionally. Discard the bay leaves. Remove the meat to a platter; tent with foil and let it rest for 20 minutes. Remove the potatoes and keep them warm. Reheat the pan juices and add the olives, parsley, and thyme. Cut the strings around the roast to remove the rack of bones. Carve into 6 servings. Spoon the sauce over each rib, and serve. Put extra sauce in a gravy boat to have at the table.

Chicken Stuffing Casserole

This casserole probably won't need salt because of the sodium content of the stuffing mix, soup, and green beans. You may wish to add freshly ground pepper, however.

Serves 4–6

⅓ cup butter

1 small yellow onion, chopped

2 celery stalks, chopped

1 6- to 8-ounce package of stuffing mix

1⅔ cup chicken broth or water

4 boneless skinless chicken breast halves, cut into 1" chunks

1 10¾-ounce can condensed cream of mushroom soup

⅓ cup sour cream

1 14½-ounce can green beans, drained

OPTIONAL: 1 cup Cheddar cheese, grated

1. Preheat oven to 350°F.

2. Melt the butter in a deep 3½-quart ovenproof nonstick skillet; add the onion and celery and sauté until softened, about 5 minutes. Pour the sautéed vegetables into a bowl and stir in the stuffing mix and its seasoning packet, if there is one. Add the broth or water and stir to combine; set aside to allow the liquid to be absorbed.

3. Spread the chicken cubes evenly in the bottom of the skillet. Mix the soup with the sour cream and spoon it evenly over chicken. Spread the green beans evenly over the soup mixture, and then sprinkle stuffing mixture evenly over all. Bake, uncovered, for 45 minutes or until the chicken in cooked through. Add the cheese at the 30-minute mark, if using, then bake an additional 15 minutes, or until the cheese is melted.

One More Thing

You can punch up the flavor of the Chicken Stuffing Casserole a bit more by sprinkling a 2.8-ounce can of French-fried onions over the top before you bake it. If you want a fresher taste, you can make your own by sautéing thin strips of onions in vegetable oil until they are crispy, about 3 minutes.

Chipotle Chili

Serves 4

1 pound lean ground beef
1 tablespoon chili powder
1 medium yellow onion, diced
2 cloves garlic, minced
1 15-ounce can red kidney
    beans, rinsed and drained
1 cup chipotle salsa
1 cup frozen whole kernel
    corn
1 14-ounce can beef broth
Salt and freshly ground
    pepper to taste

This chili is also good if you use leftover roast beef or pork instead of the hamburger. Serve the chili with crackers and cheese, peanut butter or toasted cheese sandwiches, or cornbread.

Add the ground beef and chili powder to a deep 3½-quart nonstick skillet; brown the meat over medium-high heat, breaking it apart as it cooks. When the meat is almost cooked through, add the onion; lower the heat to medium and sauté the onion until transparent. Drain off any excess fat. Add the garlic and sauté for 30 seconds. Stir in the kidney beans, salsa, corn, and broth. Bring to temperature and simmer for 15 minutes. Taste for seasoning and add salt and pepper if desired.

Ham and Sweet Potato Casserole

Serves 4

1 12-ounce bag frozen steam-
    in-the-bag California-
    blend vegetables
1 large egg
2 tablespoons milk, divided
3 tablespoons dry
    breadcrumbs
⅛ teaspoon freshly ground
    black pepper
¾ pound fully cooked ham,
    ground
1 15-ounce can cut sweet
    potatoes, drained
Nonstick cooking spray
½ cup condensed Cheddar
    cheese soup

You can improvise the condensed Cheddar cheese soup by mixing 2 tablespoons of heavy cream and a couple of drops of hot sauce into ½ cup of shredded Cheddar cheese.

1. Preheat oven to 325°F.

2. Cook the vegetables in the microwave according to package directions; drain and set aside. In a bowl, beat the egg together with 1 tablespoon of the milk. Stir in breadcrumbs, pepper, and ham; mix well. In another bowl, mash the sweet potatoes until almost smooth; spread onto the bottom and up the sides of a 9" Pyrex pie pan treated with nonstick spray. Spread the ham mixture over the sweet potatoes. Top with the vegetables. Combine the soup and remaining milk; spoon it over the vegetables. Cover with foil and bake for 45 minutes, or until heated through.

Tamale Spoon Bread Casserole

*This recipe requires one pot for the cooking and
a separate casserole dish for the baking.*

Serves 8–10

1 tablespoon extra-virgin
olive oil

1½ pounds ground chuck

1 large yellow onion,
chopped

1 clove garlic, minced

1 green pepper, seeded and
chopped

1 cup cornmeal

1 cup water

2 14½-ounce cans chopped
tomatoes, slightly
drained

1 12-ounce can whole kernel
corn

2 teaspoons salt, or to taste

1 tablespoon plus 1 teaspoon
chili powder

¼ teaspoon freshly ground
black pepper

½ cup sliced, pitted ripe olives

Nonstick cooking spray

1½ cups milk

2 tablespoons butter

1 cup grated mild Cheddar
cheese

2 eggs, slightly beaten

1. Preheat oven to 350°F.

2. Add the olive oil to a deep 3½-quart nonstick skillet and bring to temperature over medium heat; add the ground chuck and brown the meat. Add the onion, garlic, and green pepper to the skillet; cook, stirring, until the onion is slightly browned. Mix together ½ cup of the cornmeal and the 1 cup water and stir it into the skillet; cover and simmer for 10 minutes. Stir in the tomatoes, corn, 1 teaspoon of the salt, the chili powder, and pepper; simmer for 5 minutes longer. Mix in the olives and then spoon the meat mixture into a 3-quart casserole treated with nonstick spray.

3. Heat the milk over medium heat along with the remaining 1 teaspoon salt and the butter; once the milk begins to simmer, slowly whisk in the remaining ½ cup cornmeal. Lower the heat and continue to simmer while stirring or whisking until it thickens. Remove from the heat and stir in the cheese and eggs. Pour over the meat mixture. Bake uncovered for 1 hour, or until the entire casserole is hot and bubbly.

Quickest and Easiest

You can assemble this casserole the night before or earlier in the day. Cover the casserole dish with plastic wrap and refrigerate until needed. Remove the plastic wrap and bake for 75 to 90 minutes. The extra cooking time lets you bake the casserole without letting it come to room temperature before you put it in the oven.

Reuben Casserole

Serves 4–6

1¾ cup sauerkraut, rinsed
    and well drained
Nonstick cooking spray
1 pound thinly sliced corned
    beef
2 cups Swiss cheese, grated
3 tablespoons thousand
    island or Russian dressing
3 tablespoons mayonnaise
OPTIONAL: 2 fresh tomatoes,
    peeled and thinly sliced
½ cup butter, melted
1 cup rye wafers, crumbled
OPTIONAL: sprinkle of caraway
    seeds

You can bake the tomatoes in with the casserole if you prefer to have everything in one dish—just omit some of the tomato juice. Another option is to serve the casserole with fresh tomato slices or add tomato to a tossed salad.

1. Preheat oven to 350°F.

2. Put the drained sauerkraut in the bottom of a 3-quart casserole treated with nonstick spray. Add the corned beef and cheese. Spread the tomato slices in a layer over the cheese, if using. Mix the salad dressing and mayonnaise together and spread over the mixture in the casserole dish. Mix together the butter and rye wafers. Sprinkle the crumbs over the top of the casserole. If the wafers or bread that you used to make the crumbs don't contain caraway seeds, sprinkle some caraway seeds over the top of the crumbs. Bake for 30 to 45 minutes, or until the cheese is melted and the crumb topping is browned and crunchy.

Well-Drained Sauerkraut

Once you've rinsed the sauerkraut and drained it in a colander, it's a good idea to dump it into a clean cotton towel. Roll up the towel around the sauerkraut and then twist the towel to wring out even more of the liquid.

Chapter 12
Soups

Beef and Blackberry Soup

Serves 6–8

3 tablespoons peanut or extra-virgin olive oil

2 stalks celery, diced small

2 large carrots, peeled and diced small

1 large yellow onion, diced

1½ pounds boneless chuck roast

2 cups beef broth

2 cups water

1 tablespoon honey

1 cup blackberries

2 large sweet potatoes, peeled and diced

Salt and freshly ground black pepper to taste

OPTIONAL: 2 large russet potatoes, peeled and diced

Serve this soup with cornbread or corn muffins. Have honey at the table for those who want to spread it on their cornbread or muffins, or want to use it to sweeten their soup.

1. Add the oil to a 6-quart Dutch oven and bring to temperature over medium heat. Add the celery and carrots; sauté for 3 to 5 minutes, or until tender. Add the onions and sauté until the onions are transparent.

2. Trim the fat from the roast and cut it into bite-sized pieces. Add to the meat to the Dutch oven and brown it for a few minutes. Add the broth, water, honey, blackberries, sweet potatoes, salt, and pepper. Bring to a boil. Lower the heat and simmer, covered, for 1 hour, or until the meat is tender. Taste for seasoning and add more honey, salt, and pepper, if needed.

3. Add the potatoes, if using. Cover and simmer for an additional 30 minutes, or until the potatoes are cooked.

Name Game

A boneless "English-cut" chuck roast is the perfect cut to use in a slow-cooked beef dish; it cooks up to pull-apart tender. The boneless cut is sometimes called an English roll. That cut of chuck roast also can be referred to as a cross rib roast, cross rib pot roast, Boston cut, English cut roast, English roast, thick rib roast, bread and butter cut, or beef chuck cross rib pot roast.

Mock Turtle Soup

This soup is the perfect opportunity to use up leftover meat you have stored in the freezer. Served with a salad and crusty bread or toast, it makes a hearty meal.

Serves 8–10

¼ pound salt pork or bacon, diced
2 stalks celery, finely diced
2 large carrots, peeled and finely diced
1 medium yellow onion, diced
3 cloves garlic, minced
¼ cup butter
½ cup all-purpose flour
3 cups beef broth
1 cup chicken broth
1 15-ounce can diced tomatoes
½ teaspoon dried basil
½ teaspoon dried marjoram
½ teaspoon dried thyme
1 bay leaf
1 teaspoon freshly ground black pepper
1 tablespoon dried parsley
1 4-ounce halibut fillet
1 cup cooked roast beef, shredded
1 cup cooked chicken, shredded
½ cup cooked crabmeat, shredded
2 tablespoons fresh lemon juice
¼ teaspoon hot sauce, or to taste
1½ tablespoons Worcestershire sauce
⅛ teaspoon ground cloves
½ cup dry sherry
4 hard-boiled eggs, peeled and finely diced

1. Add the salt pork or bacon to a Dutch oven and sauté it over medium heat long enough to render the fat. Add the celery and carrots, and sauté for 3 to 5 minutes, or until tender. Add the onion and sauté until transparent. Add the garlic and sauté another 30 seconds. Melt the butter into the sautéed vegetables. Stir in the flour and cook until the roux turns the color of peanut butter, stirring constantly.

2. Gradually add the beef broth, whisking it in to mix thoroughly with the roux. Stir in the chicken broth and tomatoes. Stir in the basil, marjoram, thyme, bay leaf, pepper, and parsley. Bring to a boil, and boil for 1 minute. Reduce the heat and simmer until the mixture begins to thicken.

3. Add the halibut. Cover and simmer for 10 minutes. Remove the halibut and flake it. Stir in the fish, beef, chicken, crabmeat, lemon juice, hot sauce, Worcestershire sauce, and ground cloves. Reduce the heat; simmer until the meat reaches serving temperature. Stir in the sherry and diced eggs. Serve hot.

Chicken and Corn Soup
with Mini Dumplings

Serves 4–6

2 tablespoons butter

1 stalk celery, finely chopped

1 large carrot, peeled and
   finely chopped

1 small yellow onion,
   chopped

1 clove garlic, minced

4 cups chicken broth

1 17-ounce can creamed corn

1 large egg, beaten

Pinch salt

¾–1 cup all-purpose flour

1 cup cooked chicken,
   shredded

2 hard-boiled eggs, peeled
   and sliced

OPTIONAL: fresh chopped
   parsley for garnish

This is a simplified version of a Pennsylvania Dutch soup. In that version, the mini dumplings are known as rivels. The literal meaning of rivel is "lump."

1. Melt the butter in a deep 3½-quart nonstick skillet or large saucepan over medium heat. Add the celery and carrot; sauté for 3 to 5 minutes, or until soft. Add the onion and sauté until transparent. Add the garlic and sauté for an additional 30 seconds. Stir in the broth and corn. Lower the temperature and allow the soup to simmer while you mix up the dumplings.

2. In a small bowl, mix the egg together with the salt and enough flour to make a dry dough. Working with 1 tablespoon of the dough at a time, rub it between your hands over the pan so that pieces of the dough drop into the soup. After all of the mini dumplings have been added to the pan, simmer the soup for an additional 10 minutes, or until the dumplings are tender. Serve with slices of hard-boiled egg floating on top of the soup. Garnish with parsley, if desired.

Chicken and Corn Egg Drop Soup

In step 2, omit the flour and use 2 large eggs instead of 1. Beat the eggs together with a pinch of salt. A little at a time, drizzle the eggs into the simmering soup and cook until the eggs are set.

Artichoke Soup

With this soup, you almost spend more time opening cans than you do cooking.
It doesn't get simpler than this, but it tastes like you worked on it all day.

Add all ingredients except the salt and pepper to a large saucepan. Stir to combine. Bring to a simmer over medium heat; reduce the heat and simmer, uncovered, for 15 minutes. Taste for seasoning and add salt and pepper, if needed.

Serves 8

1 10¾-ounce can condensed
   cream of mushroom soup
1 10¾-ounce can condensed
   cream of celery soup
3¼ cups milk
1 5-ounce can shrimp,
   drained
1 cup carrots, peeled and
   finely shredded
1 14-ounce can artichoke
   hearts, drained and
   chopped
½ teaspoon curry powder
Pinch allspice
¼ teaspoon onion powder
Salt and freshly ground black
   pepper to taste

Sauerkraut Soup

To save time, get frozen small white onions.
Thaw them before you add them to the soup.

1. Bring the water to boil in a 4-quart Dutch oven over medium-high heat. Add the caraway seeds, chervil, onions, celery, carrots, sauerkraut, and sugar. Reduce the heat and simmer, covered, for 15 minutes.

2. Stir in the green beans. Slice the hot dogs or smoked sausage into ½" pieces and stir into the soup along with the tomato and potato soup. Cook, covered, for 15 minutes, stirring occasionally. Taste for seasoning and add salt and pepper, if needed.

Serves 8–10

3 cups water
½ teaspoon caraway seeds
½ teaspoon dried chervil
16 small white onions
4 stalks celery, diced
4 large carrots, peeled and
   thinly sliced
1 14-ounce can sauerkraut,
   undrained
1 tablespoon granulated
   sugar
1 8-ounce package frozen
   green beans, thawed
2 pounds hot dogs or fully
   cooked smoked sausage
1 large tomato, diced
2 10¾-ounce cans cream of
   potato soup
Salt and freshly ground black
   pepper to taste

Butternut Squash Soup
with Kielbasa and Wild Rice

Serves 6–8

1 1½- to 2-pound butternut squash

2 tablespoons extra-virgin olive oil

6 cups chicken broth

1 large yellow onion, diced

1 cup uncooked wild rice

1 pound kielbasa, cut into ¼" slices

1 12- or 16-ounce package frozen whole kernel corn, thawed

Salt and freshly ground black pepper to taste

Water as needed

1 cup heavy cream

OPTIONAL: 1 tablespoon fresh parsley, chopped

If you prefer, you can substitute cooked pork, chicken, or turkey for the kielbasa.

1. Preheat the oven to 400°F.

2. Cut the squash in half and remove the seeds. Place the squash halves skin-side down on a baking sheet and drizzle the meat with 1 tablespoon of the olive oil; bake for 1 hour. Remove from the oven and let cool completely. Peel the squash and add it to a blender or food processor along with 2 cups of the chicken broth; purée until smooth and set aside.

3. Add the remaining 4 cups of the broth and ½ of the chopped onions to a Dutch oven and bring to a simmer over medium heat. Stir in the rice; cook for 1 hour, or until the rice is tender and most of the liquid is absorbed, stirring occasionally with a fork. Remove the rice from the pan and set aside.

4. Add the remaining 1 tablespoon of oil to the Dutch oven and bring it to temperature over medium heat. Add the kielbasa slices; brown them for 3 minutes. Add the remaining onions and corn; season with salt and pepper and sauté for 3 minutes. Add the squash purée; reduce the heat to medium-low, cover, and simmer for 20 minutes, checking occasionally and adding water, if needed. Skim off any fat on the surface, stir in the rice, and continue to cook for 10 minutes. Remove from the heat and stir in the cream. Taste for seasoning, and add salt and pepper, if needed. Serve garnished with parsley, if desired.

Microwave-Roasted Butternut Squash

Instead of baking the butternut squash, you can fix it in the microwave. Wash the squash, slice in half lengthwise, remove the seeds, and place it cut-side down in a shallow microwave-safe pan. Add water to about ¾-inch deep. Microwave on high for 8 to 10 minutes, or until the squash is tender.

Pumpkin Soup

Canned pumpkin actually packs more nutrients than raw fresh pumpkin, so this is one shortcut you absolutely shouldn't feel guilty about! Serve with cornbread or peanut butter sandwiches.

Serves 4–6

2 tablespoons butter
1 stalk celery, finely diced
1 large carrot, peeled and
    finely diced
1 medium yellow onion,
    minced
1 medium apple, peeled,
    cored, and minced
1 15-ounce can pumpkin
    purée
3 cups chicken broth
1 10-ounce package frozen
    whole kernel corn,
    thawed
OPTIONAL: diced cooked ham,
    to taste
Salt and freshly ground
    pepper to taste
OPTIONAL: toasted pumpkin
    seeds, shelled

1. Melt the butter in a small Dutch oven over medium heat. Add the celery and carrot; sauté for 3 to 5 minutes, or until tender. Add the onion and apple; sauté until the onion is transparent. Stir in the pumpkin and chicken broth. Bring to a boil; reduce heat and simmer for 10 minutes. Use a stick blender to purée the soup if you wish.

2. Add the corn and the ham (if using); simmer for 8 minutes, or until the corn is tender. Taste for seasoning and add salt and pepper if needed. Garnish with pumpkin seeds, if desired.

Pumpkin Soup Variations

Omit the corn in the Pumpkin Soup recipe and stir in ½ cup of peanut butter and a little brown sugar instead. Or, season the soup by adding 1 teaspoon smoked paprika, ⅛ teaspoon ground cumin, and a pinch of cayenne pepper. Turn any variation into a cream soup by stirring in ½ cup of heavy cream, or more to taste.

Sweet Potato Soup
with Ginger

Serves 6–8

2 tablespoons extra-virgin
   olive oil
2 stalks celery, finely diced
1 large carrot, peeled and
   finely diced
1 large yellow onion, minced
1 clove garlic, minced
2 teaspoons fresh ginger,
   grated
5 cups chicken broth
4 medium sweet potatoes,
   peeled and diced
1 cup heavy cream
Salt and freshly ground
   pepper to taste
OPTIONAL: ¼ cup dry sherry
OPTIONAL: fresh chives,
   chopped, to taste

*This soup is hearty enough to serve as a meal, or serve it alongside
a ham or turkey sandwich for a soup and sandwich lunch.*

1. Melt the butter or oil in a deep 3½-quart nonstick skillet or large sauce-pan over medium heat. Add the celery and carrot; sauté for 3 to 5 minutes, or until soft. Add the onion and sauté until transparent. Add the garlic and ginger, and sauté for an additional 30 seconds.

2. Pour 3 cups of the chicken broth into the pan along with the diced sweet potatoes. Bring to a boil; reduce heat, cover, and simmer for 10 minutes, or until the sweet potatoes are cooked through. Periodically check the simmering pot to make sure it doesn't boil dry. Mash the sweet potatoes with a fork or blend them with a stick blender.

3. Stir the remaining broth and cream into the soup. Bring to temperature. Taste for seasoning and add salt and pepper if needed. Stir in the sherry and garnish with chopped chives, if desired.

Taking the Blender to the Pot

A stick blender is also sometimes referred to as an immersion blender or a hand blender. They're available in electric and cordless rechargeable-battery models. You can purée soups with ease, and they're also excellent for making sauces. To clean, simply put the blades into some soapy water and run the appliance, then run in clear water.

Pork Steak and Cabbage Soup

You can ladle this soup over some shredded Cheddar or American cheese, allow time for the cheese to melt, and stir everything together.

Serves 8–10

3 tablespoons extra-virgin olive oil

2 stalks celery, finely diced

1 1-pound bag baby carrots

1 large yellow onion, diced

1 clove garlic, minced

2 pounds boneless pork steak

4 large russet or red potatoes, peeled or unpeeled, and diced

4 cups chicken broth

1 large head of cabbage, cored and shredded

OPTIONAL: 1½ teaspoons juniper berries

OPTIONAL: ½ cup dry white wine or beer

OPTIONAL: shredded Cheddar cheese, to taste

1. Add the oil to a 6-quart Dutch oven and bring to temperature over medium heat. Mince or shred 4 or 5 of the baby carrots and add them to the pan along with the celery; sauté for 3 to 5 minutes, or until soft. Add the onion and sauté until transparent. Add the garlic and sauté for an additional 30 seconds. Trim the pork of most of the fat; cut into small strips or dice. Add the pork and potatoes; stir-fry for 3 to 5 minutes, or until the potatoes just begin to take on a golden brown color.

2. Deglaze the pan with some of the chicken broth, and then add the remaining broth. Bring the broth to a boil; reduce the temperature and simmer, covered, for 45 minutes. Cut the remaining carrots into 3 or 4 pieces each and add to the pan.

3. Add the cabbage in stages. Stir in ½ cup, cover the pan and allow to steam for 5 minutes, stir the cabbage into the soup, and repeat until all the cabbage has been added. Add the juniper berries and wine or beer, if using. Cover and simmer for 45 minutes, stirring occasionally. Add water if additional cooking liquid is needed. Serve topped with some shredded Cheddar cheese, if desired.

Best Options

This hearty soup tastes even better after it's been refrigerated overnight and warmed up the next day. The traditional version doesn't have the extra carrot pieces in it; omit them if you wish. Serve the soup with pumpernickel or whole grain bread and beer.

Mulligatawny Soup

This soup is traditionally served garnished with lots of freshly ground black pepper along with the chopped cilantro.

Serves 8

8 chicken thighs
1 stalk celery, cut in half
1 large carrot, peeled and cut in 4 pieces
1 small yellow onion, quartered
8 cups water
1 tablespoon ghee
1 medium yellow onion, diced
2 stalks celery, finely diced
4 large carrots, peeled and finely diced
2 cloves garlic, minced
¼ teaspoon turmeric
½ teaspoon ground coriander
¼ teaspoon dried red pepper flakes
½ teaspoon dried cumin
½ teaspoon ground cardamom
½ teaspoon ground dried ginger
Salt and freshly ground black pepper to taste
4 cups chicken broth
OPTIONAL: fresh chopped cilantro, to taste

1. Add the chicken thighs, celery and carrot pieces, onion quarters, and 4 cups of the water to a Dutch oven. Bring to a simmer over medium heat; reduce the heat, cover, and simmer for 1 hour. Strain the broth into a bowl and set aside. Discard the cooked vegetables. Once the chicken has cooled enough to handle it, remove the meat from the bones, discarding the skin and the bones; set aside.

2. Meanwhile, melt the ghee in the Dutch oven over medium heat. Add the diced celery and carrot; sauté for 3 to 5 minutes, or until soft. Add the diced onion and sauté until transparent. Add the garlic and sauté for an additional 30 seconds.

3. Stir the turmeric, coriander, red pepper flakes, cumin, cardamom, ginger, salt, and pepper into the sautéed vegetables. Stir in the chicken broth and the remaining 4 cups of water. Bring to a boil; reduce the heat, cover, and simmer for 30 minutes. Add the cooked chicken; simmer uncovered, stirring occasionally, for an additional 5 minutes to bring the meat to temperature. Taste for seasoning and add additional salt, if needed. Serve garnished with additional freshly ground black pepper and chopped cilantro if desired.

Fat Adds Flavor—and Calories

Fat is tasty, but it adds extra calories to a dish. If you favor lean over flavor, you can either remove the skin before you cook the thighs or refrigerate the broth to make it easier to skim the fat off the top.

Pho

This is a simplified, Americanized version of this recipe, substituting brown sugar for the yellow rock sugar found in Asian markets.

1. Trim the roast of any fat; cut the meat into 2" × 4" pieces and add them to a 4-quart slow cooker. Peel and quarter 2 of the onions. Cut the ginger into 1" pieces. Add the onion and ginger to the slow cooker along with the star anise, cloves, cinnamon stick, salt, broth, and enough water to cover the meat by about 1 inch. Cook on low for 6 to 8 hours, or until the beef is pull-apart tender.

2. About 30 minutes before serving, peel the remaining onion; cut it into paper-thin slices and soak them in cold water. Cover the noodles with hot water and allow to soak for 15 to 20 minutes, or until softened and opaque white; drain in colander.

3. Remove the meat from the broth with a slotted spoon; shred the meat. Strain the broth through fine strainer, discarding the spices and onion; return the strained broth to the slow cooker along with the shredded meat. Set the slow cooker on the high setting and bring the broth to a rolling boil. Stir the fish sauce and brown sugar into the broth.

4. Taste and adjust seasoning if necessary. If you desire a stronger, saltier flavor, add more fish sauce. Add more brown sugar to make the broth sweeter, if desired. If the broth is too salty, add some additional water.

5. Blanch the noodles in stages. Add ¼ of the noodles to a strainer and submerge in the boiling broth, being careful not to allow the slow cooker to boil over. The noodles will collapse and lose their stiffness in about 15 to 20 seconds. Pull the strainer from the broth, letting the excess broth drain back into cooker, and empty the noodles into bowls, allowing each serving to fill about ⅓ of the bowl. Ladle some of the hot broth and beef over each serving of noodles. Garnish with the onion slices, green onions, and chopped cilantro, and finish with freshly ground black pepper.

Serves 8–10

3-pound English-cut chuck roast
3 medium yellow onions
4-inch piece ginger
5 star anise
6 whole cloves
1 3" cinnamon stick
¼ teaspoons salt
2 cups beef broth
Water as needed
4 tablespoons fish sauce
1 tablespoon light brown sugar
1½–2 pounds small dried banh pho noodles
3 or 4 green onions, green part only, cut into thin rings
⅓ cup fresh cilantro, chopped
Freshly ground black pepper to taste

Cock-a-Leekie

This is the Scottish version of a chicken soup. Feel free to add carrots to the soup if you desire more vegetables with your meal. Serve it alongside or over buttered biscuits for true comfort food goodness.

1. Add the chicken, beef shanks, bacon, broth, thyme, and bay leaf to a large Dutch oven. Add enough water to cover the meat. Bring to a boil over medium-high heat; cover, reduce heat, and simmer for 1 hour, or until the chicken is cooked through and tender.

2. Use a slotted spoon to remove the chicken from the pot. Set aside and allow to cool. Bring the broth to a boil over medium heat. Add the barley. Boil for 10 minutes, stirring occasionally.

3. Remove the chicken from the bones. Discard the skin and bones, and shred the chicken. Use a slotted spoon to remove the beef shanks from the pot; set aside and allow to cool.

4. Add the leeks to the pan. Reduce heat, cover, and simmer for 10 minutes. Remove the beef from the bones, discarding the bones and any fat. Add the chicken and beef to the pan. Cover and simmer for 5 minutes to bring the meat to temperature. Taste for seasoning and add salt and pepper, if needed. Garnish with parsley if desired.

Matzo Balls

Matzo balls are good in almost any chicken soup. To make six servings, mix 2 tablespoons of chicken fat, 2 large eggs, ½ cup matzo meal, 1 teaspoon salt, and 2 tablespoons chicken broth. Cover and refrigerate for at least 20 minutes. Roll the mixture into 12 balls. Cook, covered, in boiling water or broth for 30 to 40 minutes.

Fish Soup
with Lettuce

Pick up some spring or California rolls and serve them alongside this soup for a complete, light meal. Tastes vary, so have the salt, soy sauce, toasted sesame oil, and green onions at the table and let each person season his or her own soup.

Add the peanut oil to a deep 3½-quart nonstick skillet or wok and bring to temperature over medium heat. Add the garlic and stir-fry for 30 seconds. Add the broth and bring to a simmer. Add the ginger and fish, cover, and simmer for 5 minutes. Use a slotted spoon to remove the ginger slices, and stir in the lettuce. Cook for another 2 minutes. Add the salt, soy sauce, and toasted sesame oil to taste. Garnish with the chopped green onions.

Serves 4

1 tablespoon peanut oil
2 cloves garlic, minced
4 cups chicken broth
½" fresh ginger, thinly sliced
1 pound whitefish fillet, sliced thin
1 head iceberg lettuce, chopped
Salt to taste
Soy sauce to taste
Toasted sesame oil to taste
3 green onions, chopped

Thai-Inspired Chicken Soup

This soup is an excellent use for leftover cooked chicken breast. If you don't have any on hand and want to add raw meat, allow extra simmering time to let the chicken cook through.

1. Add the chicken broth, ginger, garlic, shallot, and lime leaves to a 6-quart Dutch oven. Bring to a boil over medium heat. Peel the bottom 5 inches of the lemongrass stalks, chop, and add to the broth. Reduce the heat, cover, and simmer for 10 minutes. Strain the broth and discard the solids.

2. Return broth to the pan. Stir in the curry paste, sugar, coconut milk, and fish sauce. Bring to a simmer over low heat. Add the chicken, peppers, and lime juice. Cover and simmer for 10 minutes, or until the peppers are tender. Taste for seasoning and add salt and pepper if needed. Serve garnished with the chopped cilantro, if desired.

Serves 6–8

6 cups chicken broth
½" fresh ginger, thinly sliced
2 cloves garlic, minced
3 shallots, sliced
7 dried Kaffir lime leaves
3 stalks fresh lemongrass
1 teaspoon Thai red curry paste
1 tablespoon granulated sugar
1 14-ounce can coconut milk
3 tablespoons Thai fish sauce
2 cups cooked chicken breast, diced
2 small jalapeño peppers, seeded and thinly sliced
2 tablespoons fresh lime juice
Salt and freshly ground black pepper to taste
OPTIONAL: fresh chopped cilantro, to taste

Persian Lentil and Rice Soup

Serves 8–10

2 tablespoons extra-virgin olive oil

1 large yellow onion, thinly sliced

1 tablespoon dried parsley

4 cups chopped tomatoes

10 cups chicken broth

2 teaspoons dried mint, crushed

1 cup lentils

⅛ cup fresh lemon juice

¼ cup uncooked basmati rice

½ cup bulgur wheat, medium grind

2 tablespoons tomato paste

½ teaspoon granulated sugar

2 teaspoons sumac

2 teaspoons advieh (recipe follows)

Salt and freshly ground black pepper to taste

If you prefer to have meat in your soup, add boiled chicken with the ingredients in step 3.

1. Add the oil to a 6-quart Dutch oven and bring to temperature over medium-high heat. Add the onion, and sauté until transparent. Stir in the parsley and tomatoes; sauté a few minutes and then add the chicken broth, mint, lentils, and lemon juice. Bring to a boil; reduce the heat, cover, and simmer for 30 minutes.

2. Add the rice to a blender or food processor; pulse several times to break it into a coarse powder. Add the broken rice and bulgur; cover and simmer for 75 minutes.

3. Stir in the remaining ingredients. Simmer until the soup is heated through. Taste for seasoning, adding more salt and pepper if necessary.

Advieh

To make this Persian seasoning mix, add a tablespoon of edible dried rose petals, a tablespoon ground cinnamon, ¼ teaspoon cardamom seeds, ¼ teaspoons black peppercorns, ⅛ teaspoon turmeric, ½ teaspoon freshly ground nutmeg, ½ teaspoon cumin seeds, and ¼ teaspoon coriander seeds to a blender or spice grinder; grind to a powder. Store in an air-tight container.

Chapter 13
Stews

Brunswick Stew

This stew is made with chicken or rabbit. The cooking times are the same whether you use fresh or thawed frozen vegetables.

Serves 6

2 slices bacon, diced

3 tablespoons all-purpose flour

1 teaspoon salt

½ teaspoon pepper

Pinch cayenne pepper

1 4-pound chicken or rabbit, cut into serving pieces

Giblets, if using chicken

3 small yellow onions, thinly sliced

1½ cups boiling water

4 tomatoes, diced

1 red bell pepper, seeded and diced

½ teaspoon dried leaf thyme, crushed

2 cups lima beans

2 cups corn kernels

½ cup okra, sliced

2 tablespoons fresh parsley, chopped

1 tablespoon Worcestershire sauce

Add the bacon to a slow cooker; cook on the high setting to render the fat. Remove the bacon and set aside. Put the flour, salt, pepper, and cayenne in a gallon-size food-storage bag; add the rabbit or chicken, close the bag, and shake to coat the pieces with the seasoned flour. Add the meat to the pan and brown in the rendered fat. Add the onion, cover, and steam until the onions are transparent, about 5 minutes. Add the water, tomatoes, red pepper, and thyme to the slow cooker. Cover; cook on low for 6 to 8 hours, or until the meat is cooked through and tender. Add the remaining ingredients along with the reserved bacon; cover and cook on high for 25 minutes, or until the vegetables are tender.

Pot-au-feu

Pot-au-feu is French for "pot on the fire." This recipe is a slow-cooker adaptation of the French boiled dinner, with ingredients added so that the potatoes sit atop the meat and steam during the cooking process.

Serves 8

2 tablespoons butter
1 1-pound bag baby carrots
2 large yellow onions, sliced
4 stalks celery, finely diced
2 cloves garlic, left whole
1 bouquet garni
2-pound boneless chuck
    roast, cut into 1" pieces
8 chicken thighs
1 pound Western-style pork
    ribs
1 tablespoon coarse sea salt
4 small turnips, peeled and
    quartered
1 medium rutabaga, peeled
    and cut into eighths
Water as needed
8 medium red or Yukon
    gold potatoes, cut into
    quarters

1. Add the butter to a 6½-quart slow cooker set on high heat. Finely dice 10 of the baby carrots and 2 of the onion slices. Add the diced carrots and onion and the celery to the slow cooker; cover and cook for 15 minutes. Add the garlic, bouquet garni, beef, chicken, and pork; sprinkle the salt over the meat and then layer in the remaining onion slices, remaining carrots, turnips, and rutabaga. Add enough water so that the water level comes just to the top of the vegetables. Arrange the potatoes on top of the rutabaga. Reduce the heat setting to low, cover, and cook for 8 hours.

2. For a casual supper, you can ladle servings directly from the crock. For a more formal dinner, use a slotted spoon to arrange the vegetables and potatoes around the outside of a large serving platter with the meats arranged in the center; ladle a generous amount of the broth over all. Strain the remaining broth; pour the strained broth into a gravy boat to have at the table.

3. Serve with toasted French bread rubbed with garlic and have coarse sea salt, cornichons, Dijon mustard, grated horseradish, pickled onions, sour cream, and whole grain mustard at the table.

Bouquet Garni

Create the bouquet garni by wrapping 2 bay leaves, 1 teaspoon dried thyme, 1 tablespoon dried parsley, 1 teaspoon black peppercorns, and 4 cloves in cheesecloth or in a muslin spice bag.

Seafood Stew

*2 tablespoons extra-virgin
olive oil, plus extra for
serving*
*2 medium yellow onions,
diced*
4 garlic cloves, minced
*1 pound smoked sausage,
sliced into chunks*
½ teaspoon dried thyme
*¼ teaspoon dried oregano,
crushed*
1 bay leaf
*8 large Yukon gold potatoes,
diced*
8 cups chicken broth
1 pound kale, chopped
OPTIONAL: Water as needed
*2 pounds perch, cod, or bass
fillets, skin and pin bones
removed*
*2 28-ounce cans boiled baby
clams, drained*
*Sea salt and freshly ground
black pepper to taste*
*OPTIONAL: ¼ cup fresh flat-leaf
parsley, chopped*

*You can add a Portuguese touch to this dish by substituting linguiça or
chorizo sausage for the smoked sausage. Regardless, serve the stew with
warm garlic bread so you can sop up the broth.*

1. Bring the oil to temperature in a 4- to 6-quart Dutch oven over medium heat. Add the onions, garlic, and sausage; stirring frequently, sauté for 5 minutes, or until the onions are transparent. Add the thyme, oregano, bay leaf, and potatoes, stirring everything to mix the herbs and coat the potatoes in the oil. Pour in the chicken broth; bring to a simmer. Add the kale; cover and simmer for 10 minutes, or until the potatoes are nearly tender.

2. Add the fish; cook for another 3 minutes. Add water if additional liquid is needed to cover the fish. Add the drained clams, and cook for an additional 3 minutes, or until the fish is cooked and the clams are brought to temperature. Taste for seasoning, and add salt and pepper if needed. Garnish with chopped parsley, if desired, and drizzle with extra-virgin olive oil.

Why Water Is Optional

The heat at which you cook a dish makes a difference in how much of the liquid will evaporate during the cooking process. Some vegetables in a dish also sometimes absorb more liquid than do others. If such evaporation or absorption occurs, the broth will become concentrated. Thus, water only reintroduces more liquid; it doesn't dilute the taste.

Southern Chicken Stew

*The sugar in this dish offsets the acidity of the tomatoes. If
you're using apple juice instead of wine, you may want to wait
until the dish is cooked to see if the sugar is needed.*

Serves 8

3 tablespoons bacon fat
*1 3-pound chicken, cut into
    serving pieces*
2 cups water
*1 28-ounce can diced
    tomatoes*
2 large yellow onions, sliced
½ teaspoon granulated sugar
*½ cup dry white wine or
    apple juice*
*1 10-ounce package frozen
    lima beans, thawed*
*1 10-ounce package frozen
    whole kernel corn,
    thawed*
*1 10-ounce package frozen
    okra, thawed and sliced*
1 cup breadcrumbs, toasted
*3 tablespoons Worcestershire
    sauce*
*Salt and freshly ground black
    pepper to taste*
OPTIONAL: hot sauce to taste

1. Bring the bacon fat to temperature in a 6-quart Dutch oven over medium heat. Add the chicken pieces and fry them until lightly browned. Add the water, tomatoes, onions, sugar, and wine or apple juice. Bring to a simmer; cover and simmer for 75 minutes, or until the chicken is cooked through. Use a slotted spoon to remove the chicken and set it aside until it's cool enough to handle. Then, remove the chicken from the bones and discard the skin and bones. Shred the chicken meat and set aside.

2. Add the lima beans, corn, and okra to the pot. Bring to a simmer and cook uncovered for 30 minutes. Stir in the shredded chicken, bread-crumbs, and Worcestershire sauce. Simmer for 10 minutes, stirring occasionally, to bring the chicken to temperature and thicken the stew. Taste for seasoning and add salt and pepper, if needed, and hot sauce, if desired.

African Peanut and Chicken Stew

2 tablespoons peanut oil

2 3-pound chickens, cut into serving pieces

1 large yellow onion, sliced

½ teaspoon dried dill

2 bay leaves

Water as needed

½ cup peanut butter

3 tablespoons cornstarch

½ cup cold water

Salt and freshly ground pepper to taste

OPTIONAL: 3–6 cups cooked long-grain rice

OPTIONAL: 5 bananas, peeled and cut lengthwise, then browned in butter

OPTIONAL: unsweetened pineapple chunks

OPTIONAL: 4 ounces unsweetened coconut, toasted

½ cup roasted peanuts, finely chopped

When served with all of the optional condiments, African Peanut and Chicken Stew is a one-pot meal and dessert rolled into one.

1. Add the oil to a 6-quart Dutch oven and bring it to temperature over medium heat. Add the chicken pieces, skin-side down, and brown them for 5 minutes. Add the onion, dill, bay leaves, and enough water to almost cover the chicken. Bring to a boil, reduce heat and simmer, covered, for 45 minutes. Remove the chicken from the pot and keep warm; discard the skin, if desired. Remove and discard the bay leaves.

2. Add ½ cup of the hot liquid from the Dutch oven to the peanut butter; mix well, and then pour the resulting peanut butter sauce into the pan. In a small bowl, mix the cornstarch and cold water together; remove any lumps. Whisk the cornstarch mixture into the broth in the pan, continuing to stir or whisk until the broth thickens. If you prefer a thicker sauce, mix more cornstarch in cold water and repeat the process.

3. Taste the sauce for seasoning and add salt and pepper, if needed. The traditional way to serve this dish is to place the chicken over some cooked rice. Ladle the thickened pan juices over the chicken and rice. Top with fried bananas, pineapple, and toasted coconut (if using), and chopped peanuts.

Toasted Coconut

To toast coconut, preheat oven to 350°F. Spread the coconut out over a jellyroll pan. Place the pan in the oven and, watching it carefully, bake the coconut for 5 minutes, or until it's a very light golden brown.

Green Chili Stew

Serve this stew with a salad and corn chips. It also works as an enchilada filling. To accommodate different tastes, use mild green chili peppers in the stew and have hot green salsa at the table.

Melt the butter in a 4-quart Dutch oven over medium heat. Add the onion and sauté for 5 minutes, or until the onion is transparent. Stir in the oregano, garlic, and chili powder. Whisk in the flour to make a roux, and cook it until it's lightly browned. Whisk in the chicken broth a little at a time, whisking until smooth. Bring to a boil and boil for 1 minute. Reduce heat, and stir in the pork and canned chilies. Simmer gently, stirring occasionally, until thickened. Taste for seasoning and add salt and pepper if desired.

Serves 6–8

½ cup butter
1 large yellow onion, diced
½ teaspoon dried oregano
½ tablespoon granulated garlic
1 tablespoon chili powder
¼ cup all-purpose flour
4 cups chicken broth
1 28-ounce can heat-and-serve pork
3 7-ounce cans mild or hot green chilies, drained and chopped
Salt and freshly ground black pepper to taste

Spiced Armenian Lamb Stew

Serve this rich stew over rice or couscous along with a cucumber salad and your choice of bread.

1. Melt the butter in a 6-quart Dutch oven and bring to temperature over medium heat. Add the onions; sauté for 3 minutes. Pushing the onions to the side of the pan, add the lamb and brown the meat in the butter. Stir the paprika, pepper, allspice, and cinnamon into the meat and onions. Add salt to taste.

2. Push the meat and onions to the side and sauté the tomato paste for 2 minutes, then stir it into the meat and onions. Slowly pour the water into the pan. Stir to dissolve the tomato paste into the water. Bring the water to a boil, then reduce the heat, cover, and simmer for 45 minutes, or until the meat is tender. Add the red wine, cover, and simmer for 15 more minutes. Taste for seasoning and add salt and pepper, if needed.

Serves 4–6

2 tablespoons butter
1 large yellow onion, diced
2 pounds lean, boneless leg of lamb, cut into 1" cubes
½ teaspoon paprika
½ teaspoon freshly ground black pepper
½ teaspoon ground allspice
¼ teaspoon ground cinnamon
Salt to taste
¼ cup tomato paste
1 cup water
2 tablespoons dry red wine

Unstuffed Tomatoes and Peppers

Rather than taking the time to make a filling and then filling the peppers and tomatoes, this dish is prepared layered in a slow cooker.

Serves 8

1 cup uncooked long-grain rice
1 cup tomato juice
1 pound ground beef
½ pound ground lamb or pork
1 large yellow onion, diced
1 tablespoon dried parsley
1 teaspoon salt
Freshly ground black pepper to taste
1 teaspoon paprika
⅛ teaspoon ground allspice
Pinch ground cinnamon
1 teaspoon granulated sugar
2 14.5-ounce cans diced tomatoes
4 green bell peppers, seeded and diced
1 cup beef broth
2 tablespoons lemon juice
Water or additional broth, as needed

1. In a large mixing bowl, combine the rice, tomato juice, beef, lamb or pork, onion, parsley, salt, black pepper, paprika, allspice, cinnamon, and sugar. Set aside.

2. Add 1 can of the diced tomatoes to a 4-quart or larger slow cooker. Add half of the meat-rice mixture. Spread the diced green peppers over the top of the meat mixture, and top the peppers with the rest of the meat. Add the remaining can of diced tomatoes. Pour in the beef broth and add the lemon juice. If needed, add additional water or broth to bring the liquid to almost the top of the solid ingredients. Cook for 6 to 8 hours on low. If too much liquid remains in the slow cooker, cook uncovered long enough to allow some of the liquid to evaporate.

Irish Lamb Stew

This is the type of dish that's easy to expand if extra people show up for dinner. Simply add extra broth, carrots, and potatoes as needed.

1. Bring the oil or fat to temperature over medium heat in a Dutch oven. Add the onion and sauté for 3 to 5 minutes, or until the onion is transparent. Add the garlic and sauté for an additional 30 seconds. Add the lamb; brown it for about 5 minutes, or until it begins to release some of its juices and some of the pieces become caramelized.

2. Sprinkle the flour over the lamb, and stir to toss the flour with the meat and fat in the pan. Stir in the broth, salt, pepper, bay leaf, marjoram, and lemon juice. Bring to a simmer, cover, and simmer for 30 minutes to 1 hour, or until the meat begins to get tender. If needed, skim off any excess fat from the top of the broth. Add the small onions, carrots, and potatoes; cover and simmer for 30 minutes, or until the carrots and potatoes are cooked through. Serve sprinkled with parsley, if desired.

Serves 6–8

4 tablespoons extra-virgin olive oil or bacon fat

1 large yellow onion, chopped

1 clove garlic, minced

2½ pounds lean lamb shoulder, cut in bite-sized pieces

2 tablespoons all-purpose flour

1½ cups chicken broth

Salt to taste

¼ teaspoon pepper

1 bay leaf

¼ teaspoon dried marjoram

2 teaspoons lemon juice

1 cup frozen pearl onions, thawed

4 large carrots, peeled and cut in chunks

4 large russet potatoes, peeled and diced

OPTIONAL: 1½ tablespoons fresh parsley, finely chopped

Puerto Rican Chicken Stew

*The consistency of this dish is a compromise: It's
thicker than a stew but moister than a paella.*

Serves 4

2 teaspoons dried oregano,
    crushed
¼ teaspoon freshly ground
    black pepper
2 teaspoons paprika
¼ teaspoon salt
1 3½-pound chicken, cut into
    serving pieces
4 tablespoons extra-virgin
    olive oil
1 ounce salt pork or bacon,
    diced
1 medium yellow onion, diced
1 medium green bell pepper,
    seeded and diced
2 ounces ham, diced
1 medium tomato, diced
½ pound chorizo or smoked
    sausage
¼ cup small pimiento-stuffed
    olives
1 tablespoon capers, rinsed
    and drained
1 tablespoon Annatto Oil
    (page 113)
2 cups converted rice
3 cups water
½ cup frozen peas

1. Add the oregano, black pepper, paprika, and salt to a large resealable plastic bag; shake to mix the spices. Add the chicken and shake to coat the chicken in the spices.

2. Add the olive oil to a large Dutch oven and bring to temperature over medium heat. Add the salt pork or bacon, onion, and green pepper. Sauté for 3 to 5 minutes, or until the onion is transparent and the green pepper begins to get tender. Stir in the ham and tomato; reduce heat to low, cover, and simmer for 10 minutes. Stir in the chorizo or smoked sausage, and then add the chicken, skin-side down, with as many of the chicken pieces touching the pan bottom as possible. Cover and simmer for 30 minutes.

3. Add the olives, capers, annatto oil, rice, and water; bring to a simmer, cover, and simmer for 15 minutes. Add the peas; cover and simmer for another 5 minutes, or until the chicken is cooked through and the rice is tender. Taste for seasoning and add salt and pepper, if needed.

Romanian Veal with Vegetables Stew

*This recipe lets you stretch a small amount of expensive veal into
lots of servings. This stew is especially good if each bowl is
garnished with a dollop of drained yogurt or sour cream.*

1. Add the flour, salt, and pepper to a large food-storage bag; shake to mix. Add the veal cubes and toss to coat in the seasoned flour. Melt the butter in an ovenproof 6-quart Dutch oven over medium heat. Add the veal, and brown for 5 minutes. Add the onions and sauté, stirring frequently, for 5 minutes, or until the onions are transparent. Add the garlic and sauté for an additional 30 seconds.

2. Preheat oven to 350°F.

3. Add the beef broth, wine, and half of the cabbage; cover and simmer until the cabbage wilts, then add all the remaining ingredients. Bring to a boil, cover, and bake for 1 hour, stirring the stew about every 20 minutes. The stew is done when the meat and all of the vegetables are cooked through and tender.

Serves 8

3 tablespoons all-purpose flour
½ teaspoon salt
¼ teaspoon freshly ground black pepper
1 pound boneless veal shoulder, cut into 1" cubes
2 tablespoons butter
1 medium yellow onion, sliced
2 small cloves garlic, minced
½ cup beef broth
½ cup dry red wine
1 small head cabbage, cored and thinly sliced
2 teaspoons dried parsley
1 tablespoon tomato paste
2 large carrots, peeled and sliced
1 14.5-ounce can diced tomatoes
1 large green pepper, seeded and cut into strips
2 cups eggplant, diced
2 cups zucchini, diced
1 cup leeks (white part only) well-rinsed and thinly sliced
2 small turnips, diced
1 cup celery root, diced
2 small parsnips, diced
1 14.5-ounce can French-style green beans, drained
¼ cup seedless green grapes
¼ teaspoon dried thyme
¼ teaspoon dried marjoram

French Veal Stew

This stew is sometimes served over rice cooked with lots of onions in it, but a tossed salad with lemon vinaigrette will complement the gremolata's citrus addition to the stew.

Serves 6–8

4 pounds veal stew meat, cut into 2" pieces
1 pound veal bones, sawed into pieces
Water as needed
8 tablespoons butter
1 large carrot, peeled and finely diced
1 celery stalk, finely diced
2½ cups veal or chicken broth
1 large white onion, peeled and stuck with a whole clove
1 tablespoon dried parsley
½ bay leaf
Pinch dried thyme, crushed
8 ounces fresh button or cremini mushrooms, cleaned and sliced
5 tablespoons all-purpose flour
1 tablespoon lemon juice
1 1-pound bag frozen white pearl onions, thawed
3 egg yolks
½ cup heavy cream
OPTIONAL: *gremolata*

1. Add the veal and veal bones to a 4-quart Dutch oven. Add enough cold water to cover the meat; bring to a boil over high heat. Reduce temperature and simmer for 3 minutes, or until a heavy scum rises to the top of the pan. Drain the meat and bones in a colander and rinse to remove the scum.

2. Wipe out the Dutch oven. Melt 2 tablespoons of the butter over medium heat. Add the carrot and celery; sauté for 5 minutes, or until tender. Add the veal and veal bones back into the pan along with the broth and onion studded with a clove, parsley, bay leaf, and thyme. If needed, add enough water to bring the liquid level up to the top of the meat. Bring to a boil; reduce heat, cover, and simmer for 1½ hours, or until the veal is tender. Skim any scum from the surface and discard. Taste for seasoning and add salt, if needed; let the meat rest in the broth, uncovered, for 30 minutes. Pour the contents of the pan into a colander set over a large bowl to hold the broth.

3. Melt 2 tablespoons of the butter in the Dutch oven over medium heat. Add the mushrooms to the pan and sauté for 5 minutes, stirring occasionally. Return the broth to the pan, adding water if necessary to bring the broth to 4 cups.

4. Melt the remaining 4 tablespoons of butter in a small microwave-safe bowl. Whisk in the flour and lemon juice. Once the broth begins to boil, whisk in the flour mixture, stirring constantly for 2 minutes, or until the broth begins to thicken. Stir in the pearl onions. Reduce the heat and simmer uncovered while you prepare the final touches.

5. Discard the clove-studded onion and veal bones. Add the veal meat to the Dutch oven. In a small bowl, whisk the egg yolks together with the cream. Slowly whisk in a cup of the thickened broth from the pan to temper the eggs. Remove the pan from the heat, then slowly whisk the egg mixture into the remaining thickened broth in the pan. Set the pan back over low heat and stir gently to allow the egg yolks to cook into the sauce, being careful not to allow the sauce to return to a simmer. Taste for seasoning; add salt and pepper, if needed. If desired, stir some of the gremolata into the stew before you garnish each serving with it.

Gremolata

Gremolata is a garlic-citrus condiment for stews. Remove the zest from an orange and a lemon; blanch in 4 cups of water for 10 minutes. Drain and rinse in cold water. Pat dry, then finely chop it along with 1 garlic clove and ¼ cup fresh flat-leaf parsley. Sprinkle over the stew, to taste.

Lobster Chowder

Serve this rich chowder alongside a green salad and buttered biscuits, dinner rolls, or common crackers.

Serves 4

2 ounces smoked slab bacon, cut into ¼" dice

2 medium leeks, white part only, rinsed and cut to ½" dice

4 medium russet or red potatoes, peeled and diced

4 cups water, lobster or fish stock, or chicken broth

2 tablespoons unsalted butter

Freshly ground black pepper to taste

1 pound cooked lobster, cut into bite-sized pieces

1 cup heavy cream

Sea salt to taste

OPTIONAL: *pinch cayenne pepper or dash of hot sauce*

OPTIONAL: *fresh chives, snipped*

1. Add the diced bacon to a 4-quart Dutch oven and fry it over moderate heat until golden and nearly crisp. If the bacon renders more than 2 tablespoons of fat, pour off the excess. Add the leeks, stir to coat them in the bacon fat, and sauté for 2 minutes. Stir in the potatoes and reduce the heat to low; cover, and cook for 10 minutes, stirring frequently to prevent browning, or until the potatoes are tender. Mash some of the potatoes with a fork, if desired. Add the water, stock, or broth; bring to a simmer, cover, and cook for 5 minutes.

2. Whisk the butter into the broth. Once the butter is melted, add the pepper, lobster, and cream. Stir gently and cook on low to bring all the ingredients to temperature. Taste for seasonings, and add sea salt, additional black pepper, and a pinch of cayenne pepper or a dash of hot sauce, if desired. Remove the pan from the stove, cover, and allow the chowder to ripen for 15 or 20 minutes before serving. Ladle into warmed shallow soup bowls; sprinkle with snipped chives, if desired.

Healthy Alternatives

If you don't want to use heavy cream in the Lobster Chowder recipe, decrease the amount of water, stock, or broth by a cup and add 2 cups of milk. Do not use half-and-half because it has a tendency to curdle.

Simplified Bouillabaisse

Using tomato juice or chicken broth lets you customize this simple fish stew without the tedium of creating fish stock, cleaning and steaming clams, and all of those other steps the purists insist you go through.

1. Add the oil to a Dutch oven and bring to temperature over medium heat. Add the yellow and green onions; sauté for 5 minutes, or until transparent. Add the garlic and sauté for another 30 seconds. Add the tomato juice or broth, tomatoes, wine, water, bay leaf, pepper, tarragon, thyme, and parsley; bring to a boil. Reduce the heat, cover, and simmer for 1 hour. Remove the bay leaf. At this point, this broth can be refrigerated and reheated later to finish the dish.

2. Add the fish pieces; simmer for 10 minutes, or until the fish is opaque and cooked through. Stir in the shrimp, clams, and mussels; simmer for 2 or 3 minutes to bring all the ingredients to temperature. Serve with toasted garlic toast, if desired.

Garlic Toast

Preheat the oven to 400°F. Slice French bread into ¼"-thick slices. Brush both sides of the bread with extra-virgin olive oil, place flat on a baking sheet, and bake for 10 minutes, or until crisp and lightly browned. While the toast is still warm, rub a cut clove of garlic over the top of each slice. Allow 2 slices per serving.

Serves 8

⅓ cup extra-virgin olive oil
1 large yellow onion, sliced
1 bunch green onions (4 to 5 stalks), sliced
1 clove garlic, minced
2 cups tomato juice or chicken broth
1 14.5-ounce can diced tomatoes
1 cup Chardonnay or other dry white wine
2 cups water
1 bay leaf
½ teaspoon freshly ground black pepper
1 teaspoon dried tarragon, crumbled
½ teaspoon thyme, crushed
1 tablespoon parsley, crushed
1 pound white fish, cut into 1" pieces
1 pound frozen cooked shrimp, thawed
2 3.53-ounce pouches of whole baby clams
1 10-ounce can boiled mussels, drained
OPTIONAL: garlic toast

Marsala Beef Stew

Serves 8

2 tablespoons extra-virgin olive oil

1 tablespoon butter or ghee

3 pounds English-cut chuck roast, cut into bite-sized pieces

1 large carrot, peeled and finely diced

1 celery stalk, finely diced

1 large yellow onion, diced

3 cloves garlic, minced

8 ounces button or cremini mushrooms, cleaned and sliced

½ cup dry white wine

1 cup Marsala wine

½ teaspoon dried rosemary

½ teaspoon dried oregano

½ teaspoon dried basil

Water as needed

Salt and freshly ground black pepper to taste

Serve this rich stew over cooked rice, polenta, mashed potatoes, or toast alongside a tossed salad.

1. Add the oil and melt the butter in a 4-quart Dutch oven over medium-high heat. Add 10 pieces of the beef to the pan and brown for 5 minutes, or until the meat takes on a rich dark outer color. Reduce the heat to medium and add the carrot and celery; sauté for 3 to 5 minutes, or until soft. Add the onion and sauté until the onion is transparent. Add the garlic and sauté for an additional 30 seconds. Stir in the mushrooms; sauté until tender.

2. Add the remaining meat, the wines, rosemary, oregano, and basil to the pan. Add water, if needed, to bring the liquid level to just over the top of the meat. Reduce the heat, cover, and simmer for 1½ hours or until the meat is tender. Taste the broth. Simmer uncovered long enough to reduce the broth if it tastes weak. Add salt and pepper, if needed. Allow the stew to rest, uncovered, off of the heat for a 30 minutes, then return it to the stovetop over low heat to bring it back to temperature.

Contrary to Popular Opinion

Searing meat does not seal in the juices, but it does intensify the flavor of a dish by adding another flavor dimension. Therefore, while it isn't necessary to sear all of the meat, it is a good idea to do so with some of it before you add the liquid and begin to simmer a stew.

Chapter 14
Legumes and Grains

Sweet and Hot Chili

The longer you simmer chili, the richer the flavor.

Serves 8–10

1 pound ground chuck

1 pound ground pork

2 large yellow onions, diced

6 cloves garlic, minced

1 teaspoon whole cumin seeds

2 tablespoons chili powder

¼ teaspoon oregano

1 28-ounce can diced tomatoes

¼ cup ketchup

¼ teaspoon cinnamon

¼ teaspoon ground cloves

2 tablespoons light brown sugar

2 15-ounce cans kidney beans, rinsed and drained

1 14-ounce can reduced-sodium beef broth

OPTIONAL: 1 tablespoon Worcestershire sauce

Water, if needed

Salt and freshly ground black pepper to taste

OPTIONAL: hot sauce to taste

1. Add the ground chuck, pork, onion, garlic, cumin seeds, chili powder, and oregano to a Dutch oven; cook over medium heat until the beef and pork are browned and cooked through. Drain off any excess fat and discard.

2. Stir in the tomatoes, ketchup, cinnamon, cloves, brown sugar, kidney beans, beef broth, and Worcestershire sauce (if using). Bring to a simmer; reduce the heat, cover, and simmer for 1 hour. Stir the chili occasionally, and add water if needed. Taste for seasoning and add salt and pepper, if needed, and hot sauce, if desired. You may also wish to add more brown sugar or chili powder according to your taste.

Or, If You Prefer . . .

If you want to make the chili in a slow cooker, follow step 1, and then add the cooked meat mixture, tomatoes, ketchup, cinnamon, cloves, brown sugar, kidney beans, beef broth, and Worcestershire sauce (if using) to the slow cooker. Add water if need to bring the liquid level to the top of the beans and meat. Cook on low for 6 to 8 hours.

Sauerkraut and Bean Soup

*Keep with Eastern Europe tradition and serve this
dish with hearty dark or whole-grain bread.*

1. Add the bacon fat, lard, or oil to a Dutch oven and bring it to temperature over medium heat. Add the celery and carrot; sauté for 3 to 5 minutes, or until soft. Add the onion and sauté until transparent. Add the garlic and sauté for an additional 30 seconds.

2. Brown some of the pork butt. Add the remaining meat, the broth, and enough water to bring the liquid level to just above the meat. Stir in the paprika and bring to a simmer; reduce heat, cover, and simmer for 1 hour.

3. Mash half of the beans. Add the sauerkraut and beans into the meat. Add water, if needed; cover and simmer for 1 hour, or until the meat is tender. Season with salt and pepper. Serve with a dollop of sour cream, if desired.

Serves 6–8

2 tablespoons bacon fat, lard, or peanut oil
1 large carrot, peeled and shredded
1 celery stalk, finely diced
1 large yellow onion, diced
3 cloves garlic, minced
1 pound boneless pork butt, trimmed of fat and cut into bite-sized pieces
1 14-ounce can reduced-sodium beef broth
Water as needed
2 teaspoons paprika
1 2-pound bag sauerkraut, rinsed and drained
2 15-ounce cans of pink or pinto beans, rinsed and drained
Salt to taste
Freshly ground black pepper
OPTIONAL: sour cream to taste

Southwest Pinto Beans
with Pork and Corn

*This is an adaptation of a Southwestern dish that uses dried pinto beans and
chicos (a type of dried sweet corn). You can prepare this version in minutes
rather than in hours. Serve it with corn bread or corn chips and a salad.*

Add the bacon to a deep nonstick skillet or large saucepan; fry over medium heat until it begins to brown. Add the onion and sauté until transparent. Add the garlic and chopped pepper (if using), and sauté for 1 minute. Stir in the beans, corn, and pork. Bring to a simmer and reduce the heat; simmer for 5 to 10 minutes to bring the beans, corn, and pork to temperature and to marry the flavors. Taste for seasoning and add salt and pepper, if needed.

Serves 4–6

4 slices bacon, diced
1 large yellow onion, diced
3 cloves garlic, minced
OPTIONAL: chopped jalapeño or other hot pepper to taste
1 15-ounce can pinto beans, rinsed and drained
1 12-ounce bag frozen whole kernel corn, thawed
1 28-ounce can heat-and-serve pork in pork broth
Salt and freshly ground black pepper to taste

Puerto Rican Chicken and Beans

Puerto Rican cooking has Spanish, African, Taíno (pre-Columbian inhabitants of the Bahamas), and American influences.

Serves 8

¼ pound salt pork or bacon, diced

1 large carrot, peeled and shredded

1 celery stalk, finely diced

1 large yellow onion, diced

3 cloves garlic, minced

½ pound Spanish or Mexican chorizo sausage, diced or thinly sliced

½ pound ham, chopped

8 chicken thighs

4 cups water, or more, as needed

2 teaspoons Worcestershire sauce

Hot sauce to taste

4 large russet potatoes, peeled and diced

1 small head cabbage, cored and thinly sliced

2 cups kale, tough stems removed, and thinly sliced

4 turnips, diced

1 15-ounce can white beans, rinsed and drained

Salt and freshly ground black pepper to taste

1. Add the salt pork or bacon to a Dutch oven; cook over medium heat until the fat is rendered from the bacon. Add the carrot and celery; sauté for 3 to 5 minutes, or until soft. Add the onion and sauté until transparent. Add the garlic and sauté for an additional 30 seconds. Stir in the sausage; continue to stir while it fries for a few minutes, then stir in the ham. Add the chicken to the pan, skin-side down, pushing the other ingredients to the side so that as much of the chicken as possible touches the pan bottom. Cover and cook for 10 minutes. Add the water, Worcestershire sauce, and hot sauce, and bring to a simmer; reduce the heat, cover, and simmer for 35 to 45 minutes, or until the chicken is cooked through. Remove the chicken from the pan and set aside.

2. Add the potatoes, cabbage, kale, and turnips to the pan. Stir to combine with the other ingredients. Cover and simmer for 30 minutes.

3. Shred the chicken, discarding the skin and bones. Stir the shredded chicken into the pan.

4. Stir the beans into the pan. Add additional water if needed to prevent the pan from boiling dry. Cover and simmer for 10 minutes. Taste for seasoning, and add salt and pepper as needed.

Or, If You Prefer . . .

If you or someone at your table insists on eating the chicken skin, you can skip step 3. Proceed straight to step 4, and add the thighs to the top of the stew after you've stirred in the beans.

Falafel

Make the falafel into patties for sandwiches, or into walnut-sized balls to serve them in a salad (accompanied by toasted pita) instead. Use water instead of the chicken broth for a meatless meal.

1. Add the garbanzo and fava beans to a large bowl. Add enough water to the bowl to cover the beans; cover and let soak overnight.

2. Drain the beans and run through the fine blade in a meat grinder or add to a food processor and pulse until they're a fine mash. Return the beans to the bowl, and combine with the onion, garlic, broth, sesame seeds, garbanzo flour, bulgur, parsley, salt, cumin, coriander, baking powder, cayenne, and black pepper. Cover and let stand for 1 hour.

3. Preheat oil in a deep fryer to 375°F. Form the falafel mixture into 1½" round patties about ⅓" thick). Deep-fry for 4 minutes, or until brown and crunchy on the outside.

4. Fill the pita rounds with falafel patties, tomato, onion, lettuce, cucumber slices, and yogurt.

Cayenne Choices

You can throw in a pinch of cayenne pepper to enhance the flavor or up to ½ teaspoon of it to add a hot punch.

Makes 24 patties, enough for 6 or 8 sandwiches

1 cup dried garbanzo beans
1 cup dried shelled fava beans
Water as needed
1 medium yellow onion, minced
3 cloves garlic, minced
1 cup chicken broth or water
½ cup sesame seeds
½ cup garbanzo flour
¼ cup fine bulgur
¼ cup fresh parsley, finely chopped
2 teaspoons salt
2 teaspoons ground cumin
2 teaspoons ground coriander
2 teaspoons baking powder
Cayenne pepper to taste
¼ teaspoon freshly ground black pepper
Vegetable oil, as needed
6–8 pita rounds
6–8 slices tomato
6–8 slices yellow onion
1½–2 cups lettuce, shredded
12–16 cucumber slices
1½–2 cups plain yogurt

Spanish Bean Soup

½ pound dried white beans
Water as needed
¼ pound salt pork or bacon, diced
½ pound Spanish chorizo, diced or thinly sliced
1 stalk celery, finely chopped
1 large carrot, peeled and shredded
1 large yellow onion, diced
3 cloves garlic, minced
½ pound smoked ham, diced
4 chicken thighs
1 cup chicken, pork, or ham broth
4 cups water
2 teaspoons Worcestershire sauce
Hot sauce to taste
4 large russet potatoes, peeled and diced
4 turnips, quartered, and sliced
1 small head cabbage, cored and shredded
2 cups kale, remove the tough stems and thinly slice
Salt and freshly ground pepper to taste

Many claim that the leftovers taste even better than the original servings. You can add a ham bone in step 2 to enhance the flavor.

1. Put the dried beans in an 8-quart stock pot or Dutch oven. Add enough water to cover the beans; cover and let soak overnight.

2. Drain the beans in a colander. Wipe out the pot and add the salt pork or bacon; cook over medium heat to render the fat. Add the chorizo, celery and carrot; sauté for 3 to 5 minutes, or until soft. Add the onion and sauté until transparent. Add the garlic and sauté for an additional 30 seconds. Stir in the smoked ham. Add the beans and chicken. Stir in the broth, water, Worcestershire, and hot sauce. Bring to a simmer; cover and simmer for 1 hour, stirring occasionally. Add more water, if needed to keep the pot from boiling dry.

3. Remove the chicken and set aside. Stir the soup well and then stir in the potatoes and turnips. Add the cabbage and kale; cover and simmer for 15 minutes. Shred the chicken, discarding the skin and bones. Stir the chicken into the soup. Add additional water, if needed. Bring to a simmer, cover, and simmer for 45 minutes to 1 hour, or until the beans are tender. Taste for seasoning and add salt and pepper if desired.

Try This with Leftover Bean Soup

Add ½ teaspoon (or more) of cider vinegar and granulated sugar to taste to a bowl of reheated soup. If you want an improvised baked beans effect, stir in a little ketchup, too. Top with minced onion.

Mushroom and Barley Soup

To stretch this recipe to 10 servings instead of 8, use all 10 cups of beef broth. Either way, the final result will be a rich soup that, when served along with a salad and a dinner roll or toasted whole grain bread, is a worthy main course.

1. Put the dried mushrooms in a small bowl and pour the 1 cup of warm water over them. Set aside to soak for 30 minutes.

2. Add the 2 cups of water to a 6-quart Dutch oven or stockpot and bring to a boil over medium-high heat. Stir in the barley; reduce the heat, cover, and simmer for 15 minutes, or until all liquid is absorbed. Stir in the butter.

3. Use a slotted spoon to remove the mushrooms from the soaking liquid; dice the mushrooms and then stir them into the butter-barley mixture.

4. Add the broth, carrots, potatoes, celery, green beans, and parsley. Stir well to separate the grains of barley. Bring to a simmer, cover, and cook for 1 hour, or until the barley is tender. Season with salt and pepper to taste. Ladle the soup into bowls and top each serving with a dollop of sour cream, if desired.

Or, If You Prefer . . .

You can use the mushroom soaking liquid in place of some of the broth; just strain it first to remove any grit or sand from the mushrooms.

Serves 8–10

1 ounce dried porcini or oyster mushrooms
1 cup warm water
2 cups water
1 cup pearl barley
¼ cup butter
8–10 cups beef broth
2 large carrots, peeled and diced
2 large russet potatoes, peeled and diced
1 stalk celery, diced
1 10-ounce package cut frozen green beans, thawed
1 teaspoon dried parsley
Salt and freshly ground pepper to taste
OPTIONAL: sour cream to taste

Russian Beef Stroganoff
with Kasha

Serves 4–6

1 14-ounce can reduced-
sodium beef broth

¼ cup water

½ teaspoon salt

½ teaspoon freshly ground
black pepper

4 tablespoons butter

1 cup kasha

1 large egg, beaten

2 large yellow onions, diced

2 pounds beef sirloin,
trimmed of fat and cut
into thin strips

8 ounces fresh button or
cremini mushrooms,
cleaned and sliced

Additional salt and freshly
ground black pepper to
taste

½ cup sour cream, plus extra
for serving

OPTIONAL: fresh chopped dill
to taste

Tastes vary, so have extra sour cream at the table for those who want it.

᪐

1. In a 4-cup microwave-safe container, bring the broth, water, salt, pepper, and 2 tablespoons of the butter to a boil; you'll need to microwave it on high for 2 to 3 minutes.

2. While the broth is coming to a boil, add the kasha and egg to a deep 3½-quart nonstick skillet or wok over medium-high heat. Use a nonstick-skillet-safe utensil to stir, flatten, and chop the kasha; do this until the egg is cooked, and then pour in the boiling broth. Reduce the heat to low, cover, and simmer for 10 minutes, or until the liquid is absorbed and the kernels are tender. Transfer the cooked kasha to a bowl; set aside and keep warm.

3. Wipe out the skillet or wok. Add the remaining 2 tablespoons butter and melt over medium-high heat. Add the onion and beef strips. Stir-fry until the onions are transparent and the beef is cooked and releasing its juices. Add the mushroom slices and stir-fry to wilt them. Taste for seasoning and add salt and pepper, if desired. Remove from the heat and stir in the sour cream. Serve ladled over a serving of kasha, or mix the kasha into the stroganoff if you prefer. Garnish with fresh dill, if desired.

Alternative Recipe: Steak and Stroganoff

You can serve mushroom-kasha stroganoff alongside broiled or grilled steaks. Omit the beef strips and stir-fry the onions and mushrooms in butter, and then stir in a cup of beef broth and a can of condensed mushroom soup. When it's heated through, stir in the sour cream.

Italian Barley Soup

This is a meatless soup, but you can add leftover beef to it if you wish. With or without the meat, serve it with a salad and some dinner rolls to make it a complete meal.

1. Add the broth and water to a Dutch oven or stockpot; bring to a boil over medium-high heat. Reduce the heat, and stir in the barley, celery, carrots, onion, garlic, wine, lemon peel, pepper, and salt. Cover and simmer for 2 hours, stirring frequently to prevent the barley from sticking to the bottom of the pot.

2. Stir in the basil, oregano, parsley, bay leaves, rosemary, tomatoes, and tomato paste. Cover and simmer for 1 hour, stirring occasionally. Add the drained tomato juice (if using canned diced tomatoes) or water if needed to keep the pot from boiling dry. Remove the bay leaves and discard. Taste for seasoning and adjust, if necessary. Serve topped with the grated cheese to taste.

Instead of Wine

To give gravy a fruity taste reminiscent of wine, stir in some redcurrant jelly or a little balsamic vinegar and sugar before you thicken it. Currants are small berries, similar to gooseberries. If you go the balsamic route, adding a little sugar moderates the intense taste of the vinegar.

Serves 8

6 cups beef broth
2 cups water
¾ cup barley
4 stalks celery, finely diced
4 large carrots, peeled and grated
1 large yellow onion, diced
4 cloves garlic, minced
½ cup dry red wine
1 1" × ½" piece of lemon peel
½ teaspoon freshly ground black pepper
Salt to taste
1 teaspoon dried basil
½ teaspoon dried oregano, crushed
1 tablespoon dried parsley
2 bay leaves
½ teaspoon dried rosemary
2 tomatoes, diced, or 1 15-ounce can diced tomatoes, drained and juices reserved
Water as needed
4 tablespoons tomato paste
Freshly grated Parmigiano-Reggiano or Romano cheese to taste

Tuscan Bean Soup

*Beans that are soaked overnight are supposed to be easier to digest.
This recipe shows an alternative to soaking the beans over night.*

Serves 8–10

*8 ounces dry white kidney,
cannelloni, or Great
Northern beans*

*10 cups water, or more as
needed*

*1 tablespoon extra-virgin
olive oil*

2 stalks celery, diced

*3 large carrots, peeled and
diced*

*3 medium yellow onions,
diced*

4 cloves garlic, minced

*1 pound crosscut beef shanks,
1" to 1½" thick*

*1 14-ounce can reduced-
sodium beef broth*

4 smoked ham hocks

1 bay leaf

*½ teaspoon dried thyme,
crushed*

*½ teaspoon dried rosemary,
crushed*

*¼ teaspoon freshly ground
black pepper*

Salt to taste

*4 cups torn fresh spinach
leaves*

1. Rinse the beans and add them to a 6-quart Dutch oven along with 6 cups of the water. Bring to a boil; reduce the heat and simmer, uncovered, for 2 minutes. Remove from the heat, cover, and let stand for 1 hour. Drain the beans in colander; set aside.

2. Wipe out the pan. Add the oil and bring to temperature over medium heat. Add the celery and carrot; sauté for 3 to 5 minutes, or until soft. Add the onion and sauté until transparent. Add the garlic and sauté for an additional 30 seconds.

3. Add the beef and cook it in the hot oil for about 5 minutes, or until browned. Add the drained beans and the remaining 4 cups water, the beef broth, ham hocks, bay leaf, thyme, rosemary, pepper, and salt; bring to a boil. Reduce the heat, cover, and simmer for 1½ hours, stirring occasionally and adding more water if necessary.

4. Remove the bay leaf, ham hocks, and beef; set aside to cool. Remove the meat from the bones, cut it into bite-sized pieces, and stir it into the soup. Discard the bones and bay leaf. Cover and simmer for another 30 minutes, or until the beans and meats are tender. Skim off any fat from the surface of the soup. Stir in the spinach. Heat through and serve.

Cassoulet

This dish is traditionally baked in layers—beans and vegetables, tomato sauce, and then some of the meat; the layers are repeated until all ingredients are used up. This version mixes everything together to keep the cooking to one pot.

2 pounds white beans
Water as needed
¼ pound salt pork or bacon, diced
2 tablespoons butter
2 tablespoons extra-virgin olive oil
8 chicken thighs
2 pounds pork shoulder roast, trimmed of fat and cut into bite-sized pieces
1 large yellow onion, diced
2 large carrots, peeled and shredded
2 stalks celery, finely diced
6 cloves garlic, minced
¼ pound Polish sausage, sliced
2 small yellow onions, peeled
4 whole cloves
1 ham bone or 2 smoked ham hocks
1 lamb shank
1 1-pound bag baby carrots
4 cups chicken broth
10 cups water, or as needed
1 cup tomato purée
Salt and freshly ground pepper to taste

1. Add the beans to a large ovenproof Dutch oven or stockpot. Add enough water to cover the beans; cover the pan and let soak overnight.

2. Preheat the oven to 350°F. Drain the beans in a colander and set aside. Wipe out the pan. Add the salt pork or bacon, butter, and oil to the pan; cook over medium heat until the butter is melted. Stir to entirely coat the bottom of the pan. Remove from the heat. Line the chicken pieces across the bottom of the pan, skin-side down. Add the pork, diced onion, carrot, celery, garlic, and Polish sausage in layers. Bake for 45 minutes to brown the meat.

3. Remove the pan from the oven. Stick two cloves into each of the onions. Add the beans, onions, ham bone or ham hocks, lamb shank, carrots, chicken broth, and enough of the water to cover the beans. Bring to a simmer; cover and cook for 1½ hours, stirring occasionally and adding more water, if necessary. Remove the chicken, ham bone or ham hocks, and lamb shank from the pot and set aside to cool.

4. Stir in the tomato purée, salt, and pepper. Cover and simmer for 30 minutes. Remove the chicken, ham, and lamb from the bones; discard any skin, fat, or bones. Stir the meat into the beans, adding more water if needed. Cover and bake for 1½ hours, checking every 30 minutes to make sure more water isn't needed.

Rule of Thumb: Cooking Beans

You can usually count on using 7 cups of liquid for each pound of beans. The amount you use can vary according to how hot you keep the simmering liquid and how many times you remove the lid to stir the beans.

Barley and Mushroom Casserole

This is a delicious way to use leftover chicken. Most other seasonings go well with the basil and parsley, but you can adjust the seasoning in this recipe according to how the chicken was cooked, if necessary.

Serves 8

6 tablespoons butter

1 large carrot, peeled and shredded

1 stalk celery, finely diced

2 medium yellow onions, diced

2 cloves garlic, minced

1 pound button or cremini mushrooms, cleaned and sliced

1 cup pearl barley

½ tablespoon dried basil

½ tablespoon dried parsley

3 cups chicken broth

2 cups cooked chicken, shredded or diced

Salt and freshly ground black pepper to taste

1. Preheat the oven to 375°F.

2. Melt the butter in an ovenproof 4-quart Dutch oven over medium heat. Add the carrot and celery; sauté for 3 to 5 minutes, or until soft. Add the onion and sauté until transparent. Add the garlic and sauté for an additional 30 seconds. Add the mushroom slices; sauté for 5 minutes or until they begin to brown. Stir in the barley, basil, parsley, broth, chicken, salt, and pepper; bring to a boil. Remove from the heat, cover, and bake for 50 minutes, or until the barley is tender. Serve hot.

Ham and Beans Salad

This recipe turns some leftover cooked ham into a delicious luncheon salad.

Serves 4

¼ cup extra-virgin olive oil

3 tablespoons balsamic vinegar

1 tablespoon red onion or shallots, minced

1 clove garlic, minced

1 tablespoon fresh parsley, minced

2 stalks celery, diced

2 large carrots, peeled and shredded

1 cup cooked ham, diced

1 15-ounce can cannelloni or white beans, rinsed and drained

Salt and freshly ground black pepper to taste

4 or more cups lettuce or salad mix

In a mixing bowl, make the dressing by whisking together the oil and vinegar; then stir in the onion or shallots, garlic, parsley, celery, carrots, ham, and beans. Cover and let stand for at least 1 hour. Taste for seasoning, and add salt and pepper, if needed. Divide the lettuce or salad mix between 4 plates and top with equal amounts of the dressing.

Quinoa Salad

*You can make this quinoa salad the night before
and then assemble the salad for lunch the day.*

1. Cover the quinoa with water; rub the grains between the palms of your hands for several seconds, drain, and repeat the process once.

2. Bring the water to a boil in a saucepan; add the quinoa, salt, and oil. Lower heat, cover, and simmer for 20 minutes, or until all of the water is absorbed. Remove the pan from the heat and allow the cooked quinoa to cool, and then fluff with a fork. Stir in the artichoke hearts, olives, spinach, tomatoes, and parsley.

3. To make the citrus vinaigrette, whisk together the lemon zest, balsamic vinegar, orange juice, oil, oregano, mint, basil, salt, and pepper. Taste for seasoning and adjust, if necessary, by adding more vinegar, oil, or salt and pepper. Divide the salad between two plates of the baby spinach leaves. Dress with the citrus vinaigrette and serve with the pine nuts and crumbled feta cheese sprinkled over the top.

Serves 2

- 2 cups quinoa
- 4½ cups water
- 1 teaspoon sea salt
- 2 tablespoons extra-virgin olive oil
- ½ cup sliced marinated artichoke hearts
- ¼ cup sliced, pitted Kalamata olives
- 2 tablespoons fresh spinach, finely chopped
- 1 cup cherry tomatoes, cut in half
- 2 tablespoons flat-leaf parsley, finely chopped
- 1 tablespoon freshly grated lemon zest
- ¼ cup balsamic vinegar, or more to taste
- ¼ cup orange juice
- ¼ cup extra-virgin olive oil, or more to taste
- 1 teaspoon dried oregano
- 1 teaspoon dried mint
- 1 teaspoon dried fresh basil
- Sea salt and freshly ground black pepper to taste
- 2 cups fresh baby spinach
- 2 tablespoons toasted pine nuts
- ½ cup feta cheese, crumbled

Homemade Granola

Yields 12 cups

¾ cup cold-pressed, organic coconut oil

½ cup honey

4 cups old-fashioned rolled oats

2 cups sweetened shredded coconut

2 cups slivered or whole almonds

1 cup raw, unsalted cashews

1½ cups small-diced dried apricots

1 cup small diced dried figs

1 cup dried cherries

1 cup dried cranberries

Coconut oil contains no trans fat, but it does contain lauric acid. When it is consumed, lauric acid transforms to monolaurin, which is believed to strengthen the immune system. Coconut oil proponents also claim it stimulates the metabolism.

1. Preheat the oven to 250°F.

2. Add the oil and honey to a large microwave-safe bowl. Microwave until the oil is liquid and can be whisked into the honey. Mix in the oats, coconut, almonds, and cashews using a wooden spoon to stir until all dry the ingredients are coated. Pour onto a 13" × 18" × 1" sheet pan. Stirring with a spatula every 15 minutes, bake for 75 minutes, or until the mixture turns a nice, even, golden brown. Remove the granola from the oven and allow to cool, stirring occasionally. Toss with the apricots, figs, cherries, and cranberries. Store in an airtight container for up to two weeks.

Alternate Recipe: Maple-Walnut Granola

Substitute chopped walnuts for half of the almonds and the cashews. Use ½ cup of maple syrup and ¼ light brown sugar instead of the honey and raisins instead of dried apricots.

Chapter 15
Pasta

Lobster Ragu

Serves 6–8

1½ pounds dried pappardelle or fettuccine

3 tablespoons extra-virgin olive oil

3 stalks celery, diced

3 large carrots, peeled and diced

2 medium red onions, sliced

Salt and freshly ground black pepper to taste

8 ounces tasso, salt pork, or bacon, diced

8 ounces cremini mushrooms, cleaned and sliced

8 ounces portabello mushrooms, cleaned and sliced

8 ounces button mushrooms, cleaned and sliced

2 tablespoons tomato paste

2 teaspoons dried oregano

2 teaspoons dried thyme

1 tablespoon dried parsley

1 cup red wine

4 cups beef broth

2 1¼-pound cooked lobsters

¼ cup fresh basil, chopped

Tasso is a Cajun ham that comes from the shoulder (pork butt), which makes it a fattier cut of meat with a great deal of flavor. If you're not sure how to cook a whole lobster, refer to the Lobster Bake recipe on page 286.

1. In a Dutch oven or deep pot, cook the pasta in boiling water according to the package directions until al dente. Drain in a colander, set aside, and keep warm.

2. Wipe out the Dutch oven; add the oil and bring to temperature over medium heat. Add the celery and carrot; sauté for 3 to 5 minutes, or until soft. Add the onion and sauté until transparent. If using tasso, sauté for 1 minute; if using salt pork or bacon, sauté for 3 minutes, or until it renders some of its fat. Add all the mushrooms; stirring frequently, cook until all of the mushroom liquid is rendered out. Push the mushrooms to the sides of the pan; add the tomato paste and sauté for 2 minutes, then stir it into the mushrooms along with the oregano, thyme, parsley, wine, and broth, scraping the bottom of the pot to loosen any browned bits as you stir. Reduce the heat and simmer for 20 minutes. Toss the drained pasta into the reduced ragu sauce.

3. Remove the meat from the lobster shells; chop into large pieces. Gently stir the lobster meat into the pasta and ragu sauce. Garnish with the chopped basil.

Lobster Shell Uses

Freeze the lobster shells and use them later to make a broth to add to your favorite seafood stew or soup. Lobster broth is delicious, and it's easy to make—just simmer the shells with a roughly chopped onion, a few bay leaves, and enough water to cover everything for about 45 minutes.

Lamb and Pasta Salad

*Tomatoes are essential for this Greek-inspired salad. If you don't
have fresh ones on hand, you can use 1 cup of drained canned
diced tomatoes or use cherry tomatoes cut in half.*

1. Cook the pasta according to the package directions. Drain and transfer to a large bowl.

2. Add 3 tablespoons of the oil to a small skillet and bring to temperature over medium heat. Add the yellow onion and sauté for 3 to 5 minutes, or until transparent. Add the onion to the bowl with the pasta along with the green onions, olives, cheese, tomato, parsley, and lamb. Toss to combine.

3. In a small bowl, whisk together the cup of extra-virgin olive oil, mayonnaise, garlic, and dill; add this mixture to the large bowl, and toss with the pasta and lamb. Taste for seasoning and add salt and pepper to taste. Chill for at least 1 hour before serving.

Serves 8–10

1 pound dried penne pasta

3 tablespoons olive oil

2 medium yellow onions, peeled and thinly sliced

½ cup green onions, chopped

½ cup green olives, pitted and chopped

½ cup feta cheese, crumbled

2 large ripe tomatoes, diced

3 tablespoons fresh parsley, chopped

1 pound leftover roast lamb, cut into thin strips

1 cup extra-virgin olive oil

2 tablespoons mayonnaise

2 cloves garlic, minced

1½ teaspoon fresh dill, minced

Salt and freshly ground black pepper to taste

Italian Pasta and Bean Soup

This recipe calls for more carrots than are traditionally used in Italian bean soup. You can cut that number if you prefer.

Serves 8–10

2 cups dried cannelloni or small white beans

6 cups water

2 pounds smoked ham hocks

1 bay leaf

2 cloves garlic, minced

1 small yellow onion, diced

1 1-pound bag baby carrots, cut into thirds

¼ cup lovage or celery leaves, chopped

½ cup tomato sauce

Pinch dried red pepper flakes

¼ teaspoon dried oregano

Pinch dried rosemary

½ teaspoon dried basil

1 teaspoon dried parsley

½ teaspoon granulated sugar

6 cups water

1 cup chicken broth

Salt and freshly ground black pepper to taste

OPTIONAL: 1 cup cooked pork, shredded

1 cup dried small pasta, such as orzo or stars

1. Add the beans and water to a 4-quart Dutch oven or stew pot and bring to a boil; cover, turn off the heat, and let sit for 1 hour. Drain the beans, discarding the water.

2. Return the beans to the pan along with all of the other ingredients except the cooked pork (if using) and the pasta. Bring to a simmer over medium heat; reduce the heat, cover, and simmer for 1½ to 2 hours, or until the beans are very tender. Remove the bay leaf and discard. Remove the ham hocks and set aside to cool.

3. Remove the meat from the ham hocks and cut it into bite-sized pieces. Add the ham hock meat along with the cooked pork (if using) and the pasta to the pan. Cover and cook for 15 minutes, stirring occasionally, or until the pasta is tender.

Souped-Up Spaghetti

Spaghetti is a classic dish, and this variation retains the characteristic taste but mixes up the textures.

1. Add the ground beef, onion, sweet pepper, celery, carrot, and garlic to a 4-quart Dutch oven. Cook over medium heat until the vegetables are tender and the meat is no longer pink, stirring frequently. Drain off and discard excess fat.

2. Stir in the undrained tomatoes, water, spaghetti sauce, sugar, Italian seasoning, and red pepper flakes; bring to a boil. Add the spaghetti. Reduce the heat to a gentle boil and cook uncovered for 12 to 15 minutes, or until the spaghetti is tender. Taste for seasoning and add salt and pepper, if desired. Serve immediately, garnished with parsley, if desired.

Sneaky Additions

Thanks to the spaghetti sauce, you can add a bag of frozen vegetables to the Souped-Up Spaghetti; add the vegetables 10 minutes into the pasta cooking time in step 2. This is a great trick for anyone who has a picky eater at the table.

Serves 6–8

1 pound lean ground beef
1 medium yellow onion, chopped
1 small green sweet pepper, seeded and chopped
1 stalk celery, chopped
1 medium carrot, peeled and chopped
4 cloves garlic, minced
2 15-ounce cans diced tomatoes, undrained
2½ cups water
1 13- to 15-ounce jar spaghetti sauce
1 tablespoon granulated sugar
½ teaspoon dried Italian seasoning, crushed
Dash dried red pepper flakes
2 ounces dried spaghetti, broken into 2" pieces
Salt and freshly ground black pepper to taste
OPTIONAL: fresh chopped parsley to taste

Pepperoni Pasta

Serves 4

6 ounces dried spaghetti,
broken in half

1 tablespoon butter

8 ounces fresh button or
cremini mushrooms,
cleaned and sliced

3 ounces pepperoni, thinly
sliced or cubed

6 cups lightly packed fresh
spinach, stems removed
and torn

¼ cup Parmigiano-Reggiano
cheese, grated

2 tablespoons fresh basil,
chopped

1 teaspoon lemon juice

Salt and freshly ground
pepper to taste

To keep this a one-pot meal, this recipe uses the same pot to cook the pasta, sauté the mushrooms and other ingredients, and mix it all together before plating.

1. Prepare the pasta according to the package directions. Drain; set aside, and keep warm. Wipe out the pan. Add the butter and cook over medium heat until melted; add the mushrooms and pepperoni and sauté for 5 minutes, or until the mushrooms are just tender. Drain off and discard any excess fat. Stir in the spinach and cook for 1 minute or until spinach begins to wilt, stirring occasionally. Remove from heat.

2. Add the pasta to the pan and toss to combine with the pepperoni mixture, half of the cheese, the basil, and lemon juice. Taste for seasoning and add salt and pepper, if desired. Divide between 4 plates and sprinkle with the remaining cheese.

One-Pot Kielbasa Dinner

If fresh Roma tomatoes aren't available, you can use a 15-ounce can of diced tomatoes instead. Just add the undrained canned tomatoes and cook for 5 minutes before you add the pasta; this will reduce and thicken the sauce.

Serves 6

2 cups dried rotini or rotelle pasta (about 6 ounces)
1 tablespoon olive oil
1 medium yellow onion, cut into wedges
1 pound cooked kielbasa, halved lengthwise and sliced diagonally
2 cloves of garlic, minced
1 small zucchini, cut into matchstick-sized strips
1 yellow or orange pepper, seeded and diced
1 teaspoon dried Italian seasoning, crushed
Pinch cayenne pepper
8 Roma tomatoes (about 1 pound), cored and chopped
Salt and freshly ground black pepper to taste

1. Cook the pasta according to the package directions. Drain; set aside and keep warm.

2. Wipe out the pan, add the oil, and bring to temperature over medium-high heat. Add the onion and sauté for 1 minute. Add the kielbasa, stirring often to keep the onion from burning. Cook for 5 minutes, or until the onion is transparent. Add the garlic and sauté for an additional 30 seconds. Stir in the zucchini, yellow or orange pepper, Italian seasoning, and cayenne pepper; cook and stir for 5 minutes. Stir in the tomatoes and cooked pasta. Cook until heated through, stirring occasionally. Taste for seasoning and add salt and pepper, if desired.

Shrimp and Fettuccine

You can cut some of the fat in this dish by using 1 cup of evaporated skim milk instead of the chicken broth and heavy cream. Pattypan squash is a small summer squash with lovely scalloped edges.

Serves 4

8 ounces garlic-basil or tomato-basil flavored dried fettuccine

1 tablespoon extra-virgin olive oil

6 ounces baby pattypan squash, halved or quartered

1 small red onion, diced

1 clove garlic, minced

8 ounces small shrimp, peeled and deveined

½ cup chicken broth

½ cup heavy cream

OPTIONAL: ½ teaspoon hot sauce

4 ounces cream cheese, cut up into small pieces

3 tablespoons fresh basil, chopped

2 teaspoons lemon peel, grated

1 teaspoon fresh mint, chopped

Salt and freshly ground black pepper to taste

1 small head radicchio, torn

1 cup cherry tomatoes, cut in half

Freshly grated Parmigiano-Reggiano to taste

1. Cook the fettuccine according to package directions. Drain, set aside, and keep warm. Wipe out the pan; add the oil and bring to temperature over medium heat. Add the squash, onion, and garlic; sauté for 3 minutes, or until the onion and squash begin to soften. Add the shrimp; sauté for 3 minutes, or until the shrimp are opaque.

2. Reduce the heat and stir in the chicken broth, cream, and hot sauce (if using). Remove from heat; whisk in the cream cheese, stirring until the cheese is melted into the sauce. Stir in the cooked fettuccine, basil, lemon peel, mint, salt, and black pepper. Add the radicchio and cherry tomatoes; stir until the radicchio is wilted. Serve topped with freshly grated Parmigiano-Reggiano to taste.

Herb Help

Fresh herbs, especially basil, are the most tasty and aromatic when they're raw or only exposed to heat for a short time. On the other hand, dried herbs take some time to draw out the flavor. Therefore, if you're using dried herbs in the Shrimp and Fettuccine recipe, consider adding them when you sauté the shrimp.

Mexican-Style Baked Pasta

This dish is a salsa-spiked, macaroni and cheese-style dish.
Use mild or hot salsa, according to your preference.

Serves 6

12 ounces dried bow tie pasta
3 tablespoons butter
1 medium yellow onion, diced
1 red sweet pepper, seeded
   and chopped
⅓ cup all-purpose flour
½ teaspoon salt
1 teaspoon dried cilantro,
   crushed
½ teaspoon ground cumin
3 cups milk
6 ounces Colby cheese, cubed
6 ounces Monterey jack
   cheese, grated
1 cup bottled salsa
⅔ cup halved pitted green
   and/or ripe olives
Chili powder to taste

1. Preheat oven to 375°F.

2. Cook the pasta. Wipe out the pan; melt the butter over medium heat. Add the onion and sweet pepper and sauté for 5 minutes. Stir in the flour, salt, cilantro, and cumin. Whisk in the milk and cook until thickened and bubbly.

3. Reduce heat to low; add the Colby cheese and half of the Monterey jack cheese. Stir until the cheese is melted. Add the drained pasta, salsa, and olives to the pan; stir to combine. Sprinkle with the remaining Monterey jack cheese. Sprinkle lightly with chili powder. Bake, uncovered, for 20 minutes, or until bubbly around edges and heated through. Let stand 5 minutes before serving.

Skillet Ravioli

Simply change the type of pasta sauce that you use and you easily change the taste of this dish. Try roasted red pepper or roasted garlic sauce instead of the traditional marinara.

Serves 4

2 cups pasta sauce of your
   choice
¼ teaspoon granulated sugar
⅓ cup water
Salt and freshly ground
   pepper to taste
1 9-ounce package frozen
   ravioli
1 large egg, lightly beaten
1 15-ounce carton ricotta
   cheese
¼ cup grated Romano or
   Parmigiano-Reggiano
   cheese, or more, if desired
1 10-ounce package frozen
   chopped spinach, thawed
   and drained

1. Add the pasta sauce, sugar, and water to a 10-inch skillet. Bring to boil over medium-high heat. Taste and add salt and pepper, if desired. Stir in the ravioli. Reduce the heat; cover and cook, stirring occasionally, for about 5 minutes or until the ravioli are tender.

2. Add the egg, ricotta cheese, and ½ cup of the grated cheese to a bowl and stir to combine. Top the ravioli with the spinach and then spoon the cheese mixture on top of the spinach. Cover and cook over low heat for about 10 minutes, or until the cheese layer is set.

Slow-Cooked Chicken and Mushrooms

Serve this dish with a tossed or spinach salad and garlic bread.

Serves 4–6

2 cups cleaned and sliced fresh button or cremini mushrooms

1 14½-ounce can diced tomatoes with Italian herbs

1 red sweet pepper, seeded and diced

1 medium yellow onion, thinly sliced

¼ cup dry red wine or beef broth

2 tablespoons quick-cooking tapioca

2 tablespoons balsamic vinegar

3 cloves garlic, minced

2½ pounds chicken breasts, skin removed

¼ teaspoon salt

¼ teaspoon paprika

¼ teaspoon freshly ground black pepper

1 9-ounce package fresh or frozen cheese tortellini or ravioli

OPTIONAL: freshly grated Parmigiano-Reggiano cheese to taste

1. Add the mushrooms, undrained tomatoes, red pepper, onion, wine or broth, tapioca, balsamic vinegar, and garlic to a 4- or 6-quart slow cooker. Stir to combine. Place the chicken pieces on top of the sauce. Sprinkle the salt, paprika, and black pepper over the chicken. Cover and cook on low for 8 to 9 hours.

2. Remove the chicken pieces and keep warm. Add the tortellini or ravioli to the sauce; cover and cook on high for 10 to 15 minutes, or until the pasta is done. Arrange the chicken pieces on a serving platter and top with the pasta and sauce. Top with grated cheese, if desired.

Meatball and Vegetable Soup

Serve this soup with Texas toast, garlic bread, or toasted cheese sandwiches.

Add the broth, meatballs, beans, undrained tomatoes, and vegetables to a 4-quart Dutch oven over medium-high heat. Bring to a boil and stir in the pasta. Return to boiling; reduce heat and simmer, uncovered, for about 10 minutes, or until the pasta is cooked. To serve, ladle the soup into bowls. If desired, serve sprinkled with freshly grated Parmigiano-Reggiano cheese.

Serves 6–8

3 14-ounce cans beef broth

1 16-ounce package frozen cooked meatballs, thawed

1 15-ounce can Great Northern or cannellini beans, rinsed and drained

1 14.5-ounce can diced tomatoes with Italian herbs; undrained

1 10-ounce package frozen mixed vegetables, thawed

1 cup dried small pasta, such as orzo

OPTIONAL: freshly grated Parmigiano-Reggiano to taste

Tortellini Soup

Opening a few cans is the most labor involved in making this dish.
The result tastes like you've been cooking all day.

Add the oil to a large saucepan or Dutch oven; bring to temperature over medium heat. Add the onion and sauté for 3 minutes, or until transparent. Stir in the broth, tomatoes, and spinach; bring to a boil. Stir in the tortellini; lower the heat, cover, and simmer for the amount of time suggested on the tortellini package. Serve topped with grated cheese, if desired.

Serves 4–6

1 tablespoon extra-virgin olive oil

1 small yellow onion, finely chopped

2 14-ounce cans of chicken broth

1 can of stewed Italian-style tomatoes, coarsely chopped

1 13.5-ounce can chopped spinach, drained

1 16-ounce package fresh or frozen tortellini

OPTIONAL: freshly grated Parmigiano-Reggiano cheese

Seafood Pasta

Serves 4–6

1 pound dried linguine

2 tablespoons extra-virgin olive oil

2 celery stalks, diced

1 small yellow onion, diced

4 cloves garlic, minced

½ teaspoon dried basil

¼ teaspoon dried dill

¼ teaspoon dried fennel

Salt to taste

½ teaspoon freshly ground black pepper

Pinch dried red pepper flakes

1 16-ounce can diced tomatoes

½ cup white wine or chicken broth

4 tablespoons butter

1 pound grouper, salmon, or snapper, cut into bite-sized pieces

1 10-ounce can of boiled baby clams or 6.5-ounce can of whole shelled mussels

½ pound shrimp, peeled and deveined

¼ cup fresh parsley, chopped

Herbs can add a distinctive touch to your cooking. Try a variety of fresh herbs in this recipe to create a wide range of different flavors.

1. In a Dutch oven or stockpot, cook the pasta to al dente according to package directions. Drain, set aside, and keep warm.

2. Wipe out the pan. Add the oil and bring to temperature over medium heat. Add the celery; sauté for 3 to 5 minutes, or until soft. Add the onion and sauté until transparent. Add the garlic and sauté for an additional 30 seconds. Stir in the dried herbs, salt, pepper, crushed red pepper, and tomatoes. Add the wine or broth; bring to a simmer and then add the butter, fish, and clams or mussels. Cover and simmer for about 5 minutes. Add the shrimp; simmer until the shrimp are firm and pink in color. Serve over the pasta, topped with chopped parsley.

Spaghetti Pizza

If you prefer, you can bake this pizza in a 9" × 13" nonstick baking pan or 14" nonstick deep-dish pizza pan.

1. Preheat oven to 375°F.

2. In an ovenproof Dutch oven, cook the spaghetti according to package directions. Drain the pasta and return it to the pan. Stir the pasta together with the pasta sauce, sugar, eggs, half of the mozzarella cheese, the soppressata, Parmigiano-Reggiano, heavy cream, dried parsley, salt, and pepper. Arrange the mushroom slices over the top of the spaghetti mixture, and arrange the pepperoni over the top of the mushrooms. Sprinkle the remaining mozzarella cheese over the top.

3. Cover and bake for 45 minutes. Remove the cover, and bake for an additional 20 minutes, or until the cheese on top is melted, bubbling, and lightly browned. Remove from the oven and let set for 10 minutes before serving.

Serves 10–12

1 pound dried spaghetti
2 cups pasta sauce
½ teaspoon granulated sugar
6 large eggs, lightly beaten
1 pound mozzarella cheese, grated
6 ounces soppressata sausage, cut into ¼" dice
4 ounces freshly grated Parmigiano-Reggiano cheese
¼ cup heavy cream
1 tablespoon dried parsley
Salt to taste
½ teaspoon freshly ground pepper
8 ounces fresh button or cremini mushrooms, cleaned and sliced
6 ounces pepperoni, thinly sliced

Simplified Baked Lasagna

Serves 8–10

1 pound lean ground beef

1 tablespoon dried minced onion

1 teaspoon dried oregano, crushed

1 teaspoon dried minced garlic

Salt and freshly ground black pepper to taste

1 2-pound, 13-ounce jar pasta sauce

½ teaspoon granulated sugar

½ cup water

1 pound mozzarella cheese, grated

1 16-ounce container of cottage cheese

OPTIONAL: freshly grated Parmigiano-Reggiano cheese

1 pound dried lasagna noodles

This recipe requires a stovetop pan and a separate baking pan, but you don't have to cook the lasagna noodles before you bake them in the lasagna, nor do you have to peel and dice the onions or garlic.

1. Add the hamburger, onion, oregano, garlic, salt, and pepper to a Dutch oven; brown the hamburger over medium heat, stirring it with the other ingredients in the pan and breaking apart the hamburger as it cooks. When the hamburger is cooked through, drain off any excess fat. Stir in the pasta sauce and sugar. Pour the water in the emptied pasta sauce jar; cover and shake to rinse out the jar. Add the water to the pan and stir into the hamburger-sauce mixture. Remove the pan from the heat; stir in half of the grated mozzarella cheese and the cottage cheese.

2. Preheat oven to 350°F.

3. To assemble the lasagna, ladle in enough of the sauce to cover the bottom of a 9" × 13" nonstick baking pan. Sprinkle grated Parmigiano-Reggiano cheese over the top of the sauce, if desired. Add a layer of uncooked lasagna noodles, being careful not to let the noodles overlap. Repeat layering until all of the noodles are in the pan and covered. Sprinkle the remaining grated mozzarella cheese over the top, along with some additional Parmigiano-Reggiano cheese, if desired. Cover with foil and bake for 45 minutes. Remove the foil and bake for an additional 15 minutes, or until the cheese on top is melted, bubbling, and lightly browned. Remove from the oven and let set for 10 minutes before serving.

Sausage Lasagna

If you prefer to skip the "browning the hamburger" step, you can instead substitute a pound of diced cooked smoked sausage. Use all of the other ingredients; however, because you will not be heating the pasta sauce before you assemble the lasagna, bake the lasagna covered for 1 hour and then uncovered for 15 minutes.

Chapter 16
Rice

Jambalaya

*There are as many versions of Jambalaya as there are Southern
cooks. Originally created as a dish to use up leftovers, it's a versatile
recipe that you can adjust according to your tastes.*

Serves 6–8

3 tablespoons bacon fat or
peanut oil

1 1-pound bag baby carrots

4 stalks celery, diced

2 green bell peppers, seeded
and chopped

1 large yellow onion, diced

6 green onions, chopped

3 cloves garlic, minced

½ pound smoked sausage,
thinly sliced

½ pound cooked ham, diced

2 15-ounce cans diced
tomatoes, drained

1 28-ounce can heat-and-
serve pork or chicken,
undrained

3 cups chicken broth

1 tablespoon dried parsley

1 teaspoon dried thyme

½ teaspoon hot sauce, or to
taste

¼ cup Worcestershire sauce

2 cups long-grain rice,
uncooked

Water as needed

1 pound shrimp, peeled and
deveined

Salt and freshly ground
pepper to taste

1. Add the bacon fat or oil to a Dutch oven or stockpot and bring it to temperature over medium heat. Shred 8 of the baby carrots. Add the shredded carrots, the celery, and the green peppers to the pan; sauté for 3 to 5 minutes, or until soft. Add the yellow and green onions and sauté until transparent. Add the garlic and sauté for an additional 30 seconds. Stir in the smoked sausage and stir-fry for 3 minutes; add the ham and stir-fry for 1 minute. Chop the remaining carrots and add them to the pan.

2. Stir in the tomatoes, pork or chicken, broth, parsley, thyme, hot sauce, and Worcestershire sauce. Bring to a boil, and then stir in the rice; reduce the heat, cover, and simmer for 20 minutes. Fluff the rice; add additional water, if needed. If the shrimp are large, cut them in half; otherwise, add the shrimp to the pot, cover, and cook for another 3 to 5 minutes, or until the shrimp are cooked. If excess moisture remains in the dish, uncover and cook until it's evaporated, stirring often to keep the rice from sticking. Taste for seasoning and add salt and pepper, if needed.

Pressure-Cooked Long-Grain Brown Rice

For 6 servings, add 1 cup long-grain brown rice, 2 cups of water or broth, 1 tablespoon oil, and 1 teaspoon salt to a pressure cooker over high heat, lock the lid, and bring to high pressure. Adjust the burner to maintain low pressure for 20 minutes. Remove pan from the heat and let sit for 10 minutes or until the pressure is released and you can remove the lid; fluff the rice with a fork and serve.

Shrimp Etouffée

The secret of a good Shrimp Etouffée is in the sauce, which requires a dark roux. It takes a little extra work, but it's worth the effort. Serve the results over cooked rice.

Serves 6

3 tablespoons bacon fat or peanut oil

3 tablespoons all-purpose flour

1 small green pepper, seeded and chopped

3 stalks celery, diced

OPTIONAL: 1 large carrot, peeled and shredded

1 large yellow onion, diced

4 green onions, chopped

3 cloves garlic, minced

3 tablespoons tomato sauce

1¼ cups beef broth

1 cup dry white wine

2 bay leaves

¼ teaspoon dried basil

¼ teaspoon dried thyme

1 teaspoon hot sauce, or to taste

1½ pounds shrimp, peeled and deveined

Salt and freshly ground pepper to taste

3 cups cooked rice

OPTIONAL: ¼ cup fresh parsley, chopped

1. Add the bacon fat or oil and flour to a Dutch oven or stockpot over medium heat. Cook, stirring constantly so the roux doesn't burn, for 15 minutes, or until the roux is the color of peanut butter.

2. Stir in the green pepper, carrot (if using), celery, and yellow and green onions. Sauté for 10 minutes, or until the vegetables are tender. Add the tomato paste, broth, and wine, stirring constantly until the mixture thickens. Add the bay leaves, basil, thyme, and hot sauce; stir to combine. Cover, reduce the heat, and simmer for 45 minutes.

3. Add the shrimp and simmer for 20 minutes, uncovered. Remove and discard the bay leaves. Taste for seasoning and add salt and pepper, additional hot sauce, and herbs, if needed. Serve over cooked rice, garnished with chopped fresh parsley, if desired.

Cooked Long-Grain White Rice

For 8 servings, add 3 cups long-grain rice, 4½ cups water or broth, and salt to taste to a large saucepan; bring to a boil over medium-high heat. Reduce heat to medium-low, cover, and cook for 15 minutes. Remove the lid, add butter or extra-virgin olive oil to taste, and fluff with a fork until the butter or oil is mixed into the rice and all of the liquid is absorbed.

Red Beans and Rice

Purists insist that this dish requires pickled pork. If you're not one of them, you can double the smoked sausage or substitute cooked pork.

Serves 6–8

3 15-ounce cans kidney beans, rinsed and drained

2 cups water or chicken broth, or more as needed

1 medium yellow onion, diced

1 bunch green onions, cleaned and chopped

7 cloves garlic, minced

2 tablespoons dried parsley

1 stalk celery, diced

½ cup ketchup

1 green bell pepper, seeded and diced

1 tablespoon Worcestershire sauce

2 teaspoons hot sauce, or to taste

2 whole bay leaves

¼ teaspoon dried thyme

1 pound smoked sausage, sliced

1 pound pickled pork, cut into cubes

Salt and freshly ground black pepper to taste

3–4 cups cooked rice

Add all of the ingredients except the cooked rice to a 4-quart Dutch oven or stockpot. Add additional water if needed to bring the liquid level to just above the other ingredients in the pot. Cover and simmer for 1 hour, stirring occasionally and checking to make sure the pan doesn't boil dry. Taste for seasoning; add salt and pepper, if needed. Serve over the cooked rice.

Pickled Pork

Add ¼ cup mustard seed, ½ tablespoon celery seeds, 1 tablespoon hot sauce, 2 cups white vinegar, ½ bay leaf, ½ tablespoon kosher salt, 6 peppercorns, and 3 smashed cloves of garlic to a nonreactive pan; boil for 3 minutes. Allow to cool, then pour over 1 pound of cooked cubed pork and cover. Pickled pork will keep in the refrigerator for up to three days.

Gumbo

For the broth, backwoods cooks save up chicken gizzards and necks until they have 2 pounds of each, then simmer them in 3 or 4 quarts of water. You can find filé powder at www.thespicehouse.com if your local grocery store doesn't carry it.

Serves 6–8

4 tablespoons lard or peanut oil

4 tablespoons all-purpose flour

4 stalks celery, chopped

1 large yellow onion, diced

1 green bell pepper, seeded and diced

3 cloves garlic, minced

1 15-ounce can diced tomatoes

¼ teaspoon dried thyme

¼ teaspoon dried basil

3 bay leaves

2 tablespoons filé powder

2 tablespoons Worcestershire sauce

1 teaspoon hot sauce, or to taste

8 cups chicken broth

1 pound smoked sausage, sliced

2 cups cooked chicken, shredded

Salt and freshly ground pepper to taste

4½ cups cooked long-grain rice

1. Add the lard or oil and flour to a Dutch oven or stockpot over medium heat. Cook, stirring constantly so the roux doesn't burn, for 15 minutes, or until the roux is the color of peanut butter.

2. Stir in the celery, onions, green pepper, garlic, and tomatoes; cook, stirring constantly, until the vegetables are tender. Add the remaining ingredients except the sausage, chicken, salt, pepper, and rice and simmer covered over medium heat for 30 to 45 minutes, or until the mixture thickens.

3. Stir in the sausage and chicken; simmer uncovered for an additional 15 minutes. Taste for seasoning; add salt and pepper, if needed. Serve hot over about ¼ cup of rice per serving.

Cooked Short- or Medium-Grain Rice

For 4½ cups of cooked rice, rinse and drain 1½ cups of rice and add to a large saucepan along with 2½ cups of water and salt to taste. Cover and let set for 30 minutes. Bring to a boil over high heat, reduce heat to medium-low, and cook covered for 15 minutes. Turn off the heat. Leave covered for 10 minutes or until ready to serve, for up to 1 hour.

Dirty Rice

This dish gets its name from the appearance the chopped chicken livers add to the rice. If you prefer a milder liver taste, use ½ pound chicken livers and ½ pound chicken gizzards instead of all livers.

Serves 4

2 tablespoons bacon fat or peanut oil

1 small green bell pepper, seeded and diced

2 stalks celery, chopped

1 medium yellow onion, diced

1 clove garlic, minced

½ pound lean ground pork

½ pound Italian sausage

3 cups chicken broth

1 pound chicken livers

½ tablespoon Worcestershire sauce

Cayenne pepper to taste

1 tablespoon dried parsley

1 cup uncooked long-grain rice

Water, if needed

2 green onions, chopped

Salt and freshly ground pepper to taste

1. Add the bacon fat or oil to a Dutch oven or stockpot and bring to temperature over medium heat. Add the green pepper and celery; sauté for 3 minutes. Add the yellow onion; sauté for 5 minutes, or until the onions are transparent and the vegetables are tender. Add the garlic and sauté for 30 seconds. Stir in the ground pork and sausage; fry until the meat is lightly browned. Drain off and discard any excess fat.

2. Stir in the chicken broth and bring to a boil. Add the chicken livers, cover, and lightly boil for 30 minutes. Use a slotted spoon to remove the chicken livers; set them aside to cool.

3. Stir in the Worcestershire sauce, cayenne, parsley, and rice; bring to a boil. Reduce heat to medium-low, cover, and cook for 15 minutes.

4. Chop the chicken livers. Stir into the rice-sausage mixture. Cover and simmer for 20 minutes; stir occasionally to keep the rice from sticking. Add water if additional moisture is needed. Stir in the green onion. Taste for seasoning; add salt and pepper, if needed.

Hopped-Up Hoppin' John

Hoppin' John is a Southern dish traditionally eaten on New Year's Day.
This version is hopped up by adding carrots to make it a one-dish meal.

Serves 6–8

½ pound thick-cut bacon, diced
1 stalk celery, minced
1 1-pound bag baby carrots
1 large yellow onion, diced
2 15-ounce cans black-eyed peas, rinsed and drained
3 cups cooked long-grain rice
4 cups chicken broth
Salt and freshly ground black pepper to taste

Add the bacon to a Dutch oven or stockpot; cook over medium heat until the fat begins to render out of the bacon. Add the celery; sauté for 2 minutes. Shred 4 of the baby carrots and add them to the pan with the celery; sauté for 1 minute. Add the onion and sauté for 5 minutes, or until transparent. Dice the remaining baby carrots by slicing them each into 4 or 5 pieces. Stir in the diced carrots, black-eyed peas, rice, and chicken broth. Bring to a simmer; cover, reduce heat, and simmer for 10 minutes or until the carrots are tender and the black-eyed peas are warmed through. Turn off the heat and let set, covered, for 10 minutes. Taste for seasoning; add salt and pepper if needed.

Spanish Rice

Adding a pinch or two of brown or granulated sugar when you add the water
enhances the flavor of this dish and cuts the acidity of the tomatoes.

Serves 4

1 pound hamburger
1 medium yellow onion, diced
1 green pepper, seeded and diced
1 teaspoon chili powder
1½ cups water
Pinch light brown or granulated sugar
½ cup tomato sauce
1 tablespoon butter
1 cup uncooked short- or medium-grain rice
2 tablespoons Worcestershire sauce
Hot sauce to taste
¼ teaspoon dried thyme
Salt and freshly ground black pepper to taste

Add the hamburger, onion, green pepper, and chili powder to a deep 2-quart or larger nonstick skillet; fry the hamburger over medium to medium-high heat, stirring frequently to prevent the vegetables from burning and to break apart the hamburger. When the hamburger is browned and the onions are transparent, drain off and discard any excess fat. Stir in the water, tomato sauce, butter, rice, Worcestershire sauce, hot sauce, and thyme; bring to a boil. Reduce heat to low, cover, and simmer for 25 minutes, or until the rice is tender. Taste for seasoning and add salt and pepper, if needed.

Stuffed Peppers

Serves 8

8 medium green bell peppers
Nonstick cooking spray
2 pounds lean ground beef
2 cups cooked rice
3 large eggs
3 cloves garlic, minced
1 large yellow onion, diced
4 tablespoons butter
Salt and freshly ground black
    pepper to taste
OPTIONAL: pinch allspice or
    nutmeg
1 cup tomato sauce
2 tablespoons white or white
    wine vinegar
1 tablespoon granulated
    sugar
1 cup chicken broth

This recipe is an excellent way to use up leftover rice.
It's also delicious if you use cooked brown rice.

1. Preheat oven to 350°F.

2. Cut the tops off of the green peppers. Remove the seeds from the peppers and discard. Set the peppers in a 9" × 13" nonstick baking pan and set the tops aside.

3. Add the ground beef, cooked rice, eggs, garlic, onion, butter, salt, black pepper, and allspice or nutmeg (if using) to a large bowl; mix well. Divide the meat filling mixture between the green peppers; place the tops on each.

4. In the bowl, mix together the tomato sauce, wine or vinegar, sugar, and broth. Pour into the pan holding the stuffed green peppers.

5. Treat one side of a large piece of heavy-duty aluminum foil with nonstick cooking spray. Put the foil atop the baking pan, treated side down; crimp the edges to form a seal. Bake for 45 minutes. Remove the foil, being careful to avoid being burned by the escaping steam. Return to the oven and bake for an additional 15 minutes, or until the peppers are tender and the filling is cooked through.

Stuffed Pepper Options

You can substitute a cup of breadcrumbs or cracker crumbs for the cooked rice. Or, replace some of the rice in the meat mixture with peeled and chopped hard-boiled eggs. Or, use a mixture of ground beef and ground pork or lamb.

Paella

Paella, named after the style of pan it's cooked in, is made up primarily of rice, saffron, and olive oil. Saffron is expensive; you can substitute ground turmeric, which will give the dish a similar yellow color but will alter the taste a bit.

Serves 6–8

½ cup extra-virgin olive oil or olive oil

1 red bell pepper, seeded and diced

2 medium yellow onions, diced

2 cloves garlic, minced

1 pound boneless chicken thighs, skin removed and diced

½ pound ground pork

1 cup smoked ham, diced

1 cup chorizo, sliced

2 cups uncooked Arborio or converted rice

3 cups chicken broth

⅛ teaspoon saffron threads, crushed

2 tablespoons annatto oil (page 113)

1 teaspoon paprika

Salt to taste

1 cup frozen peas, thawed

½ pound shrimp, peeled and deveined

1 6.5 can mussels, rinsed and drained

1 10-ounce can boiled baby clams, rinsed and drained

1 cup dry white wine

1 lemon, thinly sliced

1. Bring the oil to temperature over medium-high heat in a 15" paella pan or deep skillet. Stir in the red bell pepper and onion; sauté for 5 minutes, or until the onions are transparent. Add the garlic, chicken, and ground pork; stir-fry until the meat is lightly browned. Stir in the ham, chorizo, and rice; sauté until the rice begins to color.

2. Add the chicken broth and bring to a boil. Stir in the saffron, annatto oil, paprika, and salt. Reduce the heat to medium; cover, and cook for 10 minutes, rotating the pan or stirring the contents of the pan occasionally. Check the rice; cover and cook until the rice is tender.

3. Stir in the peas, shrimp, mussels, clams, and wine. Cover and cook for 5 minutes, or until the shrimp is opaque and the mussels and clams are warm. Garnish with lemon slices and serve.

Arborio Rice

Arborio rice is an Italian medium-grain rice. It has a high starch content, which creates a creamy base. This is why the firmer rounded grains are often used in paella and risotto dishes in Mediterranean cuisine.

Sweet-and-Sour Pork

Serves 4

1 tablespoon peanut oil
1 pound lean pork, cut into bite-sized pieces
1 teaspoon garlic powder
1 13½-ounce can pineapple tidbits
Water as needed
¼ cup white vinegar
1 teaspoon soy sauce
OPTIONAL: 2 tablespoons granulated sugar
1 cup uncooked converted white rice
1 green bell pepper, seeded and diced
1 tomato, diced
1 16-ounce bag frozen stir-fry vegetables mix, thawed

This is a variation of a recipe that first appeared on the back of the Uncle Ben's Converted Rice package in 1987. Adjust the sugar in the recipe according to whether the pineapple you use is canned in syrup or its own juice.

1. Bring the oil to temperature over medium-high heat in a nonstick wok or large skillet. Add the pork and garlic powder; stir-fry for 5 minutes, or until the pork is browned.

2. Drain the pineapple, reserving the juice. Set aside the pineapple tidbits. Add water to the pineapple juice to bring the total amount of liquid to 2½ cups. Add to the wok or skillet along with the vinegar, soy sauce, and sugar (if using). Bring to a boil; reduce heat to low, cover, and simmer for 20 minutes.

3. Remove the cover and stir in the rice. Cover and simmer for another 25 minutes, or until all of the liquid is absorbed and the pork is tender. Stir in the green pepper, tomato, and stir-fry vegetables mix. Cover and cook on low for 5 minutes. Uncover and stir-fry until the vegetables are cooked to crisp-tender. Serve immediately.

Baked Chicken Supreme

If your casserole dish can't withstand a 425ºF baking temperature, you can bake this casserole at a lower oven temperature; simply extend the baking time as needed, allowing for up to 1 hour, for example, if you bake it at 350ºF.

1. Preheat oven to 425ºF.

2. Add the butter and onion to a 2-quart microwave- and ovenproof casserole dish. Microwave on high for 30 seconds, or until the butter is melted. Stir, cover, and microwave on high at 30-second intervals until the onion is transparent. Stir in the flour, salt, and pepper, and then whisk in the half-and-half a little at a time. Once you have a smooth, lump-free mixture, stir in the remaining ingredients. Bake uncovered for 30 minutes.

Serves 6–8

¼ cup butter
1 small yellow onion, diced
⅓ cup all-purpose flour
½ teaspoon salt
⅛ teaspoon freshly ground
    black pepper
1 cup half-and-half
1 cup chicken broth
2 8.8-ounce pouches Uncle
    Ben's Long Grain & Wild
    Ready Rice
2 cups cooked chicken, cubed
⅓ cup pimiento, chopped
⅓ cup fresh parsley, chopped
¼ cup almonds, chopped

Southwestern Chicken and Rice Casserole

You can assemble this dish the night before, refrigerate it, and then bake it the next day. Just increase the cooking time to 45 minutes.

1. Preheat oven to 425ºF.

2. Bring the oil to temperature over medium heat in an ovenproof Dutch oven; add the onion and sauté for 5 minutes, or until transparent. Stir in the rice and vermicelli mix (including the seasoning packet); cook and stir for 2 minutes. Stir in the broth and water; bring to a boil. Reduce the heat, cover, and simmer for 20 minutes.

3. Stir in the chicken, tomatoes, peppers, basil, chili powder, cumin, and black pepper. Cover and bake for 25 minutes. Sprinkle with the cheese. Let stand for 5 minutes before serving.

Serves 6

1 tablespoon extra-virgin
    olive oil
1 medium yellow onion, diced
1 6.9-ounce package chicken-
    flavored rice and vermicelli
    mix
1 14-ounce can chicken broth
2 cups water
2 cups cooked chicken or
    turkey, chopped
1 15-ounce can diced
    tomatoes
3 tablespoons canned green
    chili peppers, drained and
    diced
1 teaspoon dried basil, crushed
1½ teaspoons chili powder
⅛ teaspoon ground cumin
⅛ teaspoon freshly ground
    black pepper
2 ounces Cheddar cheese,
    shredded

Chicken and Broccoli Casserole

Serves 8

1 tablespoon butter

1 teaspoon vegetable oil

1 cup fresh button
mushrooms, cleaned and
chopped

1 small yellow onion, diced

1 pound boneless, skinless
chicken breasts, cut into
bite-sized pieces

2 cloves garlic, minced

1 10¾-ounce can cream of
mushroom soup

1 cup pasteurized processed
cheese spread or
Velveeta, cubed

13.2 ounces Uncle Ben's
Whole Grain Brown or
Original Long Grain
Ready Rice

1 12-ounce bag frozen
broccoli florets, thawed
and drained

1 8-ounce can sliced water
chestnuts, drained

½ cup sour cream

¼ teaspoon freshly ground
black pepper

4 ounces Cheddar cheese,
shredded

½ cup breadcrumbs or
crushed croutons

*This is another casserole that can be prepared the night before,
covered and refrigerated, and then baked the next day. Simply
add 10 minutes to the initial baking time.*

1. Preheat the oven to 400°F.

2. Add the butter and oil to an ovenproof Dutch oven and bring it to temperature over medium-high heat; swirl the pan to blend the butter and oil. Add the mushrooms; cook and stir for 2 minutes. Add the onion and chicken; stir-fry until the chicken is just cooked through. Stir in the garlic, and stir-fry for another 30 seconds. Add the undiluted mushroom soup and the cheese spread or Velveeta. Stir until the cheese is melted.

3. Remove the Dutch oven from the heat. Stir in the rice, broccoli, water chestnuts, sour cream, and pepper. Bake uncovered for 15 to 20 minutes.

4. Remove from the oven and top with the Cheddar cheese and breadcrumbs or crushed croutons. Return to oven and bake for 10 minutes, or until the cheese is melted and the breadcrumbs or crushed croutons are lightly browned.

Stovetop Cooking Brown Rice

For 3 cups of cooked brown rice, bring 4 cups of salted water or chicken broth to a boil over medium heat. Stir in 1 cup whole grain brown rice. Adjust the heat so that the liquid maintains a gentle boil. Cook for up to 1 hour, stirring frequently and adding more liquid if necessary to keep the rice covered, or until tender. Drain; plunge in cold water to stop the cooking process.

Shrimp and Rice Casserole

You can omit the peas in this recipe if your family
doesn't like them. Serve with a tossed salad instead.

Serves 6

2 cups water
½ tablespoon salt
1 pound medium shrimp,
    peeled and deveined
2 tablespoons butter
½ green bell pepper, seeded
    and chopped
1 small Vidalia onion, diced
3 cups cooked rice
1 10¾-ounce can condensed
    cream of mushroom soup
8 ounces sharp Cheddar
    cheese, grated
1 cup frozen baby peas,
    thawed
Salt and freshly ground black
    pepper to taste

1. Preheat oven to 325°F.

2. Add the water to an ovenproof Dutch oven and bring to a boil over medium-high heat. Add the salt and shrimp; boil for 1 minute. Drain immediately and set the shrimp aside.

3. Wipe out the Dutch oven and melt the butter in it; add the green pepper and onion, and sauté for 5 minutes, or until the onion is transparent. Stir in the rice, soup, 1½ cups of the cheese, the shrimp, and peas. Add salt and pepper to taste. Top with the remaining cheese. Bake uncovered for 30 minutes, or until the cheese is melted and bubbly.

Chicken and Green Bean Casserole

This dish is also good if you substitute a cup of
cooked wild rice for half of the cooked rice.

Serves 6

2 tablespoons butter or
    vegetable oil
1 medium yellow onion, diced
3 cups cooked chicken, diced
2 14½-ounce cans green
    beans, drained and rinsed
1 8-ounce can water
    chestnuts, drained and
    chopped
1 4-ounce jar pimientos,
    chopped
1 10¾-ounce can condensed
    cream of celery soup
1 cup mayonnaise
2 cups cooked rice
4 ounces sharp Cheddar
    cheese, grated
Pinch salt

1. Preheat oven to 350°F.

2. Add the butter or oil to an ovenproof Dutch oven and bring it to temperature over medium heat. Add the onion; sauté for 5 minutes, or until translucent. Stir in the remaining ingredients and mix until thoroughly combined. Bake uncovered for 20 to 25 minutes, or until bubbly. Let stand for a few minutes before serving.

Chapter 17
Casseroles and Pot Pies

Three-Pork Pie

Serves 8

3 tablespoons butter

1 medium yellow onion, diced

½ pound bulk pork sausage

3 tablespoons all-purpose flour

¼ cup milk or heavy cream

1 tablespoon dried parsley

¼ teaspoon dried sage or thyme

¼ teaspoon savory

¼ teaspoon freshly ground black pepper

1 28-ounce can heat-and-serve pork

1 14-ounce bag baby potatoes and vegetables blend, thawed

1 cup cooked ham, cubed

1 15-ounce package refrigerated peel-and-unroll-style pie crusts

The ham and pork are already salty, which is why there is no salt called for in this recipe. Because tastes are different, be sure to have the saltshaker at the table for those who want more.

1. Preheat oven to 375°F.

2. Add the butter and onion to a large microwave-safe bowl. Cover and microwave on high for 1 minute. Stir to mix the melted butter with the onion. Break the sausage apart into the butter-onion mixture; stir to combine. Cover and microwave on high for 3 1-minute segments, stirring between each minute. If the sausage has lost its pink color, continue to step 3; if it hasn't, cover and microwave on high for 1 more minute.

3. Sprinkle the flour over the sausage mixture in the bowl, then stir to combine. Stir in the milk or heavy cream. Cover and microwave on high for 1 minute. Whisk in the parsley, sage or thyme, savory, and black pepper until the mixture is smooth and there are no lumps. Stir in the canned pork and broth. Cut the baby potatoes in the vegetable blend into quarters, if desired, and then stir the entire bag and the ham into the mixture.

4. Divide the pork mixture between two 9½" deep-dish pie plates. Top each filled pie plate with a pie crust. Cut vents into the crust. Place the pie plates side-by-side on a large jellyroll pan (a safety measure to catch any drippings should a pan boil over). Bake for 45 minutes, or until the crust is golden brown. Let set for 10 minutes, then cut and serve.

Blending Starch and Vegetables

You can substitute 1 cup of thawed frozen corn and 1 cup of thawed frozen hash brown potatoes for the potato-vegetable blend. You can also replace the sage or thyme, savory, and pepper with ¾ teaspoon of Mrs. Dash Original Blend. Also, if you only need 4 servings, you can freeze half of the filling mixture to use later.

Steak and Mushroom Pie

Serve this pie with a tossed salad topped with a sour cream–based salad dressing, like bleu cheese or ranch.

1. Preheat oven to 375°F.

2. Add the bacon, butter, onion, and mushrooms to a large microwave-safe bowl. Cover and microwave on high for 1 minute. Stir to mix the melted butter with the other ingredients. Cover and microwave on high for 3 1-minute segments, stirring between each minute. If the bacon has lost its pink color, continue to step 3; if it hasn't, cover and microwave on high for another minute.

3. Add the garlic and sprinkle the flour over the mushroom mixture in the bowl, then stir to combine. Slowly stir in the wine or broth. Cover and microwave on high for 1 minute. Whisk in the parsley and seasoning blend until the mixture is smooth and without lumps. Slowly stir in the remaining broth. Cut the baby potatoes in the vegetable blend into quarters, if desired, then stir the entire bag and the beef into the mixture.

4. Pour the beef mixture into a 9½" deep-dish pie plate. Top the filled pie plate with an pie crust. Cut vents into the crust. Place the pie plate on a jellyroll pan (a safety measure to catch any drippings should the pan boil over). Bake for 45 minutes, or until the crust is golden brown. Let set for 10 minutes, and then cut and serve.

Recipe Adjustments

Adjust the seasoning in this recipe according to the seasonings used in your cooked beef. For example, if you're using leftover Beef Bourguignon, use Burgundy instead of Madeira and simply add additional freshly ground black pepper to taste instead of the Mrs. Dash Original Blend.

Serves 4

4 slices bacon, cut into small dice
2 tablespoons butter
1 small yellow onion, diced
8 ounces fresh button or cremini mushrooms, cleaned and sliced
2 cloves garlic, minced
3 tablespoons all-purpose flour
½ cup Madeira wine
1 teaspoon dried parsley
1 teaspoon Mrs. Dash® Original Blend
½ cup beef broth
½ 14-ounce bag baby potatoes and vegetables blend, thawed
1 cup cooked sirloin steak or roast beef, shredded or cubed
1 refrigerated peel-and-unroll-style pie crust

Upside-Down Beef Pot Pie

Serves 4

¼ cup plus 2 tablespoons butter

1½ cups all-purpose flour

1 cup Cheddar cheese, grated

2 teaspoons granulated sugar

2 teaspoons baking powder

½ teaspoon salt

1½ cups milk

1 medium yellow onion, diced

2 baby carrots, shredded

½ stalk celery, finely diced

2 cups cooked beef, diced or shredded

1 cup frozen peas and carrots, thawed

1 cup diced cooked potatoes

1 cup beef gravy

OPTIONAL: 1 teaspoon Dijon mustard

OPTIONAL: 2 teaspoons mayonnaise

This recipe is a delicious way to use leftover roast beef and potatoes. The Dijon mustard and mayonnaise are optional flavor enhancers.

1. Preheat oven to 350°F.

2. Add ¼ cup of the butter to a large microwave-safe bowl; microwave on high for 30 seconds, or until the butter is melted. Pour the butter in an 8" square baking dish. Add the flour, cheese, sugar, baking powder, salt, and milk to the bowl; stir until blended. Pour into the baking dish.

3. Add the remaining 2 tablespoons of butter, the onion, carrots, and celery to the bowl. Cover and microwave on high for 1 minute; stir to combine the vegetables with the melted butter. Cover and microwave on high for 1 more minute, or until the onion is transparent. Stir in the beef, thawed peas and carrots, potatoes, gravy, and, if using, the mustard and mayonnaise. Pour the beef mixture over the batter. Do not stir. Bake for 1 hour, or until the beef topping is bubbly.

Armenian Meat Pie

Armenian meat pies are traditionally made using individual serving-sized rounds of dough that are filled and folded over. This recipe streamlines that process by turning it into what resembles one large double-crust, deep-dish pizza without cheese.

Serves 8

2 pounds lean ground beef
1 medium yellow onion, diced
1 green bell pepper, seeded
    and diced
2 cloves garlic, minced
1 teaspoon paprika
½ teaspoon ground allspice
Salt and freshly ground black
    pepper to taste
Pinch cayenne pepper
1 15-ounce can diced
    tomatoes, drained
2 tablespoons tomato paste
1 tablespoon dried parsley
1 teaspoon dried mint
Extra-virgin olive oil as
    needed
2 13.8-ounce cans
    refrigerated pizza crust

1. Preheat oven to 400°F.

2. Add the ground beef, onion, green pepper, garlic, paprika, allspice, salt, pepper, and cayenne to a large microwave-safe bowl. Stir to combine and break the meat apart. Cover and microwave on high for 3 minutes. Uncover and stir. Cover and microwave on high for 3 to 5 minutes, or until meat is cooked through. Drain off any excess fat. Stir in the drained tomatoes, tomato paste, parsley, and mint. Taste for seasoning and adjust.

3. Brush the bottom of a 14" nonstick deep-dish pizza pan or 9" × 13" nonstick baking pan with a generous amount of olive oil. Using the tips of your fingers, press one can of the pizza crust over the bottom of the pan. Poke holes in the bottom crust with a fork. Top with the filling. Top the filling with the other pizza crust, carefully pressing it out to the edges of the pan. Generously brush the top of the crust with extra-virgin olive oil. Cut several vents into the crust. Bake for 30 minutes, or until the crust is lightly browned on top and baked through. Let stand for 10 minutes, then cut and serve.

Hamburger Deep-Dish Pizza

To convert the Armenian Meat Pie recipe to a more traditional deep-dish pizza, substitute oregano for the mint and add 1 teaspoon of dried basil. Before you add the meat filling, cover the bottom crust with slices of or shredded mozzarella cheese to taste. You can also mix freshly grated Parmigiano-Reggiano cheese to taste into the hamburger filling.

Jamaican Meat Pie Casserole

Rather than making individual serving-sized meat pies, this recipe makes one large double-crust, deep-dish pizza-style casserole. The curry powder and jalapeño give it a taste of the islands. Serve with a salad tossed with a citrus vinaigrette to complete the theme.

Serves 8

2 pounds lean ground beef
1 large yellow onion, diced
2 green onions, finely chopped
1 jalapeño pepper, seeded and minced
2 cloves garlic, minced
1 teaspoon dried thyme
2 tablespoons curry powder
2 teaspoons paprika
Salt and freshly ground black pepper to taste
Dash cayenne pepper
2 large eggs
1 tablespoon white or white wine vinegar
½ cup breadcrumbs
½ teaspoon granulated sugar, or to taste
2 13.8-ounce cans refrigerated pizza crust

1. Preheat oven to 400°F.

2. Add the ground beef, the yellow and green onions, jalapeño, garlic, thyme, 1 tablespoon of the curry powder, 1 teaspoon of the paprika, the salt, pepper, and cayenne to a large microwave-safe bowl. Stir to combine and break the meat apart. Cover and microwave on high for 3 minutes. Uncover and stir. Cover and microwave on high for 3 to 5 minutes, or until the meat is cooked through. Drain off any excess fat. Stir in the eggs, vinegar, breadcrumbs, and sugar. Taste for seasoning and adjust if necessary.

3. Brush the bottom of a 14" nonstick deep-dish pizza pan or 9" × 13" nonstick baking pan with a generous amount of olive oil. Using the tips of your fingers, press one can of the pizza crust over the bottom of the pan. Brush the top of the crust with extra-virgin olive oil and sprinkle the remaining 1 tablespoon of curry powder over the oil. Poke holes in the bottom crust with a fork. Top with the filling. Top the filling with the other pizza crust, carefully pressing it out to the edges of the pan.

4. Generously brush the top of the crust with extra-virgin olive oil. Sprinkle the remaining 1 teaspoon of paprika over the oil. Cut several vents into the crust. Bake for 30 minutes, or until the crust is lightly browned on top and baked through. Let stand for 10 minutes, and then cut and serve.

Greek Meat and Vegetable Pie

Serve this casserole with a cucumber-yogurt salad (page 102).

1. Preheat oven to 350°F.

2. Add the onions and oil to a large microwave-safe bowl. Cover and microwave on high for 1 minute. Stir, cover, and then microwave for 2 minutes, or until transparent. Add the spinach to the bowl and toss with the onions. Microwave the broccoli according to the package directions; drain and add to the bowl along with the cheese, eggs, chicken or turkey, chives, dill, parsley, and pepper; mix well. Set aside to cool.

3. Brush the bottom of a 9" × 13" nonstick baking pan with some of the butter. Layer half of the phyllo sheets on the bottom, 1 sheet at a time, brushing each sheet with butter before adding the next sheet. Evenly spread the meat and vegetable filling over the buttered phyllo sheets. Top the filling with the remaining sheets, brushing each sheet with butter before you add the next sheet. Cut into 8 equal pieces. Bake uncovered for 1 hour, or until golden brown.

Serves 8

1 medium yellow onion, diced
2 green onions, diced
2 tablespoons extra-virgin olive oil
1 8-ounce bag baby spinach, torn
1 12-ounce bag frozen steam-in-the-bag broccoli florets
8 ounces crumbled feta cheese
2 large eggs
2 cups cooked chicken or turkey, diced
2 tablespoons fresh chives, minced
2 tablespoons fresh dill, minced
½ cup fresh parsley, minced
Freshly ground black pepper to taste
1 16-ounce package phyllo dough
½ cup butter, melted

Welsh Pork Pie

*This dish is traditionally served cold or at room temperature,
so it's an excellent dish to make ahead to serve at brunch.*

Serves 6

1½ pounds lean ground pork
1 medium yellow onion, diced
2 large eggs
Pinch cayenne pepper
¼ teaspoon dried sage
2 tablespoons Worcestershire
sauce
Salt and freshly ground black
pepper to taste
1 refrigerated peel-and-
unroll-style pie crust

1. Preheat the oven to 375°F.

2. Add the ground pork, onion, eggs, cayenne, sage, Worcestershire sauce, salt, and pepper to a deep-dish pie pan. Mix well and spread out evenly in the pan. Bake for 30 minutes. Drain off any excess fat.

3. Cover the meat mixture with the pie crust. Cut vents in the crust. Bake for 45 minutes, or until the crust is golden brown and flaky.

Stovetop Chicken Casserole

*Adjust the amount of salt in the cooking liquid for the noodles
according to the type of cooked chicken and the amount of
sodium in the soup you are using in this recipe.*

Serves 6

12 ounces dried wide egg
noodles
1½ cups frozen mixed
vegetables of your choice
1½ cups cooked chicken,
cubed
1 4½-ounce can sliced
mushrooms, drained
1 10¾-ounce can cream of
mushroom soup
1 large egg
1 tablespoon mayonnaise
2 tablespoons milk
1 cup Cheddar cheese, grated

1. In a Dutch oven, cook noodles according to the package directions. Add the vegetables during the last 3 minutes of cooking time. Drain; return the noodles and vegetable mixture to the pan.

2. Stir in the chicken, mushrooms, and half of the mushroom soup. Stir to combine and start to bring the mixture to temperature over medium-low heat. Add the egg, mayonnaise, and milk to the cream of mushroom soup remaining in the can; use a fork to mix thoroughly. Add the soup mixture to the Dutch oven and stir to combine it with the other ingredients. Cook for 5 minutes, stirring occasionally. Add the cheese and mix well. Continue to cook and stir until the cheese is melted.

Chicken Pot Pie

If you prefer, you can replace the buttermilk biscuits with pie crust.

1. Preheat oven to 400°F.

2. Melt the butter in a 4-quart ovenproof Dutch oven over medium heat. Peel the carrots; shred 1 carrot and dice the other 4. Add the shredded carrot, celery, onion, garlic, thyme, and mushrooms to the pan. Sauté until the onions are translucent.

3. Add the remaining carrots, chicken, broth, and potatoes to the pan. Bring to a simmer, reduce the heat, cover, and simmer for 20 minutes, or until the vegetables are tender and the chicken is cooked through.

4. Whisk the flour and wine together in a small bowl or measuring cup. Whisk in 1 cup of the hot broth from the pan. Strain to remove any lumps, then pour into the pan. Stir to mix. Increase the temperature to bring to a low boil. Boil and stir until the mixture thickens and the flour taste is gone, about 5 minutes. Stir in the cream and peas. Taste for seasoning and add salt and pepper, if desired.

5. In a small bowl, beat the egg with the water. Press or roll out the biscuits until they're about ¼" thick. Cut slits in the top of each biscuit to allow steam to escape while they're baking. Arrange the biscuits over the top of the pie and brush them with all of the egg mixture. Bake for 50 minutes, or until the biscuit crust is golden and the gravy is bubbling. Let stand for 10 minutes before serving.

Chicken Upside-Down Pie

Instead of baking the entire pot pie, roll out the biscuits to ¼" thickness, turn a muffin pan upside down, and shape the biscuits over the muffin pan indentations. Bake for 12 to 15 minutes, or until golden brown. For each serving, place a biscuit "bowl" inside another bowl, ladle the chicken potpie mixture into the biscuit bowl, and top with grated Cheddar cheese, if desired.

Serves 8

¼ cup butter
5 large carrots
4 stalks celery, finely diced
2 large yellow onions, diced
2 large cloves garlic, minced
1 teaspoon dried thyme
8 ounces button mushrooms, cleaned and sliced
4 boneless, skinless chicken breasts, cubed
6 cups chicken broth
4 large russet potatoes, peeled and diced
½ cup all-purpose flour
½ cup dry white wine
½ cup heavy cream
1 cup frozen baby peas, thawed
Salt and freshly ground black pepper to taste
8 large refrigerated buttermilk biscuits
1 large egg
2 tablespoons water

Tex-Mex Chicken Casserole

Serves 8–10

2 pounds skinless, boneless
    chicken breasts, cubed

2½ cups chicken broth

½ cup dry white wine

¼ cup coarsely chopped fresh
    cilantro leaves

1½ tablespoons fresh lime juice

2 cloves garlic, smashed

1 teaspoon black peppercorns

¼ teaspoon dried Mexican
    oregano

2 bay leaves

6 tablespoons butter

1 pound white button mush-
    rooms, cleaned and sliced

¼ teaspoon salt

Freshly ground black pepper
    to taste

4 tablespoons all-purpose flour

1½ cups whole milk

12 cups crusted tortilla chips

Nonstick cooking spray

2 large yellow onions, diced

2 green bell peppers, seeded
    and diced

2 jalapeño peppers, seeded
    and minced

8 ounces pepper jack cheese,
    grated

8 ounces Cheddar cheese,
    grated

2 teaspoons chili powder

1 teaspoon ground cumin

½ teaspoon paprika

¼ teaspoon freshly ground
    black pepper

½ teaspoon ground coriander

Pinch cayenne pepper

1 teaspoon garlic powder

Pinch dried red pepper flakes,
    crushed

1 cup chopped canned
    tomatoes, drained

1 4-ounce can diced green
    chilies, drained

To keep this truly a one-pot dish, everything could be stirred into and baked in the Dutch oven, but the presentation is more attractive if this casserole is made as explained in the instructions.

1. Combine the chicken, broth, wine, cilantro, lime juice, garlic, peppercorns, oregano, and bay leaves in an ovenproof Dutch oven over medium-high heat; bring to a boil. Reduce the heat to a simmer and cook, uncovered, for 10 minutes. Pour all the contents of the pan into a bowl and allow the chicken to cool in the poaching liquid.

2. Preheat oven to 350°F.

3. Wipe out the Dutch oven. Add the butter and heat on medium until melted. Add the mushrooms, salt, and pepper and cook, stirring occasionally, for 6 minutes, or until the mushrooms are browned and all the liquid has evaporated. Sprinkle the mushrooms with the flour, stir to blend, and cook for 1 minute. Slowly whisk in the milk, scraping up any bits from the bottom of the pan. Cook until the mixture begins to thicken. Stir in about 1½ cups of the chicken cooking liquid; simmer for 10 minutes, stirring occasionally. Remove from the heat.

4. Crush the tortilla chips and add them in a layer to the bottom of a 9" × 13" casserole dish treated with nonstick spray. Pour the remaining broth over the tortilla chips. Once the broth is absorbed by the crushed chips, scatter the chicken over the top of the tortilla layer. Spread the onions, bell peppers, and jalapeños in layers evenly over the chicken. Top with half of the grated cheeses.

5. Mix together the chili powder, cumin, paprika, black pepper, ground coriander, cayenne, garlic powder, and red pepper flakes; sprinkle over the cheeses. Spoon the mushroom mixture evenly over the top of the spices, then top with the tomatoes and green chilies. Cover with all the remaining cheese. Bake uncovered for 45 minutes, or until the cheese is bubbly and the casserole is heated through. Let sit for 5 minutes before serving.

Chicken à la King Pie

Adjust the seasoning in this recipe according to how well the cooked chicken and gravy are seasoned. For example, if herbs aren't needed, substitute a finely minced shallot for the Mrs. Dash Onion and Herb Blend.

Serves 4

1½ cups cooked chicken, cubed

1 4½-ounce can sliced mushrooms, drained

1 tablespoon pimiento, chopped

1 cup store-bought chicken gravy

½ cup frozen baby peas, thawed

½ cup heavy cream

½ teaspoon Mrs. Dash Onion and Herb Blend

⅛ teaspoon freshly ground nutmeg

1 15-ounce package refrigerated peel-and-unroll-style pie crusts

1. Preheat oven to 375°F.

2. In a bowl, mix together the chicken, mushrooms, pimento, gravy, peas, cream, Mrs. Dash Onion and Herb Blend, and nutmeg. Mix well.

3. Line the bottom of a 9½" deep-dish pie pan with one of the pie crusts. Add the chicken mixture to the pan. Cover the pie with the remaining crust; seal and flute the edges. Cut slits in the top of the crust. Bake for 35 minutes, or until the crust is golden brown.

Crust Tips

To prevent the crust edge from burning, wrap a strip of nonstick aluminum foil around it and crimp to secure; remove the foil after the first 20 to 30 minutes of baking. For a shinier, prize-winning look to the top crust, brush it with heavy cream or some beaten egg mixed with a little water before baking.

Turkey and Noodle Casserole

This easy recipe leaves you all evening to enjoy this satisfying comfort food.

1-pound dried extra-wide egg noodles

1 tablespoon extra-virgin olive oil

6 slices bacon or turkey bacon, chopped

2½ pounds ground turkey

1 pound white mushrooms, cleaned and sliced

1 large yellow onion, diced

Salt and freshly ground black pepper to taste

1 tablespoon dried thyme

1 cup dry white wine

2 cups chicken broth

1 cup heavy cream

¼ teaspoon freshly grated nutmeg

8 ounces Gruyère cheese, grated

1 cup plain breadcrumbs

2 tablespoons butter, melted

1. Cook the noodles in a Dutch oven according to package directions. Drain, set aside, and keep warm.

2. Preheat oven to 350°F.

3. Wipe out the Dutch oven. Add the oil and bring it to temperature over medium-high heat. Add the bacon and cook for 3 minutes to render the bacon fat and until the bacon begins to brown at the edges. Add the ground turkey; brown the turkey, crumbling it apart. Add the mushrooms and onions; stir-fry for 3 to 5 minutes, or until the onions are transparent and the meat loses its pink color. Sprinkle with the salt, pepper, and thyme.

4. Stir in the wine, deglazing the pan by scraping up any food stuck to the bottom of the pan. Stir in the broth and bring to a boil; boil for 2 minutes, stirring occasionally. Lower the heat to a simmer and whisk in the cream. Stir in the nutmeg and cheese. Stir in the noodles. Top with the breadcrumbs; drizzle the butter over the crumbs. Bake for 30 minutes, or until the crumbs are browned.

Stovetop Moroccan Turkey Casserole

This recipe is an out-of-the-ordinary way to use up leftover turkey.

1. Bring the oil to temperature over medium heat in a Dutch oven. Add the carrots; sauté for 3 minutes. Add the onions; sauté for 3 minutes. Stir in the garlic, cumin, paprika, turmeric, cinnamon, and cayenne; sauté for 30 seconds. Stir in 1 cup of the broth and bring to a boil. Stir in the couscous and dates. Remove from heat, cover, and let stand for 5 minutes, or until the liquid is absorbed.

2. Stir the remaining 1 cup of broth into the couscous mixture. Return to heat and bring to a boil. Stir in the turkey, spinach, and cereal. Reduce the heat, cover, and simmer for 3 minutes, or until the turkey is heated through and the cereal has absorbed the extra broth. Serve immediately.

Serves 6

1 tablespoon vegetable oil
2 cups baby carrots, halved
   lengthwise
6 green onions, diced
3 cloves garlic, minced
1 teaspoon ground cumin
1 teaspoon paprika
½ teaspoon turmeric
¼ teaspoon ground
   cinnamon
⅛ teaspoon cayenne pepper
2 cups chicken broth
⅔ cup quick-cooking
   couscous
6 pitted dates, quartered
3 cups cooked turkey, cubed
2 cups fresh spinach, torn
1¼ cups bran flakes cereal

Fantastic Fish Pie

Because of the generous amount of mashed potatoes that form a meringue-style mound over the fish, this recipe could easily be stretched to 6 servings.

1. Preheat oven to 375°F.

2. Treat a 9½" deep-dish pie pan with nonstick spray. Arrange the fish pieces evenly across the bottom of the pan.

3. In a bowl, mix together the stewed tomatoes, onion, garlic, basil, parsley, oregano, sugar, and cheese. Pour over the fish. Pipe or spread the mashed potatoes evenly over the top of the sauce. Sprinkle generously with paprika. Bake for 45 minutes, or until the potatoes are lightly browned and the sauce is bubbly.

Serves 4

Nonstick cooking spray
16 ounces cod fillets, cut into
   bite-sized pieces
1 14½-ounce can stewed
   tomatoes
¼ teaspoon dried minced
   onion
½ teaspoon dried minced
   garlic
¼ teaspoon dried basil
¼ teaspoon dried parsley
⅛ teaspoon dried oregano
⅛ teaspoon granulated sugar
1 tablespoon freshly grated
   Parmigiano-Reggiano
   cheese
4 cups prepared mashed
   potatoes
¼ teaspoon paprika

Enchilada Casserole

Serves 6

1 pound ground turkey
Salt and freshly ground
    pepper to taste
2 cups picante sauce or salsa
2 teaspoons ground cumin
1 8-ounce package cream
    cheese, cubed
1 10-ounce package frozen
    chopped spinach, thawed
    and squeezed dry
12 6-inch flour tortillas
1 15-ounce can diced
    tomatoes
4 ounces Cheddar cheese,
    grated

*Serve this casserole with shredded lettuce, black olives,
avocado slices or guacamole, and sour cream on the side.*

1. Preheat oven to 350°F.

2. Add the ground turkey to a microwave-safe bowl. Cover and microwave on high for 2 minutes. Use a fork to break the turkey apart. Cover, and microwave on high for an additional 2 minutes, or until the turkey is cooked through. Stir in 1 cup of the picante sauce or salsa, and 1½ teaspoons of the cumin. Microwave uncovered on high for 2 minutes, or until most of the liquid has evaporated. Add the cream cheese and stir the mixture until it is melted into the sauce. Stir in the spinach.

3. Soften the tortillas by placing them on a microwave-safe plate; cover with a damp paper towel and microwave on high for 1 minute. Spoon about ⅓ cup filling down the center of each tortilla. Roll up and place seam-side down in a lightly greased 9" × 13" nonstick baking pan.

4. Combine the tomatoes, the remaining cup of picante sauce or salsa, and the remaining ½ teaspoon cumin. Spoon over the enchiladas. Bake for 20 minutes. Sprinkle with the cheese; return to the oven and bake for 10 more minutes, or until the cheese is melted and bubbly.

Chapter 18
Comfort Food Classics

Grandma's Chicken and Dumplings

Serves 6

1 3-pound whole chicken
Salt and freshly ground black pepper to taste
1 large yellow or white onion, quartered
4 cloves garlic, crushed
2 stalks celery, halved
2 large carrots, peeled and cut in 1" pieces
Water as needed
2 tablespoons butter or extra-virgin olive oil
1 stalk celery, finely chopped
1 large carrot, peeled and shredded
1 small yellow onion, finely diced
1 clove garlic, minced
2 cups all-purpose flour
1 tablespoon baking powder
1 teaspoon salt
2 large eggs
2 teaspoons lemon juice
¾ to 1 cup milk or heavy cream
OPTIONAL: ¼–½ cup heavy cream

Some grandmas add chopped potatoes and carrots in step 3, and let things simmer until the vegetables are done before proceeding. Thawed frozen peas and carrots can be added before you spoon in the dumplings.

1. Rinse the chicken inside and out in cold, running water. Add the chicken to a Dutch oven or stockpot along with the salt, pepper, quartered onion, crushed garlic, halved celery, and carrot pieces. Add enough water to cover the chicken. Bring to a simmer over medium heat; cover, lower the heat, and simmer for 1 hour, or until the chicken is cooked through.

2. Use tongs to move the chicken to a cutting board or platter; allow to sit until cool enough to handle. Remove and discard the bones and skin. Strain the broth, discarding the vegetables.

3. Melt the butter in the Dutch oven or stockpot over medium heat. Add the chopped celery, shredded carrot, and diced onion; sauté for 2 minutes. Cover, lower the heat, and allow the vegetables to sweat for 5 minutes, or until the onion is transparent and the celery is tender. Stir in the minced garlic.

4. Measure the reserved chicken broth and add enough water to bring it to 6 cups. Pour the broth into the pan. Add the cooked chicken and stir it into the sautéed vegetables and broth. Bring to a simmer over medium heat; reduce heat to maintain the simmer.

5. To make the dumplings, mix the flour, baking powder, and salt together in a large bowl. Make a well in the center of the flour mixture and add the eggs. Use the tongs of a fork to pierce the yolks. Add the lemon juice, and lightly beat the juice into the eggs. Add the milk or cream. Mix just until the dough comes together, adding just enough liquid to moisten the batter so that it resembles biscuit dough. Using 2 spoons, carefully drop heaping tablespoonfuls of the dumpling batter into the simmering chicken and broth. Cook for 10 to 15 minutes, or until the dumplings are cooked through, firm, and puffy. If desired, stir heavy cream to taste into the broth, being careful not to break apart the dumplings. Taste for seasoning and add salt and pepper, if needed.

Macaroni and Cheese

Serves 8

4 cups dried macaroni

4 tablespoons butter

4 tablespoons all-purpose
    flour

4½ cups milk

8 ounces Cheddar cheese,
    grated

8 ounces Colby cheese, grated

8 ounces Monterey jack
    cheese, grated

Salt and freshly ground black
    pepper to taste

*Baking this dish does away with the hassles of making a white
sauce and then slowly melting the cheese into that sauce.*

1. Preheat oven to 350°F.

2. In an ovenproof Dutch oven, cook the macaroni according to the package directions. Drain; set aside and keep warm.

3. Wipe out the Dutch oven. Add the butter and melt it over medium heat. Whisk in the flour, and then slowly whisk in the milk. Add the macaroni and cheeses to the pan and stir to combine. Bake for 1 hour, or until the cheese is melted and the sauce is thickened.

Enhancing Macaroni and Cheese

To add a punch of extra flavor to Macaroni and Cheese, stir a teaspoon of Dijon mustard and a tablespoon of mayonnaise into the milk mixture before you pour it over the macaroni. For a breadcrumb topping, spread a thin layer of plain or Italian-seasoned breadcrumbs over the top of the casserole and dot the crumbs with butter or drizzle butter over them.

Red Flannel Hash

The beets in this dish turn corned beef hash into red flannel hash.

1. Add the salt pork or bacon to a large nonstick or well-seasoned cast-iron skillet; cook over medium heat until the fat begins to render from the meat. Stir in the onions; sauté for 5 minutes, or until the onion is transparent. Stir in the potatoes; stir-fry until the potatoes begin to brown. Add the corned beef, beets, parsley, Worcestershire sauce, and the half-and-half or cream. Mix well. Carefully stir-fry until the hash mixture is cooked through, or until the potatoes are done and the meat and beets are warm.

2. Lower the heat. Press the hash down into the pan to form a round cake. Fry over low without stirring for 10 minutes, or until the bottom begins to brown and form a crisp crust. Use the back of a spoon to make 4 indentations in the hash; break an egg into each indentation. Cover the skillet and cook for 3 minutes, or until the eggs are done to your taste. Taste for seasoning and add salt and pepper, if needed.

Serves 4

8 ounces salt pork or bacon, diced

2 tablespoons butter or vegetable oil

1 small yellow onion, diced

2½ cups frozen hash brown potatoes, thawed

8 ounces cooked corned beef, chopped

1 16-ounce can beets, drained and diced

1 tablespoon dried parsley

1 teaspoon Worcestershire sauce

¼ cup half-and-half or heavy cream

4 large eggs

Salt and freshly ground black pepper to taste

Turkey Casserole

Serves 8

2 tablespoons butter or extra-virgin olive oil

1 green bell pepper, seeded and diced

6 stalks celery, diced

1 medium yellow onion, diced

1 28-ounce can heat-and-serve turkey

4 large eggs, beaten

½ cup mayonnaise

1 10¾-ounce can condensed cream of mushroom soup

3 cups milk

12 slices bread, crusts removed and torn into bite-sized pieces

Salt and freshly ground black pepper to taste

4 ounces Cheddar cheese, grated

This casserole is gussied-up turkey dressing dinner. Serve it with a tossed salad and then have cranberry juice punch to drink to complete the off-season Thanksgiving feel to your meal.

1. Preheat oven to 325°F.

2. Melt the butter or add the oil to an ovenproof Dutch oven over medium heat. Add the green pepper and celery; sauté for 5 minutes. Stir in the onion and sauté for another 5 minutes, or until the onion is transparent and the other vegetables are tender. Stir in the undrained can of turkey, and before the turkey is heated through, stir in the eggs. Add the mayonnaise, soup, and milk; mix well. Fold the pieces of bread into the mixture. Cover and bake for 45 minutes.

3. Remove the cover and sprinkle the cheese over the top of the casserole. Return to the oven and bake for an additional 15 minutes, or until the cheese is melted and the casserole is set.

Cincinnati Chili

*Cincinnati Chili is served like a sauce over cooked
pasta, and then topped with onion and cheese.*

1. Add the ground beef and ¾ of the diced onion to a 4½-quart Dutch oven over medium-high heat; stir-fry until the beef is browned and the onion is transparent. Drain off and discard any excess fat. Stir in the garlic and stir-fry for 30 seconds. Add the tomato sauce, broth, chili powder, chocolate chips, vinegar, honey, pumpkin pie spice, cumin, cardamom, cloves, salt, and pepper; mix well. Bring to a simmer; lower the heat to maintain the simmer, and cook for at least 30 minutes to let the flavors mix. Shortly before serving, add the kidney beans and cook until they're heated through.

2. Serve the Cincinnati Chili meat sauce over cooked pasta, then top the chili with diced onions to taste and a generous amount of grated cheese.

Serves 8

2 pounds lean ground beef

3 large yellow onions, diced

3 cloves garlic, minced

1 16-ounce can tomato sauce

1 cup beef broth

2 tablespoons chili powder

2 tablespoons semisweet chocolate chips

2 tablespoons red wine vinegar

2 tablespoons honey

1 tablespoon pumpkin pie spice

1 teaspoon ground cumin

½ teaspoon ground cardamom

¼ teaspoon ground cloves

Salt and freshly ground black pepper to taste

2 16-ounce cans kidney beans, rinsed and drained

1 pound cooked pasta of your choice

4 cups American or Cheddar cheese, shredded

Florentine Lasagna

Serves 8

*2 10-ounce packages frozen
    spinach, thawed*
*Company's Coming Four
    Cheese Lasagna (page
    251)*

Florentine Lasagna is one way to hide a vegetable in a meal.

1. Squeeze the moisture out of the thawed spinach, and then thoroughly dry it in a salad spinner or between cotton towels.

2. Prepare the Company's Coming Four Cheese Lasagna recipe. Add the spinach in a layer between the first and second layers. Bake for 50 minutes covered and then 20 minutes uncovered. Remove from the oven, cover, and let stand 20 minutes before cutting.

Unstuffed Cabbage Rolls

Serves 8

*2 tablespoons extra-virgin
    olive oil*
6 stalks celery, diced
*6 large carrots, peeled and
    diced*
1 large yellow onion, diced
1 pound lean ground beef
2 cloves garlic, minced
1 teaspoon salt
*¾ teaspoon freshly ground
    black pepper*
1 teaspoon granulated sugar
*2 15-ounce cans diced
    tomatoes*
2 cups cooked rice
4 cups coleslaw mix
1½ cups chicken broth
1 cup dry white wine

*Use Italian-seasoned tomatoes and cooked orzo pasta instead of the
rice to give this dish a Tuscan flair. If you prefer German flavors, add a
teaspoon of caraway seeds and 2 teaspoons of brown sugar.*

1. Preheat oven to 350°F.

2. Bring the oil to temperature over medium heat in an ovenproof Dutch oven. Add the celery and carrots; sauté for 5 minutes. Add the ground beef and onion; stir-fry until the beef is browned and broken apart and the onion is transparent. Drain off and discard any excess fat. Add all remaining ingredients; stir into the beef mixture. Use the back of a spoon to press the mixture down evenly in the pan. Cover and bake for 45 minutes. Uncover and bake for an additional 15 minutes, or until most of the liquid has evaporated.

Deluxe Potato Soup

There's lots of fat (which adds lots of flavor) in this recipe, so it's not an everyday meal. But it's delicious for an occasional indulgence, especially when served over a warm buttermilk biscuit. This wonderfully thick soup freezes well, too.

1. Rinse the chicken inside and out in cold, running water. Add the chicken to a Dutch oven or stockpot along with the salt, pepper, quartered onion, smashed garlic, halved celery, and carrots pieces. Add enough water to cover the chicken. Bring to a simmer over medium heat; cover, lower the heat, and simmer for 1 hour, or until the chicken is cooked through.

2. Use tongs to move the chicken to a cutting board or platter; allow to sit until cool enough to handle. Remove and discard the bones and skin. Strain the broth, discarding the vegetables.

3. Add the bacon to the Dutch oven or stockpot and cook it over medium heat until it begins to render some of its fat. Add the chopped celery, shredded carrot, and diced onion; sauté for 5 minutes, or until the onion is transparent and the celery is tender. Stir in the potatoes and baby carrots. Fry until the potatoes just begin to brown, then stir in the cooked chicken, ham, and Canadian bacon. Measure the reserved chicken broth and add enough water to bring it to 6 cups. Pour the broth into the pan; bring to a simmer. Lower the heat, cover, and cook for 5 minutes, or until the potatoes and carrots are cooked through.

4. Add the cream cheese and Cheddar cheese, stirring gently to melt the cheeses into the broth. Stir in the heavy cream and cook about 3 more minutes to bring the cream to temperature. Taste for seasoning and add salt and of pepper, if desired.

Serves 12

1 3-pound whole chicken
Salt and freshly ground black pepper to taste
1 large yellow onion, quartered
4 cloves garlic, crushed
2 stalks celery, cut in half
2 large carrots, peeled and cut in 1" pieces
Water as needed
1 1-pound package of bacon, cut into small pieces
1 stalk celery, finely chopped
1 large carrot, peeled and shredded
1 small yellow or white onion, finely diced
8 large russet potatoes, peeled and diced
1 1-pound bag baby carrots, diced
1 7-ounce ham slice, diced
1 7-ounce package Canadian bacon, diced
1 8-ounce package cream cheese, cut into cubes
16 ounces medium Cheddar cheese, shredded
1 cup heavy cream

Scalloped Potatoes
with Ham

Serves 8

Butter

8 large russet potatoes, peeled and very thinly sliced

Salt and freshly ground black pepper to taste

1 large yellow onion, diced

6 tablespoons all-purpose flour

2 cups cooked ham, cubed

3 cups Cheddar or American cheese, grated

4 cups milk or more as needed, heated to almost boiling

This is almost a cook-without-a-recipe recipe, which makes it easy to customize. For example, you can add more cheese or onion if you like. Or change the type of cheese or add some diced bell pepper along with the onion. Make it your own.

1. Preheat oven to 350°F.

2. Generously butter the bottom of a 9" × 13" nonstick baking pan. Evenly spread ⅓ of the potatoes across the bottom of the pan and sprinkle lightly with salt and pepper. Evenly sprinkle ⅓ of the onion over the potatoes, 2 tablespoons of the flour over the onion, and dot the flour with 3 tablespoons of butter. Add 1 cup of the cooked ham in an even layer, and top that with 1 cup of the cheese. Add another layer of potatoes, salt, pepper, onion, flour, butter, ham, and cheese. Top with the remaining potatoes. Slowly pour the hot milk over the potatoes, adding enough milk to bring the liquid level to just below the top of the potatoes. Cover with foil and bake for 1 hour.

3. Remove the foil, top with the remaining 1 cup of cheese, and bake for an additional 15 minutes, or until the potatoes are cooked through, the sauce is thickened, and the cheese is melted and bubbling.

Cheese and Saltiness

Cheddar and American cheese are saltier than are most Swiss cheeses, so adjust how much you salt the potatoes according to the type of cheese you're using. Cheese is an excellent source of calcium, but you may want to opt for low-fat options if you are watching your fat intake.

Company's Coming Four Cheese Lasagna

*If you like a bubbly brown top on lasagna, put the pan under
the broiler for a few minutes when it's done baking.*

1. Add the ground beef, onion, and garlic to a deep 3½-quart nonstick skillet or large saucepan over medium heat. Stir-fry until the hamburger is browned and the onion is transparent. Drain off and discard any excess fat. Stir in the tomato juice, mushrooms, tomato paste, Worcestershire sauce, oregano, parsley, salt, and pepper. Bring to a simmer, lower the heat, and simmer uncovered for 30 minutes, stirring occasionally.

2. Preheat oven to 350°F.

3. To prepare the lasagna, treat a 9" × 13" nonstick baking pan with nonstick spray; layer half of the noodles, half of the hot prepared sauce, half of the ricotta, half of the Parmigiano, half of the Romano, and half of the mozzarella cheese and then repeat in another layer in that order. Cover with aluminum foil and let rest for 30 minutes.

4. Leave the aluminum foil cover in place and bake for 40 minutes. Remove the foil and continue baking for 15 minutes. Remove from the oven, cover, and let stand 20 minutes before cutting.

Baking a Better Lasagna

This recipe tastes best if you make the sauce in advance and refrigerate it for a day or two so the flavors can blend; the added bonus is that then when you're ready to prepare the lasagna, technically you'll only be using that one pot (well, baking pan) to make your meal.

Serves 8

1 pound lean ground chuck
1 large yellow onion, diced
3 cloves garlic, minced
4 cups tomato juice
8 ounces fresh button mushrooms, cleaned and sliced
1 6-ounce can tomato paste
1 tablespoon Worcestershire sauce
1 teaspoon dried oregano, crushed
1 teaspoon dried parsley, crushed
½ teaspoon salt
½ teaspoon fresh ground black pepper
Nonstick cooking spray
8 ounces dried lasagna noodles, uncooked
15 ounces ricotta cheese
1½ cups freshly grated Parmigiano-Reggiano cheese
1½ cups Romano cheese, freshly grated
2 cups grated mozzarella cheese

New England Boiled Dinner

*Don't tell anyone that you actually simmered this
dish and you can still call it a "boiled" dinner.*

Serves 8

2 teaspoons butter or
vegetable oil

1 3-pound boneless beef
round rump roast

2 10¾-ounce cans condensed
onion soup

1 teaspoon prepared
horseradish

1 bay leaf

1 clove garlic, minced

6 large carrots, peeled and
cut into 1-inch pieces

3 rutabagas, diced

4 large russet or red potatoes,
peeled or unpeeled, and
diced

1 2-pound head of cabbage,
cut into 8 wedges

½ cup water

¼ cup all-purpose flour

1. Bring the butter or oil to temperature in a Dutch oven over medium-high heat. Add the roast; brown on all sides. Add the soup, horseradish, bay leaf, and garlic. Bring to a simmer; lower the heat, cover, and cook for 2 hours.

2. Add the carrots and rutabagas; cover and cook for 30 minutes.

3. Add the potatoes and stir into the broth; add the cabbage wedges as a layer on top. Cover and cook for an additional 30 minutes, or until the cabbage is done.

4. Transfer the meat and vegetables to a serving platter; keep warm. Mix the water and flour together; strain out any lumps and add the mixture to the meat juices in the pan. Increase the heat to medium. When the juices in the pan reach a high simmer, whisk in the water and flour mixture. Continue to cook and stir for 5 minutes, or until the juices are thickened. Serve the resulting gravy alongside or over the meat and vegetables.

Corned Beef and Cabbage

This recipe isn't just for St. Patrick's Day. It makes a satisfying meal any time of year.

1. Trim any excess fat from the meat. Place the brisket in a 4- to 6-quart Dutch oven along with the juices and spices from the package that came with the corned beef. Add enough water to cover the brisket. Add the peppercorns and bay leaves. Bring to a boil over medium-high heat; reduce heat and simmer, covered, for 2 hours. At this point, the meat should be almost tender.

2. Add the carrots, parsnips, and onions to meat. Return to a simmer; cover and cook for 10 minutes. Add the potatoes and cabbage. Cover and cook for 20 minutes, or until the vegetables and meat are tender. Remove the bay leaves and discard. Remove the pot from the heat, cover, and let the meat rest in the broth for 10 minutes.

3. Transfer the meat to a platter and thinly slice it across the grain. Spoon the vegetables around the meat on the platter and ladle some of the broth from the pan over the meat. Strain some of the pan juices and transfer to a gravy boat to have at the table.

Serves 6

1 2- to 2½-pound corned beef brisket
Water as needed
1 teaspoon whole black peppercorns
2 bay leaves
3 medium carrots, peeled and quartered
2 medium parsnips, peeled and cut into chunks
2 medium red onions, cut into wedges
6 medium red potatoes, cleaned and quartered
1 small cabbage, cut into 6 wedges

Chicken and Noodles

*Chicken and Noodles is good served over mashed
potatoes or warm biscuits, or with crackers.*

1. Melt the butter or heat the oil in a Dutch oven over medium-high heat. Shred 1 of the carrots and dice the remaining 3; add the carrots and celery to the pan and sauté for 3 minutes. Add the onion and sauté for 5 minutes, or until the onion is transparent and the celery is tender. Add the broth, water, bay leaves, thyme, salt, and pepper; stir to combine.

2. Bring the broth mixture to a boil. Add the noodles; reduce the heat to maintain a gentle boil, and cook for the length of time specified on the noodle package, stirring occasionally. In a screw-top jar combine the milk, flour, and egg; beat lightly with a fork, then cover and shake until smooth. Remove the bay leaves and discard. Stir the milk mixture into the noodles and broth. Bring to a boil and then reduce the heat; simmer and stir until thickened and bubbly. If the mixture becomes too thick, stir in some additional milk or water. Stir in the peas and cooked chicken. Continue to cook and stir until heated through, or for about 1 to 2 minutes.

Slow-Cooked Lamb Chops

These slowed-cooked lamb chops are delicious; however, if you want to add another level of flavor, you can brown them in some oil before you add them to the slow cooker.

Serves 6

1½ pounds tiny new potatoes, scrubbed

6 medium carrots, peeled and cut into 1" pieces

6 lamb rib chops, cut 1" thick

2 cups water

½ teaspoon dried dill

½ teaspoon salt

¼ teaspoon ground black pepper

4 teaspoons butter, softened

4 teaspoons all-purpose flour

½ cup plain regular or low-fat yogurt

1. Remove a narrow strip of peel from around the center of each new potato. Place the potatoes, carrots, lamb, water, dill, salt, and pepper in a large slow cooker. Cover; cook on low-heat setting for 7 to 8 hours.

2. Transfer the lamb chops and vegetables to a serving platter; cover and keep warm.

3. For the sauce, strain the cooking liquid; skim off any fat and discard. Pour all but ½ cup of the cooking liquid back into the slow cooker; turn the heat setting to high. Whisk the butter and flour into the ½ cup of cooking liquid; remove any lumps and then whisk the flour mixture into the liquid in the slow cooker. Cook and stir over medium heat until thickened and bubbly. Stir in the yogurt. Taste for seasoning and add additional salt and pepper, if needed. Serve the chops and vegetables with the sauce.

Oven-Baked Short Ribs and Vegetables

Beef Western ribs work well for this dinner, too.

Serves 4

3 pounds beef short ribs
Salt and freshly ground black
    pepper to taste
1 1-pound bag baby carrots
4 medium russet potatoes,
    peeled and halved
1 12-ounce bag green beans,
    thawed
4 small white onions, halved
1 14-ounce can reduced-
    sodium beef broth
2 teaspoons mustard
2 tablespoons horseradish
2 tablespoons cornstarch
¼ cup cold water

1. Preheat oven to 350°F.

2. Trim off any excess fat from of the ribs, and then arrange them in a 9"
   × 13" nonstick baking pan; sprinkle with salt and pepper. Bake uncovered for 2 hours. Drain off any excess fat and discard.

3. Distribute the carrots, potatoes, green beans, and onions around the meat. In a measuring cup, whisk together the broth, mustard, and horseradish; pour over the meat. Tightly cover the pan with aluminum foil; bake for 1½ hours, or until the meat is tender. Move the meat and vegetables to a serving platter; cover and keep warm.

4. To make the sauce, strain the meat juices in the baking pan. Skim off and discard any excess fat. Add enough water to the pan juices to measure 2 cups; either return the juices to the baking pan or put in a saucepan. Bring to a boil over medium-high heat. Mix the cornstarch together with the cold water; discard any lumps. Stir the cornstarch mixture into the juices; boil for 1 minute.

Crunchy, Tasty Beans

If you prefer crisp-tender green beans, cook them separately rather than adding them to the baking pan. For this recipe, simmer them in water or broth for 5 to 7 minutes, tasting to test for desired doneness. For extra taste, sauté 1 clove of minced garlic in oil, then add the green beans, toss to coat, and pour in the liquid.

Chapter 19
Pressure Cooker

Swiss Steak Meal

Serves 6

2½ pounds beef round steak, 1" thick
1 tablespoon vegetable oil
Salt and freshly ground pepper to taste
1 medium yellow onion, diced
2 stalks of celery, diced
1 large green pepper, seeded and diced
1 cup tomato juice
1 cup beef broth or water
6 large carrots, peeled and quartered
6 medium white potatoes, scrubbed and quartered
OPTIONAL: 4 teaspoons butter

If you prefer a thick gravy, thicken the pan juices with a roux or cornstarch.

1. Cut the round steak into 6 serving-sized pieces. Add the oil and bring it to temperature over medium heat. Season the meat on both sides with salt and pepper. Add 3 pieces of the meat and fry for 3 minutes on each side to brown them. Move to a platter and repeat with the other 3 pieces of meat.

2. Leave the last 3 pieces of browned meat in the cooker; add the onion, celery, and green pepper on top of them. Place the other 3 pieces of meat on top and pour the tomato juice and broth or water over them. Place the carrots and potatoes on top of the meat. Close the lid; bring to high pressure and maintain the pressure for 17 minutes. Remove the pan from the heat and allow time for the natural release of the pressure.

3. Once the pressure has dropped, open the cooker and move the potatoes, carrots, and meat to a serving platter. Cover and keep warm. Skim any fat from the juices remaining in the pan. Set the uncovered cooker over medium heat and simmer the juices for 5 minutes. Whisk in the butter, 1 teaspoon at a time, if desired. Taste for seasoning and add additional salt and pepper, if needed. Have the resulting gravy available at the table to pour over the meat. Serve immediately.

Pressure Cooker Warning

Remember that you should never fill a pressure cooker more than ⅔ full. When in doubt about cooking times or other issues, check with the instruction manual that came with your cooker.

New England Fish Stew

To add even more impact and make this a special occasion dish, float a pat of butter on top of each portion. Using heavy cream obviously makes this a richer stew, but you can substitute milk if you prefer.

1. Add the butter to the cooker and bring it to temperature over medium heat. Add the onions; sauté for 3 minutes, or until soft. Stir in the celery, carrot, and potatoes; sauté for 1 minute. Add the fish, fish stock or clam juice, water, bay leaf, and thyme.

2. Lock the lid in place; increase to high heat and bring the pressure cooker to high pressure. Adjust the heat to maintain the high pressure and cook for 4 minutes. Reduce the pressure with your cooker's quick-release method. Remove the lid, tilting it away from you to allow any excess steam to escape.

3. Remove and discard the bay leaf. Stir in the cream or milk and corn. Taste for seasoning and add salt and pepper to taste. Simmer until the corn is cooked and the chowder is hot. Transfer to a serving tureen or individual bowls and top with additional butter, if desired. Garnish with parsley, if desired.

Newer Pressure Cooker Innovation

B/R/K pressure cookers (sold by Pleasant Hill Grain; see the appendix) have a continuously-adjustable pressure regulating valve that saves you from constantly having to monitor the pressure level; the valve maintains the pressure you set and also lets you change that pressure setting at any time during the cooking process.

Serves 4

2 tablespoons butter

1 large Vidalia onion, diced

2 stalks celery, diced

4 large carrots, peeled and diced

4 medium russet or red potatoes, peeled and cut in ½" cubes

1 pound firm-fleshed white fish fillets (like cod), cut in ½" pieces

2 cups fish stock or clam juice

1 cup cold water

1 bay leaf

½ teaspoon dried thyme

1 cup heavy cream or milk

1 cup fresh or thawed frozen corn kernels

Salt and freshly ground white or black pepper to taste

OPTIONAL: additional butter to taste

OPTIONAL: fresh chopped parsley to taste

Pork and Beans

There's enough cooked pork in this recipe to serve this as an entrée rather than as a side dish. It goes well with cornbread.

Serves 6

2 teaspoons paprika

¼ teaspoon salt

1 teaspoon garlic powder

¼ teaspoon ground black pepper

½ teaspoon onion powder

⅛ teaspoon cayenne

¼ teaspoon dried oregano

½ teaspoon dried thyme

2½ pounds pork shoulder, cut into 1½" pieces

1½ tablespoons vegetable oil

1 large yellow onion, diced

6 cups chicken broth or water

2 cups dried white beans, such as Great Northern or navy

½ pound salt pork or bacon, cut into pieces

1 15-ounce can diced tomatoes

4 cloves garlic, minced

½ cup packed light brown sugar

2 tablespoons whole grain or Creole mustard

2 teaspoons chili powder

1 bay leaf

1. Add the paprika, salt, garlic powder, pepper, onion powder, cayenne, oregano, and ¼ teaspoon of the thyme to a gallon-size plastic bag; shake to mix. Add the pork pieces and shake the bag to season the meat on all sides. Add the oil to the pressure cooker and bring it to temperature over medium-high heat. Add the pork and stir-fry for about 2 minutes per side, or until it just begins to brown. Move the meat to a plate and set aside.

2. Add the onions to the cooker; reduce heat to medium and sauté for 2 minutes, or until tender. Add the broth or water. Remove any stones or impurities from the beans, and then stir them into the liquid in the cooker, scraping up any browned bits from the bottom of the pot and stirring to incorporate them into the mixture.

3. Lock the lid into place on the pressure cooker. Bring to high pressure. Lower the heat just enough to maintain high pressure and cook for 15 minutes. Turn off the burner and leave the pan in place for 10 minutes, or long enough to allow it to return to normal pressure. Once the pressure is released, carefully remove the lid to allow excess steam to escape.

4. Add the salt pork, tomatoes, garlic, sugar, mustard, chili powder, bay leaf, the remaining ¼ teaspoon thyme, and the reserved pork to the cooker; stir to combine. Lock the lid into place; bring the pressure cooker to high pressure. Maintain high pressure and cook for 15 minutes. Remove from the heat and let set for 10 minutes, or until the cooker returns to normal pressure. Once the pressure is completely released, remove the lid.

5. Check for seasoning and add salt and pepper, if needed. Remove and discard the bay leaf. Serve.

Shrimp Risotto

A fresh tomato salad is a nice complement to this rich, creamy dish.

Serves 4

2 tablespoons extra-virgin olive oil
1 small Vidalia onion, diced
1 teaspoon fennel seeds
3 cloves garlic, minced
1½ cups Arborio rice
2 tablespoons tomato paste
Pinch saffron threads
¼ cup dry white vermouth
3 cups chicken broth
1 pound medium shrimp, peeled and deveined
Salt and freshly ground black pepper to taste

1. Add the oil to the pressure cooker and bring to temperature over medium-high heat. Add the onion and fennel seeds; sauté for 5 minutes, or until the onions are softened. Add the garlic, rice, tomato paste, and saffron; stir until the rice is evenly colored. Stir in the vermouth and broth.

2. Close and lock the pressure cooker lid; bring to high pressure and maintain it for 3 minutes. Remove from heat and use the cooker's quick-release method to release the pressure. Carefully remove the lid. Put the cooker back on the burner over medium heat and stir in the shrimp; simmer for 2 minutes, or until the shrimp are pale pink and cooked through. Taste for seasoning and add salt and pepper, if needed. Serve immediately.

Or, If You Prefer . . .

Add a vegetable to the Shrimp Risotto by stirring in 1 cup of thawed frozen baby peas when you add the shrimp.

Southern Chicken Stew

Serves 6

2 tablespoons vegetable oil

1 medium yellow onion, sliced

2 bay leaves

2 teaspoons ground allspice

1 teaspoon dried thyme

⅓ cup tomato paste

8 bone-in chicken thighs

Salt and freshly ground black pepper to taste

3½ cups water

1 jalapeño or Scotch bonnet chili, pierced

8 ounces fresh okra, trimmed and cut in half crosswise

3 large sweet potatoes, peeled and cut into large dice

1 1-pound bunch collard greens, stems removed and chopped

For a milder dish, substitute green bell pepper for the jalapeño or Scotch bonnet chili.

1. Add the oil to the pressure cooker and bring it to temperature over medium heat. Stir in the onion, bay leaves, allspice, and thyme; sauté for 5 minutes, or until the onion is soft. Increase the heat to high, stir in the tomato paste, and cook for 2 minutes, stirring and scraping until it turns brick red.

2. Remove and discard the skin on the chicken. Season the thighs with salt and black pepper to taste, and add them to the cooker; turn them to coat with the tomato and onion. Stir in the water. Add the chili, okra, potatoes, and collard greens in that order. Lock the pressure cooker lid; bring to high pressure and maintain it for 7 minutes.

3. Remove the cooker from the heat. Use the pressure cooker's quick-release method to release the pressure. Carefully open the pot. Remove and discard the bay leaves and chili. Stir and then ladle the stew into bowls and serve.

Simplified Chicken Stew

Serve this stew with warm, buttered buttermilk biscuits.

Serves 4

4 large carrots, peeled and
    sliced
1 stalk celery, finely diced
1 large yellow onion, diced
4 large russet potatoes,
    peeled and diced
4 long strips lemon zest
1 teaspoon dried dill
2 tablespoons extra-virgin
    olive oil
4 bone-in chicken breast
    halves
2 cups chicken broth
Salt and freshly ground black
    pepper to taste

1. Put the carrots, celery, onions, potatoes, lemon zest, dill, and oil in a pressure cooker. Pour the broth into the pot. Remove and discard the skin on the chicken, then nestle the chicken pieces meat-side down on top of the vegetables.

2. Lock the pressure cooker lid and bring to high pressure and maintain it for 10 minutes. Remove the cooker from the heat. Use the pressure cooker's quick pressure release. Carefully open the pot. Taste for seasoning and add salt and pepper to taste. Put 1 chicken breast in each of 4 large soup bowls and ladle some carrots, potatoes, and broth over each one.

Sausage Links Dinner

This dinner gets even better if you top each serving with a fried egg.

Serves 4

1 pound pork sausage links
1 medium sweet onion, diced
4 large russet potatoes,
    peeled and sliced thin
1 16-ounce can creamed corn
¼ teaspoon pepper
¾ cup tomato juice
Salt to taste

Add the sausage links to the pressure cooker and brown them over medium heat. Remove the sausages to a plate. Layer the potatoes, onion, and corn in the cooker. Sprinkle with the pepper. Place the sausage links on top of the corn. Pour the tomato juice over the top of the other ingredients in the cooker. Lock the lid, bring to high pressure, and maintain for 7 minutes. Remove from the heat and let set for 10 minutes, or until the pot returns to normal pressure. Taste for seasoning and add salt and additional pepper, if needed.

Spanish Chicken and Rice

2 tablespoons extra-virgin olive or vegetable oil

1 pound boneless chicken breast, cut into bite-sized pieces

1 large green pepper, seeded and diced

1 teaspoon chili powder

1 teaspoon smoked paprika

¼ teaspoon dried thyme

⅛ teaspoon dried oregano

¼ teaspoon freshly ground black pepper

Pinch cayenne pepper

1 medium white onion, diced

4 ounces fresh button or cremini mushrooms, cleaned and sliced

2 cloves garlic, minced

2 cups chicken broth

1 cup long-grain rice, uncooked

½ cup black olives, pitted and cut in half

Serve this dish with an avocado salad and baked corn chips.

Add the oil to the pressure cooker and bring it to temperature over medium heat. Add the chicken, green pepper, chili powder, paprika, thyme, oregano, black pepper, cayenne, and onion; stir-fry for 5 minutes, or until the onion is transparent and the chicken begins to brown. Stir in the mushrooms; sauté for 2 minutes. Add the garlic, broth, rice, and olives. Lock the lid and bring to high pressure; maintain for 3 minutes. Remove from the heat and allow the pressure to release naturally for 7 minutes. Quick-release any remaining pressure. Uncover and fluff with a fork. Taste for seasoning and add salt and other seasoning, if needed.

Spice It Up!

Vary the heat level of the Spanish Chicken and Rice recipe by choosing between mild, medium, or hot chili powder, according to your tastes. In addition, you can substitute jalapeño pepper for some or all of the green pepper.

Turkey Drumsticks and Vegetable Soup

Measure the turkey drumsticks to make sure they'll fit in your pressure cooker. It's okay if the end of the bone touches the lid of the cooker, as long as it doesn't block the vent.

1. Add the oil to the pressure cooker and bring to temperature over medium heat. Add the garlic and sauté for 10 seconds. Stir in the tomatoes, potatoes, carrots, onions, celery, mushrooms, oregano, rosemary, bay leaf, orange zest, salt, and pepper. Stand the two drumsticks meaty-side down in the pan.

2. Lock the lid and bring to high pressure; maintain it for 12 minutes. Remove from the heat and allow the pressure to drop naturally, and then use your cooker's quick-release method to release the remaining pressure, if needed. Remove the drumsticks, cut the meat from the bone and into bite-sized pieces, and return it to the pot. Stir in the green beans and corn; cook over medium heat for 5 minutes. Remove and discard the orange zest and bay leaf. Taste for seasoning and add salt and pepper, if needed. Serve garnished with chopped parsley or cilantro, if desired.

Or, If You Prefer . . .

Transform the Turkey Drumsticks and Vegetable Soup recipe into a turkey pot pie–style meal by substituting 4 cups of chicken broth for the tomatoes; thicken the soup with a roux, if desired, and serve it over buttermilk biscuits.

Serves 6

1 tablespoon extra-virgin olive oil

1 clove garlic, minced

2 15-ounce cans diced tomatoes

6 medium russet potatoes, peeled and cut into quarters

6 large carrots, peeled and sliced

12 pearl onions, peeled

2 stalks celery, finely diced

½ ounce dried mushrooms

¼ teaspoon dried oregano

¼ teaspoon dried rosemary

1 bay leaf

2 strips orange zest

Salt and freshly ground black pepper to taste

2 1¼-pound turkey drumsticks, skin removed

1 10-ounce package frozen green beans, thawed

1 10-ounce package frozen whole kernel corn, thawed

1 10-ounce package frozen baby peas, thawed

Fresh chopped parsley or cilantro to taste

Tex-Mex Beef Stew

Serves 8

2 tablespoons extra-virgin olive or vegetable oil

1 4-pound English or chuck roast, trimmed of fat and cut into 1" cubes

1 7-ounce can green chilies

2 15-ounce cans diced tomatoes

1 8-ounce can tomato sauce

1 large sweet onion, diced

1 green bell pepper, seeded and diced

6 cloves garlic, minced

1 tablespoon ground cumin

1 teaspoon freshly ground black pepper

Cayenne pepper to taste

2 tablespoons lime juice

2 jalapeño peppers, seeded and diced

Beef broth or water as needed

1 bunch fresh cilantro, chopped

This stew can easily be stretched to serve more than 8 if you serve it with an avocado salad and over rice, in tacos or burritos, or with whole kernel corn or baked corn chips.

Add the oil to the pressure cooker and bring it to temperature over medium-high heat. Add the beef and stir-fry for 8 minutes, or until it's well-browned. Stir in the chilies, tomatoes, tomato sauce, onion, bell pepper, garlic, cumin, black pepper, cayenne, lime juice, and jalapeño peppers. If needed, add enough beef broth or water so that all the ingredients in the cooker are covered by liquid. Lock the lid, lower the heat to medium, and bring to high pressure; maintain for 45 minutes. Let the pan remain on the burner and allow 15 minutes or more for the pressure to drop on its own. Remove the lid and stir in the cilantro. Serve immediately.

Barbecue Pot Roast

Whether you make it with beef or with pork, this barbecue is a delicious part of a casual supper when you serve it on sandwiches along with potato chips and coleslaw.

Serves 8

½ cup ketchup
½ cup apricot preserves
¼ cup dark brown sugar
¼ cup apple cider or white vinegar
½ cup teriyaki or soy sauce
Dry red pepper flakes, crushed, to taste
1 teaspoon dry mustard
¼ teaspoon freshly ground black pepper
1 4-pound boneless chuck roast or pork shoulder roast
1½ cups water for beef; 2 cups water for pork
1 large sweet onion, sliced

1. Add the ketchup, preserves, brown sugar, vinegar, teriyaki or soy sauce, red pepper flakes, mustard, and pepper to a gallon-size plastic freezer bag; close and squeeze to mix. Trim the roast of any fat, cut it into 1" cubes, and add it to the bag. Refrigerate overnight.

2. Add the appropriate amount of water and the cooking rack or steamer basket to a 6-quart or larger pressure cooker. Place half of the sliced onions on the rack or basket. Use a slotted spoon to remove the roast pieces from the marinade and place them on the onions; reserve the marinade. Cover the roast pieces with the remaining onions.

3. Lock the lid in place on the pressure cooker. Place over medium heat and bring to high pressure; maintain for 50 minutes, or 15 minutes per pound (keeping in mind that you reduce the weight of the roast when you trim off the fat). Turn off the heat and allow 15 minutes for the pressure to release naturally. Use the quick release to release any remaining pressure and then carefully remove the lid. Strain the pan juices into a bowl, and set aside. Separate the meat from the onions, and return the meat to the pan. Purée the onions in a food processor or blender.

4. Pour the reserved marinade into the cooker and use two forks to pull the meat apart and mix it into the sauce. Bring to a simmer over medium heat. Stir in the onion. Add ½ cup of the reserved pan juices (skimmed of fat) to the cooker and stir it into the meat and sauce. Reduce the heat to low and simmer for 15 minutes, or until the mixture is thick enough to serve on sandwiches.

Chicken and Spinach Curry

The chicken and spinach create a layer in the pressure cooker that keeps the pasta sauce from burning on the bottom of the pan.

Serves 6

½ cup chicken broth or water

1 pound boneless, skinless chicken, cut into 1" pieces

2 10-ounce packages frozen spinach

1½ cups store-bought pasta sauce

1 tablespoon mild curry powder

2 tablespoons applesauce

Salt and freshly ground black pepper to taste

6 cups cooked rice

OPTIONAL: fresh chopped cilantro to taste

1. Add the broth and chicken to the pressure cooker and place the still-frozen blocks of spinach on top. Mix the pasta sauce together with the curry powder and pour it over the spinach. Do not mix the sauce into the other ingredients.

2. Lock the lid in place. Bring to high pressure over medium heat; maintain pressure for 5 minutes. Quick release the pressure. Carefully remove the lid, add the applesauce, and stir well. If the moisture from the spinach thinned the sauce too much, simmer uncovered for 5 minutes, or until the sauce is the desired consistency. Taste the sauce and add salt, pepper, and more curry if needed. Serve over cooked rice. Garnish with cilantro, if desired.

Chicken Chili

Serve this chili with an avocado or tossed salad, sour cream, and baked corn tortilla chips.

Serves 4

2 tablespoons vegetable oil

2 pounds boneless, skinless chicken thighs, cut into bite-sized cubes

1 jalapeño pepper, seeded and minced

1 small red bell pepper, seeded and diced

1 small yellow onion, diced

1 clove garlic, minced

1 15-ounce can diced tomatoes

1 16-ounce can red kidney beans, rinsed and drained

1 tablespoon paprika

1 tablespoon tomato paste

1 cup chicken broth

¼ teaspoon dried thyme

¼ teaspoon dried oregano

1 teaspoon chili powder

Salt and freshly ground black pepper to taste

1. Add oil to the pressure cooker and bring it to temperature over medium heat. Add the chicken and stir-fry for 5 minutes. Add the jalapeño and red peppers; stir-fry with chicken for 2 minutes. Stir in the onion; sauté for 3 minutes, or until tender. Stir in the garlic, tomatoes, kidney beans, paprika, tomato paste, broth, thyme, oregano, chili powder, salt, and pepper.

2. Lock the lid in place. Bring to low pressure, lower the heat, and maintain pressure for 10 minutes. Remove the pan from the burner and use the quick-release method to release the pressure. Stir the chili and taste for seasoning; add additional salt, pepper, spices, or herbs, if needed.

Beef Roast Dinner

Serve this roast with a tossed salad and warm buttered dinner rolls. Have sour cream at the table. Some people also like grated horseradish on their roast.

Serves 6

1 tablespoon vegetable oil
1 stalk celery, finely diced
1 1-pound bag baby carrots
1 large yellow onion, diced
1 3-pound rump roast
Salt and freshly ground black
    pepper to taste
OPTIONAL: 1 tablespoon Dijon
    mustard
6 medium Yukon gold
    potatoes, scrubbed and
    quartered
3 cups beef broth
Water as needed
1 tablespoon butter
OPTIONAL: fresh parsley to taste

1. Add oil to the pressure cooker and bring it to temperature over medium-high heat. Add the celery. Grate 6 baby carrots and add them to the pan; sauté for 3 minutes. Add the onion, stir it into the celery and carrots, and push to the edges of the pan. Put the meat in the pan, fat-side up. Season with salt and pepper.

2. Brown for 5 minutes, then turn the roast to fat-side down. If desired, spread the mustard over the browned top of the roast. Season with salt and pepper. Spoon some of the sautéed celery, carrots, and onion over the top of the roast. Add the potatoes and the remaining carrots to the top of the meat. Pour in the broth. Add water, if needed to bring the liquid level with the ingredients in the pressure cooker.

3. Lock the lid. Bring the cooker to high pressure; lower the heat to maintain pressure for 1 hour. Turn off the heat and let the pan sit for 15 minutes to release the pressure; use the quick-release method to release any remaining pressure. Move the roast, potatoes, and carrots to a serving platter; tent with foil and keep warm.

4. Skim off and discard the fat from the pan juices. Bring to a boil over medium-high heat; reduce the heat and simmer for 5 minutes, and then whisk in the butter 1 teaspoon at a time. Pour into a gravy boat to serve with the roast. Garnish the roast platter with fresh parsley, if desired.

Making Gravy

If you prefer gravy with your roast instead of jus, increase the butter to 2 tablespoons and blend it with 2 tablespoons of all-purpose flour. When the pan juices come to a boil, begin whisking in the butter-flour paste 1 teaspoon at a time. When it's all added, boil for 1 minute and then reduce the heat; stir and simmer until the gravy is thickened.

Pork Loin Dinner

Serves 4

1 tablespoon vegetable oil

1 small yellow onion, diced

1 pound boneless pork loin, cut into 1" cubes

Salt and freshly ground black pepper to taste

½ cup dry white wine or apple juice

1 cup chicken broth

1 rutabaga, diced

1 large turnip, diced

4 small Yukon gold potatoes, scrubbed and quartered

4 carrots, peeled and diced

1 stalk celery, finely diced

½ cup sliced leeks (white part only)

½ teaspoon mild curry powder

¼ teaspoon dried thyme

2 teaspoons dried parsley

3 tablespoons fresh lemon juice

2 Granny Smith apples, peeled, cored, and diced

OPTIONAL: fresh parsley or thyme sprigs to taste

Serve this dinner with warm buttered dinner rolls and a tossed salad.

~

1. Add the oil to the pressure cooker and bring it to temperature over medium heat. Add the onion; sauté for 3 minutes. Add the pork and lightly season it with salt and pepper. Stir-fry the pork for 5 minutes, or until it just begins to brown. Add the wine or apple juice, broth, rutabaga, and turnip. Add the potatoes, carrots, celery, leeks, curry powder, thyme, parsley, and lemon juice.

2. Lock the lid into place and bring to high pressure; maintain pressure for 15 minutes. Turn off the heat and allow the pressure to drop naturally.

3. Carefully remove the lid and add the diced apples. Bring to a simmer over medium heat; reduce the heat and simmer, covered, for 5 minutes, or until the apples are tender. Serve rustic style in large bowls, garnished with fresh parsley or thyme, if desired.

Chapter 20
Main Dish Salads

Taco Salad

Serves 4

2 cups chili
1 1-pound bag salad mix
1 cup salsa
2 avocados, peeled, seeded, and sliced
4 ounces Cheddar cheese, grated
4 ounces Monterey jack cheese, grated
Baked corn tortilla chips

You can use canned or leftover chili for this recipe. Choose the salsa according to how it is seasoned and how spicy your family likes taco-style dishes.

Heat the chili on the stovetop or in the microwave. Divide the salad mix between 4 large plates or salad bowls. Spoon ½ cup hot chili over the top of each salad and top that with ¼ cup of the salsa. Arrange the avocado slices around each salad. Sprinkle 1 ounce each of the Cheddar and Monterey jack cheese over the top of each salad. Serve with baked corn tortilla chips.

Stretching the Chili

You can stretch the chili by stirring a 15-ounce can of refried beans into it when you heat it. Increase the remaining ingredients according to how many servings you need to fix. This dish can be expanded to serve as many people as you want, or you can make the servings as big as you want.

Beef and Roasted Vegetables
with Provençal Vinaigrette

Use leftover roast or steak and roasted potatoes to make this salad that will transport you and your family to the south of France.

1. Add the oil, vinegar, parsley, shallot, mustard, salt, and pepper to a glass jar; screw on the lid and shake the jar to combine the dressing. Set aside to allow flavors to meld.

2. Prepare the green beans in the microwave according to package directions; set aside. Add the potatoes and steak or roast to a large microwave-safe bowl; cover and microwave at 70 percent power for 2 minutes, or until heated through. Add the green beans to the bowl and mix with the potatoes and steak or roast. Shake the dressing jar to remix the dressing and then pour it into the bowl; stir to cover the warm meat and vegetables in the dressing. Add the salad greens, tomatoes, onion, and olives; toss to combine. Serve immediately.

Serves 4

3 tablespoons extra-virgin olive oil

1 tablespoon sherry, red wine, or champagne vinegar

1 tablespoon chopped fresh parsley

2 teaspoons minced shallot

1 teaspoon Dijon-style mustard

Salt to taste

¼ teaspoon pepper

1 12-ounce package steam-in-the-bag green beans

4 small baked or oven-roasted potatoes, quartered

2 cups leftover steak or roast beef, cubed or shredded

4 cups mixed baby salad greens

1 cup grape tomatoes

¼ cup thinly sliced red onion

16 niçoise olives, pitted

Chicken Salad
with Toasted Pecans and Green Grapes

Serves 4

⅔ cup sour cream

⅓ cup mayonnaise

½ teaspoon champagne or
  white wine vinegar

1 teaspoon granulated sugar

1 small red onion, diced

8 bread and butter pickle
  slices, minced

2 cups cooked chicken, cubed
  or shredded

1 cup grape tomatoes

1 cup green seedless grapes

1 cup pecans, toasted and
  chopped

4 cups salad mix

*The presentation for this salad is a bit more attractive if you use
cubed cooked chicken breast, and it tastes delicious when it's
made with both dark and white meat.*

1. Add the sour cream, mayonnaise, vinegar, sugar, onion, and pickles to a large bowl; stir to combine. Fold in the chicken, tomatoes, grapes, and half of the pecans.

2. To serve, put 1 cup of salad greens on each of 4 plates. Spoon equal amounts of the chicken salad over the tops of each plate of salad greens, and sprinkle the remaining pecans over the top of the chicken salad.

Toasting Pecans

To toast pecans, either dry-fry them for 5 minutes in a skillet over medium heat or bake them at 300°F for 10 to 15 minutes in a single layer on a baking sheet. Either way, be sure to stir them often and only toast them until they just begin to turn brown. Watch the nuts closely because they go from toasted to burned within seconds, and they'll continue to roast after they've been removed from the heat.

New Orleans–Style Oysters and Shrimp Salad

You can serve the pasta and the salad separately, but the contrast between the warm soft pasta and the cool crisp salad makes for a delightful dish.

1. In a Dutch oven, cook the penne according to package directions; drain, set aside, and keep warm.

2. Wipe out the Dutch oven; add the oil and bring it to temperature over medium heat. Stir in the flour and cook it until it begins to turn light brown. Add the onion; sauté for 3 minutes, or until limp. Whisk in the anchovy paste, milk, and cream. Bring to a simmer and stir in the hot sauce, Worcestershire sauce, and thyme; simmer for 10 minutes.

3. Drain the oysters and stir them and the shrimp into the cream sauce. Simmer just long enough to bring the seafood to temperature, then stir in the pasta. If the pasta mixture is too thick, stir in a little extra milk, cream, or the liquid drained from the oysters. Taste for seasoning and add salt and pepper if needed.

4. To serve, spread 1 cup of salad mix over the top of a plate, ladle the pasta mixture over the salad greens, and garnish with the chopped green onion.

Serves 8

1 pound dried penne pasta
2 tablespoons peanut or vegetable oil
2 tablespoons all-purpose flour
1 large yellow onion, diced
1 teaspoon anchovy paste
1 cup milk
1 cup heavy cream
Hot sauce to taste
1 teaspoon Worcestershire sauce
Pinch dried thyme
2 pints small oysters
2 pounds medium shrimp, cooked, peeled, and deveined
Salt and freshly ground black pepper to taste
8 cups salad mix
8 green onions, chopped

Indian Spinach Salad

Serves 8

1½ cups plain yogurt

½ cup sour cream

1 teaspoon ground cumin, pan-toasted

1 teaspoon ground coriander, pan-toasted

¼ teaspoon freshly ground black pepper

Cayenne pepper to taste

Salt to taste

1 10-ounce package frozen spinach, thawed and squeezed dry

2 large cucumbers, peeled and grated

2 tablespoons fresh mint, finely chopped

2 tablespoons fresh cilantro, finely chopped

½ cup currants or raisins

¼ cup walnuts, toasted and chopped

½ cup roasted cashews

¼ cup almonds, toasted and chopped

¼ cup pistachios, toasted

¼ cup macadamia nuts, chopped

8 cups fresh baby spinach

The assortment of nuts in this dish take the place of meat. If you don't have all the nut varieties on hand, substitute an equal amount of what you do have. You can use more or fewer nuts according to your taste.

1. In a large bowl, mix together the yogurt, sour cream, cumin, coriander, black pepper, cayenne, salt, frozen spinach, cucumbers, mint, cilantro, currants or raisins, and nuts. Taste for seasoning and add more salt, pepper, or spices, if desired. The moisture remaining in the spinach and cucumbers will determine the final texture of the salad; if it's too thick, add additional sour cream to thin it.

2. For each serving, put 1 cup of baby spinach on a plate or in a salad bowl and top with a helping of the salad.

Pan-Toasting Spices

To toast spices on the stovetop, add them to a skillet and dry sauté them over medium heat until they just begin to release their aromas. Pan toasting the spices gives them a unique flavor. Be careful not to burn the spices.

Tabouleh

This Middle Eastern dish is a meatless departure from the usual luncheon salad.

1. In a large bowl, pour the cold water over the bulgur wheat; let soak for 15 minutes. Drain off any excess water, and pour the bulgur out onto a clean cotton towel and squeeze dry.

2. Cut off the root end and remove the outer membrane of each green onion and slice the white part of each green onion into two 1" pieces; discard the remaining green tops. Remove the parsley from the stems. Add the green onions, parsley, bell pepper, celery, and mint to a food processor; pulse until finely chopped.

3. Add the oil, lemon juice, allspice, cinnamon, salt, and black pepper to the large bowl. Whisk to mix, and then whisk in the mixture from the food processor. Fold in the bulgur wheat and tomatoes. Serve over salad mix or baby spinach, if desired.

Serves 4

1 cup fine bulgur wheat
2 cups cold water
8 green onions
2 large bunches fresh parsley
1 small red bell pepper, seeded and quartered
2 stalks celery, cut into quarters
2 tablespoons fresh mint
¼ cup extra-virgin olive oil
¼ cup fresh lemon juice
¼ teaspoon ground allspice
¼ teaspoon ground cinnamon
Salt to taste
¼ teaspoon freshly ground black pepper
4 medium tomatoes, diced
OPTIONAL: 4 cups salad mix or baby spinach

Swedish Herring Salad

Serves 4

½ pound new potatoes,
    unpeeled, diced small

½ cup water

1 1-pound can pickled beets

2 hard-boiled eggs

2 6-ounce jars wine-flavored
    pickled herring

1 Granny Smith apple, cored
    and diced small

½ cup cooked roast beef,
    shredded

2 tablespoons yellow onion,
    finely diced

⅓ cup dill pickle, finely
    chopped

6 tablespoons reserved beet
    liquid

2 tablespoons white or white
    wine vinegar

2 tablespoons granulated
    sugar

Salt and freshly ground black
    pepper to taste

½ cup heavy cream

OPTIONAL: 4 cups salad mix

This isn't your everyday style of potato salad. If you're uncertain about the herrings, only use one jar and increase the amount of cooked roast beef. For a milder taste, use creamed herring.

1. Add the diced potatoes and water to a large microwave-safe bowl; cover and microwave on high for 5 minutes, or until the potatoes are tender. Drain in a colander and then return to the bowl. Drain the beets, reserving 6 tablespoons of the liquid; finely dice the beets and add to the bowl. Peel the hard-boiled eggs and set aside the yolks; dice the whites and add them to the bowl. Drain and finely chop the herring; add to the bowl along with the apple, beef, onion, dill pickle, beet liquid, vinegar, 1 tablespoon of the sugar, the salt, and black pepper. Mix well; taste for seasoning and add the remaining sugar, if desired. Whip the heavy cream until soft peaks form; fold it into the salad.

2. Serve over salad mix, if desired. Garnish with the reserved, chopped hard-boiled egg yolk.

Thai Beef Salad

*This salad takes leftover beef to a whole new level.
You can punch it up with store-bought dressing.*

Serves 4

1 small yellow onion, thinly
   sliced
¼ cup fresh lime juice
¼ cup fish sauce
10 fresh mint leaves, chopped
½ teaspoon granulated sugar
½ teaspoon red chili paste
2 cloves garlic, minced
2 cups cooked beef, cubed
4 cups salad mix
2 large cucumbers, thinly
   sliced
Fresh chopped cilantro to
   taste
4 green onions, chopped

1. Add the yellow onion, lime juice, fish sauce, mint, sugar, red chili paste, garlic, and beef to a bowl; stir to mix. Cover and chill for 30 minutes.

2. For each serving, place 1 cup of salad mix on a plate or in a salad bowl. Arrange the cucumber slices over the top of the salad mix. Spoon the beef mixture over the cucumber slices. Garnish with fresh cilantro and chopped green onion.

Macadamia and Avocado Chicken Salad

*If you don't have macadamia nut oil, you can substitute extra-virgin
olive oil or a mild vegetable oil. If you use a substitute, start with half the
oil called for in the recipe, taste, and then add more oil, if desired.*

Serves 4

½ cup macadamia nut oil
2 tablespoons white balsamic
   vinegar
½ tablespoon whole-grain
   mustard
2 green onions, white part
   only, chopped
Salt and freshly ground black
   pepper to taste
2 cups cooked chicken,
   shredded
1 red bell pepper, seeded and
   diced
1 yellow bell pepper, seeded
   and diced
4 ounces macadamia nuts,
   chopped
4 cups of mesclun greens
2 avocados, peeled, pitted,
   and sliced

Add the oil, vinegar, mustard, onion, salt, and pepper to a large bowl; whisk to combine. Add the chicken, red and yellow bell pepper, nuts, and mesclun greens or salad mix; toss to mix. Spoon the salad onto 4 individual plates and arrange ¼ of the avocado slices decoratively on the side of each plate.

Chicken and Cellophane Noodle Salad

Serves 4

1 8-ounce package
  cellophane noodles
2 cups chicken broth
4 tablespoons peanut butter
2 tablespoons hot water
5 tablespoons soy sauce
Red chili paste or cayenne
  pepper to taste
2 large cucumbers
1 tablespoon rice wine
  vinegar
½ teaspoon granulated sugar
2 teaspoons sesame oil
4 cups salad mix
2 cups cooked chicken,
  shredded
¼ cup dry-roasted peanuts,
  chopped

*You can substitute 2 cups of water and 2 chicken
bouillon cubes for the chicken broth.*

1. Add the noodles and chicken broth to a saucepan; soak the noodles for 1 hour. Place the saucepan over medium heat and bring to a simmer; simmer for 10 minutes, or until the noodles are tender. Drain off the broth. Cover and cool in the refrigerator.

2. Add the peanut butter, hot water, and red chili paste or cayenne to a small bowl; whisk to mix, adding more water if necessary to bring the mixture to the consistency of heavy cream. Pour the mixture over the noodles; toss to mix.

3. Peel, seed, and cut the cucumbers into julienne strips. In a small bowl, mix the cucumber strips together with the vinegar, sugar, and sesame oil.

4. To assemble each salad, arrange a cup of salad mix on a plate or in a salad bowl. Top with ¼ of the cellophane noodles, ¼ of the chicken, ¼ of the cucumber, and 1 tablespoon of chopped peanuts, in that order.

A Noodle by Any Other Name

Cellophane noodles—sometimes referred to as bean threads, glass noodles, and sai fun—are commonly made from bean starch. These delicate noodles easily absorb the flavors they are cooked with. You can find them in the Asian foods aisle in most supermarkets.

Chicken Waldorf Salad

This salad is better if it's refrigerated for 1 hour before serving.
The lime juice prevents the apples from turning brown.

Add the mayonnaise, sour cream, lime juice, sugar, and ginger to a bowl large enough to hold the salad; stir to combine, then fold in the apples, celery, walnuts, and chicken. Before serving, check for seasoning and add salt, pepper, and more sugar, if needed. To serve, spoon ¼ of the chicken salad over 1 cup of salad mix.

Serves 4

¼ cup mayonnaise
½ cup sour cream
½ tablespoon fresh lime juice
1 teaspoon granulated sugar
¼ teaspoon fresh ginger, grated
1 large Granny Smith apple, cored and diced
1 large Red Delicious apple, cored and diced
1 large Yellow Delicious apple, cored and diced
2 stalks celery, diced
½ cup walnuts, toasted and chopped
2 cups cooked chicken, shredded
Salt and freshly ground black pepper to taste
4 cups salad mix

Chinese Chicken Salad

Serves 6

1 3-pound rotisserie chicken
½ cup tamari sauce
½ cup macadamia nut oil
⅓ cup rice wine vinegar
1 teaspoon fresh ginger,
　grated
½ teaspoon garlic powder
1 teaspoon honey
4 cups raw broccoli florets
6 cups salad mix
4 stalks celery, diced
4 green onions, sliced on a
　slant
5 large radishes, thinly sliced
1 red bell pepper, seeded and
　sliced
½ cup unsalted macadamia
　nuts, toasted and
　chopped

*Start this meal the night before you plan to serve it. Complete step 1
the night before, step 2 1 to 2 hours before serving, and step 3
immediately before the dish hits the table.*

1. Remove the skin from the chicken and discard; remove the meat from the bones and shred it. Put the chicken in a large salad bowl. To make the dressing, put the tamari sauce, oil, vinegar, ginger, garlic powder, and honey in a jar with a tight-fitting lid; shake well to mix. Pour ¼ cup dressing over the chicken; cover and chill overnight. Cover and refrigerate the remaining dressing.

2. The next day, 1–2 hours before serving, add the broccoli florets and ⅓ cup of the dressing; stir to mix and chill. Cover and refrigerate the remaining dressing.

3. To serve, add the salad greens, celery, green onions, radishes, and red pepper to the salad bowl. Pour the remaining dressing over the salad; toss lightly to mix. Divide the greens equally among individual chilled salad plates. Top each serving with toasted macadamia nuts.

Bacon-Spinach Salad

You can use a combination of melted bacon grease and oil for the dressing.

1. Add the oil, onion, sugar, vinegar, ketchup, and Worcestershire sauce to a blender or food processor; pulse to mix.

2. To assemble each salad, arrange 2 cups of spinach on a plate and top with the mushrooms, chopped egg, bacon, and bean sprouts (if using). Drizzle a generous amount of dressing over the salad, and top with grated cheese. Refrigerate any leftover dressing.

Hot Bacon Dressing

In a nonreactive or nonstick skillet, fry 1 pound of bacon until crisp. Remove the bacon and crumble it. Remove the pan from the heat and stir ¼ cup apple cider vinegar, ¼ cup granulated sugar, 1 diced small yellow or red onion, and ⅓ cup ketchup into the bacon fat. If desired, stir the bacon back into the dressing.

Serves 4

1 cup vegetable oil
1 small yellow or red onion, diced
¾ cup granulated sugar
¼ cup apple cider vinegar
⅓ cup ketchup
1 teaspoon Worcestershire sauce
8 cups baby spinach, stems removed
8 ounces fresh button mushrooms, cleaned and sliced
4 hard-boiled eggs, peeled and chopped
8 slices bacon, cooked crisp and crumbled
OPTIONAL: fresh bean sprouts
4 ounces Cheddar cheese, grated

Chef's Salad

Serves 4

8 cups salad mix
1 small red onion, sliced or diced
2 stalks celery, diced
1 cup frozen baby peas, thawed
4 hard-boiled eggs, peeled and chopped
1 pound boiled ham, diced
8 ounces Cheddar cheese, grated
Salad dressing to taste

This salad is an easy one to pack for lunch. Put the salad in an empty container with a lid, the cheese in a snack-size baggie, and enough dressing for your salad in a small plastic container.

1. Add the salad mix, onion, celery, peas, eggs, and ham to a large salad bowl; toss to mix.

2. Divide the salad between 4 plates or salad bowls. Top each salad with grated cheese and salad dressing.

The Best Bleu Cheese Dressing Ever!

In a small bowl, stir together ⅔ cup sour cream, ⅓ cup mayonnaise, 1 teaspoon champagne vinegar, 2 teaspoons (or to taste) granulated sugar, and 1 ounce (or to taste) crumbled bleu cheese. Store leftovers in the refrigerator.

Tuna-Macaroni Salad

Serves 4

7 ounces dried elbow macaroni
4 ounces Cheddar cheese, cut into cubes
1 7-ounce can tuna, drained
¾ cup candied sweet pickles, chopped
1 small red onion, diced
1 cup salad dressing or mayonnaise
1 tablespoon granulated sugar, or to taste
Salt and freshly ground black pepper to taste
OPTIONAL: iceberg lettuce or salad mix

This salad tastes best if it's refrigerated overnight before serving. Wait until after it's completely chilled to taste for seasoning.

Cook the macaroni according to package directions; drain well. Add the cooked macaroni to a large bowl. Add the cheese, tuna, sweet pickles, onion, salad dressing or mayonnaise, sugar, salt, and pepper. Stir to combine. Cover and refrigerate overnight. Taste for seasoning before serving, and add additional sugar, salt, and pepper, if needed. Serve the salad on top of lettuce leaves or salad mix.

Chapter 21
Meals Worthy of the Extra Effort

Lobster Bake

Butter to taste

2 Idaho potatoes, scrubbed

2 ears of corn on the cob, husked

2 1½-pound live lobsters

Sea salt and freshly ground black pepper to taste

2 tablespoons extra-virgin olive oil

½ cup unsalted butter, at room temperature

4 ounces fresh button mushrooms, cleaned and sliced

1 tablespoon minced shallots

½ cup dry-style hard cider or dry white wine

Lobster bibs will add a bit of whimsy to this romantic dinner for two. Serve it with tossed salads and warmed dinner rolls.

1. Preheat oven to 450°F.

2. Rub the potatoes with a little butter and individually wrap them in foil; place on the oven rack. After the potatoes have baked for 30 minutes, rub butter on each ear of corn, individually wrap them in foil, and place on the oven rack next to the potatoes. Continue to bake for 20 minutes.

3. While the corn is baking, kill each lobster with a sharp-pointed knife stuck into the body behind the head. Remove the bands from the claws, twist the claws and knuckles off the body, and separate the claws from the knuckles. Crack them slightly by lying the flat edge of a chef's knife against them and striking a sharp blow against the knife's flat edge with the heel of your hand. Twist off each tail, carefully split it lengthwise, and remove and discard the intestinal tract. Split each lobster body. Arrange the lobster pieces in a single layer in a 9" × 13" nonstick baking pan, placing the tail and body pieces shell-side down. Sprinkle sea salt and black pepper over the exposed meat, and drizzle the oil over them. Bake for 8 minutes, or until the shells are almost uniformly red and the meat is opaque.

4. Add several pieces of the ½ cup butter, the mushrooms, and shallots to a microwave-safe dish; cover and microwave on high for 1 minute. Stir, cover, and microwave on high for another 30 seconds. After the lobsters have baked for 8 minutes, remove them from the oven, and pour the mushroom-shallots mix and the cider or wine over the lobsters. Dot with the butter pieces. Place back in the oven for 3 minutes, or until the butter has completely melted.

5. Arrange the lobster pieces on dinner plates. Unwrap the potatoes, split them each in half, and place 2 halves on each plate beside the lobster. Unwrap the corn and place an ear on each plate. Swirl the baking pan to emulsify the liquid ingredients and spoon the resulting sauce over the plates. Have additional sea salt and pepper at the table, if needed.

Baked Versus Steamed Potatoes

Food purists insist that wrapping potatoes in foil and then baking them actually steams the potatoes. If you prefer a classic baked potato, bake scrubbed unpierced potatoes directly on the oven rack. Potato size can affect baking time, but as a general rule, at 425°F bake for 40 to 50 minutes, at 375°F for 50 to 60 minutes, and at 325°F for 75 to 85 minutes.

Herbed Duck
with Parsnips

Serves 4

1 5-pound duck
2 large parsnips, diced
1 8-ounce bag baby carrots
10 ounces shallots, peeled
2 heads of garlic, cloves
　　separated but unpeeled
2 bay leaves
½ teaspoon dried rosemary
Salt and freshly ground black
　　pepper to taste
1 cup water
OPTIONAL: fresh parsley to taste

If you need something green to complete a meal, crispy duck cracklings will add a delicious dimension to a tossed salad.

1. Carve the duck so that you have 12 pieces: 2 bone-in breast pieces, 2 breast fillets, 2 legs, 2 thighs, 2 wing drumsticks, and 2 2-part wing pieces. Trim off any superfluous fatty skin pieces and reserve for later use. Freeze the neck to use later for broth, or add it to the skillet along with the other pieces.

2. Place the duck pieces skin-side down in a deep 3½-quart nonstick skillet over medium- to medium-high heat. Cook for 25 minutes, or until the skin is crispy. Watch the skillet and adjust the temperature, if necessary, to ensure that the duck doesn't burn.

3. Reduce the temperature to low and spread the parsnips, carrots, shallots, and garlic over the top of the duck pieces. Add the bay leaves and sprinkle with the rosemary, salt, and pepper. Cover and simmer for 30 minutes, or until the parsnips and carrots are tender.

4. Discard the bay leaves. Use a slotted spoon to move the duck pieces and vegetables to a serving platter. Pour off the duck fat and reserve it for later use. Place the pan back over medium heat, pour the water in the pan, and bring to a boil while stirring and scraping the bottom of the pan with a spatula. Pour the resulting sauce over the duck. Garnish with fresh parsley, if desired.

Duck Cracklings and Rendered Duck Fat

Cut fatty skin pieces from the duck into ¼" strips. Arrange them in a baking pan and bake at 350°F for 40 minutes or put them in a nonstick skillet and fry for 30 minutes over medium heat. The cracklings are done when they're crisp and the rendered duck fat is clear. Drain the cracklings on paper towels. The duck fat keeps for months when stored in a covered container in the refrigerator.

Châteaubriand Meal

*Serve Châteaubriand with a salad tossed with bleu
cheese dressing and warm dinner rolls with butter.*

Serves 4

4 Idaho potatoes, scrubbed
*1 24-ounce beef tenderloin,
    cut from the large end*
*Freshly ground or cracked
    black pepper to taste*
*1 12-ounce package frozen
    steam-in-the-bag
    Brussels sprouts*
*1 tablespoon extra-virgin
    olive oil*
*2 tablespoons olive or
    vegetable oil*
2 tablespoons butter
*8 ounces fresh button or
    cremini mushrooms,
    cleaned and sliced*
1 large shallot, minced
1 tablespoon brandy
*½ cup Madeira or other red
    wine*
Salt to taste
*OPTIONAL: additional 1
    tablespoon butter*

1. Preheat oven to 450°F. Wrap the potatoes in foil and place on the oven
    rack to bake; allow them to bake for 45 minutes to 1 hour before you
    plan to add the tenderloin to the oven.

2. Remove any membrane from the tenderloin and season all sides with
    freshly ground black pepper or roll it in cracked black pepper. Prepare
    the Brussels sprouts in the microwave according to package directions.
    Open one end of the bag and drain out any excess moisture, then pour
    in the tablespoon of extra-virgin olive oil; hold the bag opening closed
    and shake to coat the vegetables in the oil.

3. Bring a cast-iron skillet or ovenproof grill pan to temperature over
    medium-high heat. Add the oil and 1 tablespoon butter; when it begins
    to smoke, add the tenderloin and quickly sear it on one side and then
    the other. Pour the Brussels sprouts around the meat. Move the pan to
    the oven and roast for about 10 minutes for rare or about 15 minutes
    for medium. Remove the potatoes from the oven and keep warm. Move
    the tenderloin and Brussels sprouts to a serving platter; tent with alumi-
    num foil.

4. Move the pan back to the stovetop; add the remaining tablespoon of
    butter and melt it over medium heat. Add the mushrooms and shallots;
    sauté for 3 minutes, or until the mushrooms are tender. Add the brandy
    and sauté until all the liquid has evaporated. Turn the heat to low and
    pour in the wine. Simmer gently for 1 minute; taste for seasoning and
    add salt and pepper, if needed. To make a glossier sauce, whisk in the
    optional additional 1 tablespoon of butter, 1 teaspoon at a time until it's
    incorporated into the sauce. Remove the foil from the serving platter,
    carve the meat, and pour the sauce over the tenderloin and Brussels
    sprouts. Serve immediately.

Standing Rib Roast

1 3-pound standing rib roast, trimmed

Salt and freshly ground black pepper to taste

1 teaspoons herbes de Provence

3 medium yellow onions, rough chopped

1 head garlic, cloves separated but unpeeled

2 bay leaves, crumbled

1 2-pound bag baby carrots

8 medium Yukon gold potatoes, scrubbed and quartered

Extra-virgin olive oil to taste

½ cup dry red wine

Beef broth as needed

2 tablespoons butter

This meal is also good with a salad tossed with bleu cheese dressing. If you're serving it with Yorkshire Pudding, warm buttered dinner rolls are optional.

1. Preheat the oven to 425°F.

2. Place the roast rib-side down in the center of a large roasting pan. Rub the salt, pepper, and herbes de Provence into the meat. Bake for 15 minutes. Remove the pan from the oven. Lower the oven temperature to 325°F.

3. Scatter the onions, garlic, and bay leaves around the roast. Spread the carrots around the roast on top of the onions and garlic. Rub the potatoes with extra-virgin olive oil; place the potatoes evenly over the carrots. Salt and pepper the vegetables, if desired. Return to the oven and bake for 75 minutes, or until the roast reaches an internal temperature of 125°F for medium-rare.

4. Remove from the oven. Center the roast on a serving platter; remove the potatoes and most of the carrots and arrange them around the roast. Tent with foil and allow to rest for 20 to 30 minutes.

5. Strain the juices remaining in the pan, pushing against the vegetables to release the juices from them; discard the vegetables. Skim the fat from the strained juices. Set the roasting pan on the stovetop over medium heat. Add the wine to deglaze the pan, using a spatula to scrape any browned bits from the bottom of the pan. Add enough beef broth to the strained pan juices to bring it to 2 cups. Bring to a simmer and then whisk in the butter, 1 teaspoon at a time. Taste for seasoning and add salt and pepper, if needed. Serve the resulting au jus with the roast.

Beef Bourguignon

*Serve Beef Bourguignon over buttered noodles or mashed
potatoes, along with a salad and a steamed vegetable.*

Serves 8

8 slices bacon, diced
1 3-pound boneless English
    or chuck roast
1 large yellow onion, diced
4 cups Burgundy wine
2 cups beef broth or water
2 tablespoons tomato paste
3 cloves garlic, minced
½ teaspoon thyme
1 bay leaf
Salt and freshly ground black
    pepper to taste
1 large yellow onion, thinly
    sliced
16 ounces fresh button or
    cremini mushrooms,
    cleaned and sliced
½ cup plus 2 tablespoons
    butter
½ cup all-purpose flour

1. Add the bacon to a Dutch oven and fry it over medium heat until it
   renders its fat; use a slotted spoon to remove the bacon and reserve it
   for another use or use it in the tossed salads you serve with the meal.
   Trim the roast of any fat and cut it into bite-sized pieces; add the beef
   pieces to the Dutch oven and stir-fry for 5 minutes. Add the diced onion
   and sauté for 3 minutes, or until transparent. Add the Burgundy, broth
   or water, tomato paste, garlic, thyme, bay leaf, salt, and pepper; stir
   to combine. Bring the contents of the pan to temperature; reduce the
   heat, cover, and simmer for 2 hours, or until the meat is tender.

2. Add the sliced onion to a microwave-safe bowl along with 2 tablespoons of the butter; cover and microwave on high for 2 minutes. Add
   the mushrooms; cover and microwave on high for 1 minute. Stir, cover,
   and microwave on high in 30-second increments until the mushrooms
   are sautéed and the onion is transparent.

3. Stir the mushroom-onion mixture into the pan; cover and simmer for 20
   minutes.

4. In a small bowl or measuring cup, mix the remaining ½ cup of butter
   together with the flour to form a paste; whisk in some of the pan liquid
   a little at a time to thin the paste. Strain out any lumps. Increase the
   heat to medium-high and bring the contents of the pan to a boil. Whisk
   the butter-flour mixture into the meat and juices in the pan; boil for 1
   minute. Reduce the heat and simmer uncovered, stirring occasionally,
   until the pan juices have been reduced to make a gravy.

Roast Leg of Lamb

Serves 8

6 cloves garlic, minced

Salt and freshly ground black pepper to taste

3 teaspoons dried rosemary

1 4½-pound leg of lamb

24–32 small red new potatoes, scrubbed

1 1-pound bag baby carrots, halved

3 tablespoons extra-virgin olive oil

2 10-ounce packages frozen asparagus spears or cuts, thawed

1½ cups chicken broth or dry white wine

OPTIONAL: mint or redcurrant jelly to taste

Have your butcher trim the pelvic bone and as much fat as possible from a whole 6-pound leg of lamb to get the 4½ pounds you need. Roast lamb on a rack so that any fat drains away from the meat and vegetables.

1. Move the oven rack to its lowermost position. Preheat oven to 400°F.

2. Add the garlic, salt, pepper, and rosemary to a small bowl; mix well. Reserve 1½ teaspoons of the mixture. Use a sharp knife to make 1" deep incisions in the top of the leg and around the meatier parts of the leg. Rub what remains of the herb mixture into those incisions and onto all sides of the meat. Sprinkle additional salt and pepper over the outside of the meat, if desired. Set the roast topside up on a rack in a large roasting pan.

3. Prepare two large sheets of double thickness of heavy-duty aluminum foil, one large enough to hold all of the potatoes and the other large enough to hold the carrots. Add the oil and remaining garlic-herb mixture to a small bowl; mix well. Place the potatoes in the center of one of the foil pieces; drizzle with ⅓ of the oil mixture, rubbing it into the potato skins. Bring the sides of the foil up and over the potatoes and crimp it on top to form a packet; put at one end of the roasting pan. Place the carrots on the other foil piece; drizzle with ⅓ of the oil mixture. Bring the sides of the foil up and over the carrots and crimp it on top to form a packet; put at the other end of the roasting pan. Put the roasting pan in the oven for 30 minutes.

4. Remove the roasting pan from the oven; turn the roast over. Open each of the foil packets. Form one or two bowls out of doubled sheets of heavy-duty aluminum foil; add the asparagus and drizzle with the remaining oil mixture. Position in the roasting pan. Return the roast to the oven for 45 minutes, or until the thickest part of the leg reaches an internal temperature of 130°F. Remove from the oven and transfer the roast and all vegetables to a large serving platter; tent with foil and let rest for 30 minutes before carving the meat.

5. To make a meat sauce, drain as much of the fat as possible from the roasting pan, then use paper towels to blot any fat that remains in the pan. Put the roasting pan on the stovetop over medium heat. Bring to a simmer, using a spatula to scrape up any browned bits from the bottom of the pan. Simmer for 15 minutes, stirring occasionally, then whisk in mint or redcurrant jelly to taste, if desired. Serve the sauce as is or strained over the meat.

Moussaka

This is a simplified recipe that uses yogurt and cream rather than a Béchamel sauce; the extra effort comes from moving ingredients in and out of the pan and then laying the dish before you bake it.

Serves 4

7 tablespoons extra-virgin olive oil

1 medium eggplant, peeled and sliced into ½" rounds

Salt and freshly ground black pepper to taste

1 large white onion, diced

2 cloves garlic, minced

1 pound lean ground lamb or beef

½ teaspoon ground cinnamon

¼ teaspoon ground nutmeg

1 15-ounce can diced tomatoes

4 medium russet or red potatoes, peeled and thinly sliced

1 cup freshly grated Parmigiano-Reggiano

2 cups plain whole yogurt

3 eggs, lightly beaten

¾ cup light cream

OPTIONAL: additional ground nutmeg to taste

1. Preheat oven to 375°F.

2. Add 2 tablespoons of the oil to an ovenproof Dutch oven and bring to temperature over medium-high heat. Add the eggplant slices and brown them for 2 minutes on each side; remove and drain on paper towels. Lightly salt and pepper the eggplant slices.

3. Add another 2 tablespoons of oil to the same Dutch oven and bring it to temperature over medium heat; add the onion and sauté for 3 minutes, or until the onion is transparent. Add the garlic and ground lamb or beef; salt and pepper to taste and brown the meat completely, breaking it apart as it cooks. Stir in the cinnamon, nutmeg, and tomatoes; simmer uncovered for 10 minutes. Transfer the cooked meat mixture to a bowl.

4. Wipe out the Dutch oven, add the remaining 3 tablespoons of oil, and bring it to temperature over medium heat. Add the potato slices and brown them for about 5 minutes on each side, or until cooked through; spread the potatoes in an even layer across the bottom of the pan. Lightly season with salt and pepper.

5. Spread the meat over the layer of potatoes, arrange the eggplant on top of the meat, and top the meat with the Parmigiano-Reggiano.

6. Add the yogurt, eggs, and cream to a medium-sized bowl; stir to combine and pour over the Parmigiano-Reggiano. Sprinkle additional nutmeg over the yogurt sauce, if desired. Let sit for 10 minutes, and then move to the oven and bake for 40 minutes, or until golden brown and bubbly. Remove from the oven and let rest for 15 minutes before serving.

Baked Stuffed Round Steak

Serve this dish with garlic bread, cooked pasta, and antipasto or a tossed salad.

Serves 4

3 tablespoons extra-virgin olive oil

2 pounds round steak

Salt and freshly ground black pepper to taste

3 cloves garlic, minced

4 hard-boiled eggs, peeled and sliced

4 large carrots, peeled and grated

1 small yellow onion, minced

1 cup zucchini, grated and squeezed dry

2 ounces freshly grated Parmigiano-Reggiano cheese

1 25-ounce jar pasta sauce

1. Preheat oven to 350°F.

2. Rub 2 tablespoons of the oil over both sides of the round steak. Put the steak between 2 pieces of plastic wrap; pound the meat out flatter. Remove the plastic wrap and season the meat with salt and pepper. Sprinkle the garlic over the meat, then rub it into the meat. Evenly arrange the egg slices, carrots, onion, zucchini, and half of the Parmigiano-Reggiano down the center of the meat. Roll up the steak like a jellyroll, and then place it seam-side down in a 9" × 13" nonstick baking pan or casserole dish large enough to hold the meat and pasta sauce. Rub the remaining oil over the top of the meat. Place under the broiler for 15 minutes, or until the meat begins to brown and caramelize. Change the oven setting back to 350°F. Pour the pasta sauce over the meat, cover the pan, and bake for 1 hour.

3. Remove the cover from the baking pan. Sprinkle the remaining Parmigiano-Reggiano over the meat and pasta sauce; bake for an additional 30 minutes, or until the meat is tender and the cheese has melted into the bubbling sauce. Remove from the oven, tent or cover, and let rest for 15 minutes before carving the meat and serving.

Potatoes over Pasta

Instead of serving Baked Stuffed Round Steak over pasta, add 4 medium scrubbed potatoes to the baking dish when you add the pasta sauce. You'll still get your starch, but the flavor will be a welcome change from the norm.

Braciole

*The stuffing in the Braciole adds substance to this dish, but you can
also serve it with cooked pasta or garlic bread if you wish. Add a salad
and a steamed vegetable for a complete meal.*

Serves 4

4 tablespoons extra-virgin
olive oil
2 pounds flank steak
Salt and freshly ground black
pepper to taste
3 cloves garlic, minced
1 cup breadcrumbs
1 medium carrot, peeled and
shredded
½ stalk celery, minced
1 small yellow onion, minced
1 teaspoon dried oregano
¼ teaspoon dried rosemary
¼ teaspoon dried thyme
2 teaspoons dried parsley
2 ounces freshly grated
Parmigiano-Reggiano
cheese
2 large eggs
1 teaspoon granulated sugar
1 25-ounce jar pasta sauce
OPTIONAL: fresh parsley to taste
OPTIONAL: additional freshly
grated Parmigiano-
Reggiano to taste

1. Preheat oven to 350°F.

2. Rub 2 tablespoons of the oil over both sides of the steak. Put the steak between 2 pieces of plastic wrap; pound the meat to ¼" thickness. Remove the plastic wrap and season the meat with salt and pepper. Sprinkle the garlic over the meat, then rub it into the meat.

3. Add the breadcrumbs, carrot, celery, onion, oregano, rosemary, thyme, parsley, Parmigiano-Reggiano, and eggs to a bowl; mix well. Use your hands to shape the mixture into a log and place it in the center of the meat. Roll up the steak like a jellyroll so that when you slice the meat later, the slices will be against the grain of the meat; tie with butcher's twine.

4. Add the remaining 2 tablespoons of oil to an ovenproof Dutch oven; bring to temperature over medium heat. Add the meat roll; brown for 5 minutes on each side.

5. Stir the sugar into the pasta sauce, then pour it over the meat. Cover and bake for 1½ hours, or until the meat is tender. Bake uncovered for 15 minutes if necessary to thicken the sauce. Remove from the oven and let rest for 15 minutes, then move the meat to a serving platter, carve, and spoon the sauce over the meat. Garnish with fresh parsley and serve topped with additional freshly grated Parmigiano-Reggiano, if desired.

Osso Buco

This Osso Buco recipe is a hybrid, combining today's tradition of adding tomatoes and the nineteenth-century Milanese practice of using allspice and cinnamon. It's usually served with a rich risotto made with saffron, heavy cream, and Parmigiano-Reggiano.

Serves 8

1 cup all-purpose flour
Salt and freshly ground black pepper to taste
8 veal shanks, cross-cut 1½" thick
3 tablespoons extra-virgin olive oil
3 tablespoons unsalted butter
1 medium white onion, diced
1 celery stalk, diced
2 carrots, peeled and diced
1 head garlic, cut horizontally through the middle
1 bottle dry white wine
1 14½-ounce can low-sodium beef broth
1 28-ounce can whole tomatoes, hand-crushed
¼ teaspoon ground cinnamon
⅛ teaspoon allspice
2 bay leaves
¼ cup fresh flat-leaf parsley, stems removed and chopped
1 lemon, zest only
½ orange, zest only

1. Add the flour to a large plastic bag and season with a generous amount of salt and pepper; add the veal shanks to the bag and shake to coat them. Bring the oil to temperature in a large ovenproof Dutch oven over medium heat; add the butter and swirl it around the pan to melt. Remove the veal shanks from the plastic bag, tap off any excess flour, and then add them to the pan. Use tongs to turn the shanks until all sides are a rich brown caramel color. Remove the browned veal shanks to a side plate.

2. Preheat the oven to 375°F.

3. Add the onion, celery, carrots, and garlic to the Dutch oven; sauté for 10 minutes, or until the vegetables start to get some color and develop a intense aroma. Add the veal shanks back to the pan. Pour in the wine; reduce the heat and simmer for 20 minutes, or until the wine is reduced by half. Stir in the broth, tomatoes, cinnamon, allspice, and bay leaves. Cover and bake for 1½ hours. Uncover and continue to bake for an additional 30 minutes, or until the veal is tender and nearly falling off the bone. Remove and discard the bay leaves.

4. Transfer the meat to a serving platter, cover and keep warm. Put the Dutch oven over medium heat and bring the pan juices to a boil. Skim off and discard any fat. Cook for about 20 minutes, or until the sauce has thickened and coats the back of a spoon. Stir in the parsley and orange and lemon zests. Taste for seasoning and add additional salt, pepper, cinnamon, and/or allspice, if needed. Simmer for another 5 minutes, then pour over the meat and serve immediately.

Apple Pancake

Serve this for a special occasion brunch along with some brown-and-serve sausages and some cinnamon ice cream on the side.

Serves 4

4 tablespoons butter

2 tablespoons granulated sugar

⅛ teaspoon ground nutmeg

¼ teaspoon ground cinnamon

4 tart apples, peeled, cored, and sliced thin

4 eggs

1 cup milk

½ cup all-purpose flour

¼ teaspoon salt

1 teaspoon vanilla extract

1. Preheat oven to 375°F.

2. Melt butter in a 10" ovenproof skillet or German pancake pan over medium heat. Add 1 tablespoon of the sugar, the nutmeg, cinnamon, and apple slices to the pan; sauté and stir for 8 minutes, or until the apples start to soften and the sugar starts to brown.

3. Add the remaining 1 tablespoon of sugar, the eggs, milk, salt, flour, and vanilla to a bowl; whisk to combine. Gently pour the pancake batter into the pan, keeping the apples as a separate layer on bottom. Move to the oven and bake for 10 minutes, or until puffed and almost firm. Slide onto a large plate, cut into wedges, and serve.

Chicken
with 40 Cloves of Garlic

*Serve this chicken with a tossed salad and heated or toasted slices of French bread.
Squeeze the cloves of roasted garlic onto the bread; they'll spread like butter.*

Serves 8

⅔ cup extra-virgin olive oil
8 chicken drumsticks
8 chicken thighs
Nonstick cooking spray
4 stalks of celery, cut in long
    strips
2 medium yellow onions,
    diced
1 1-pound bag baby carrots
1 tablespoon dried parsley
1 teaspoon dried tarragon
½ cup dry vermouth
Salt and freshly ground black
    pepper to taste
⅛ teaspoon ground nutmeg
40 cloves garlic, unpeeled
8 medium Idaho potatoes,
    scrubbed

1. Preheat oven to 375°F.

2. Add the oil and chicken pieces to a large plastic bag; seal and turn to coat the meat on all sides. Treat the bottom of a heavy 6-quart casserole with nonstick spray. Spread the celery, onions, and carrots in layers over the bottom of the pan; sprinkle with the parsley and tarragon. Lay the chicken pieces on top of the seasoned carrots. Pour the vermouth over the chicken, and then sprinkle them with the salt, pepper, and nutmeg. Tuck the garlic cloves around and between the chicken pieces. To create an airtight seal for the casserole dish so that the steam doesn't escape, cover it with heavy-duty aluminum foil crimped around the edges of the dish and top that with the casserole lid. Move the dish to the oven.

3. Rub some of the oil remaining from coating the chicken onto the skins of the potatoes; wrap each one in foil and move to the oven beside the casserole dish. Bake for 1½ hours. Transfer the chicken, carrots, and cloves of roasted garlic to a serving platter. Strain the pan juices, skim off the fat, and serve it alongside the chicken and potatoes.

Spanakopita

Serves 10

3 tablespoons olive oil

1 large yellow onion, diced

8 green onions, white and 1 inch of green parts diced

3 cloves garlic, minced

2 pounds fresh baby spinach, trimmed, washed, and roughly chopped

1½ tablespoons fresh lemon juice

2 large eggs, lightly beaten

12 ounces crumbled feta

1 tablespoon coriander seeds, toasted and ground

½ teaspoon freshly grated nutmeg

½ pound unsalted butter, melted

1 pound package of phyllo pastry sheets

¼ cup fresh oregano, finely chopped

¼ cup fresh chives, finely chopped

½ cup freshly grated Parmigiano-Reggiano

Serve these as an appetizer or as a main course with a tossed salad. If you like, you can add a piece of cooked chicken, lobster, or crabmeat into each triangle.

1. Add the oil and yellow and green onions to a large microwave-safe bowl; cover and microwave on high for 1 minute. Stir and microwave for 1 more minute, or until the onions are transparent. Stir in the garlic and spinach; cover and microwave on high for 2 minutes. Set aside to cool, and then stir in the lemon juice, eggs, feta, coriander, and nutmeg.

2. Preheat the oven to 350°F.

3. Brush 2 baking sheets with some of the melted butter. Unroll the phyllo dough; prevent the dough from drying out and becoming brittle by keeping it covered with a damp towel until you are ready to work with it. Lay out a piece of the dough flat on a work surface; brush it with melted butter, then evenly spread some oregano and chives over it. Repeat the butter and herb step with 2 more sheets of phyllo, stacking them on top of each other. Use a sharp knife or pizza cutter to cut the sheets lengthwise into thirds to form 2½" strips. Repeat with all the remaining sheets of dough.

4. Put 1 heaping teaspoon of the spinach filling near 1 corner of each layered phyllo strip. Fold the end at an angle over the filling to form a triangle and continue to fold along the strip until you reach the end, in a manner similar to folding up a flag. Brush the top of the resulting triangle packet with butter and dust with Parmigiano-Reggiano. Place each triangle on one of the prepared baking sheets; cover while preparing the remaining pastries. Repeat until all the filling and phyllo strips are used up. Bake for 20 to 30 minutes, or until crisp and golden. Serve hot, warm, or cold.

Honey-Glazed Striped Sea Bass Dinner

The extra effort required for this meal comes more from hunting down striped sea bass than from the work required to prepare the meal. If, after checking with your local fishmonger, you can't find striped sea bass, you can substitute salmon, halibut, black sea bass, or cod.

Serves 4

4 10-ounce striped sea bass
   fillets
3 tablespoons honey
1 tablespoon soy sauce
1 tablespoon sesame oil
2 10-ounce boxes rice pilaf
1 12-ounce frozen steam-in-
   the-bag green beans
1 12-ounce frozen steam-in-
   the-bag asparagus tips
2 tablespoons butter
Salt and freshly ground black
   pepper to taste
8 teaspoons sesame seeds,
   toasted

1. Rinse the fillets and pat dry. Add the honey, soy sauce, and sesame oil to a gallon-size plastic food bag; seal and squeeze to mix well. Add the fillets to the bag, seal the bag, and, being careful not to break the fillets, turn the bag several times to coat them with the marinade. Refrigerate and let marinate for 1 hour.

2. Preheat the oven to 425°F. Place the fillets side-by-side on a jellyroll pan or baking sheet. Bake for 12 minutes, or until opaque.

3. While the fish bakes, prepare the rice pilaf, green beans, and asparagus tips according to the package directions. Drain any excess moisture from the bags holding the green beans and asparagus; add 1 table-spoon of butter to each bag, allow the butter to melt, then hold the bags closed and turn to coat the vegetables inside with the butter.

4. Add a fillet to each dinner plate, along with a helping of the rice pilaf, green beans, and asparagus. Season with salt and pepper to taste. Sprinkle 2 teaspoons of toasted sesame seeds over all of the food on each plate.

Cashew Chicken

*Bump up the flavor by serving this dish over rice
cooked in chicken broth instead of water.*

Serves 4

2 tablespoons peanut oil
1 large green pepper, seeded
    and cut into strips
1 stalk celery, finely diced
1 medium sweet onion, diced
8 boneless, skinless chicken
    thighs, cut into bite-sized
    pieces
1 tablespoon soy sauce
1 tablespoon cornstarch
½ cup chicken broth
⅛ cup dry white wine
1 teaspoon honey or
    granulated sugar
Toasted sesame oil to taste
1 cup unsalted roasted
    cashews
4 cups cooked rice
OPTIONAL: 4 cups iceberg
    lettuce, torn into bite-
    sized pieces

1. Heat a wok or large nonstick pan over medium-high heat. Add the oil, green pepper, and celery; stir-fry 2 minutes. Push to the side. Add the onion; stir-fry for 3 minutes, or until transparent. Push to the side.

2. Add the chicken; stir-fry for 4 minutes, or until cooked through. Mix the green pepper, celery, and onion in with the chicken.

3. Add the soy sauce, cornstarch, broth, wine, and honey or sugar to a small bowl; mix well and strain out any lumps; pour into the stir-fried chicken mixture. Heat and stir until the sauce is thickened and clear. Stir in the toasted sesame oil and cashews. Serve over the rice or a mixture of rice and lettuce, if desired.

Preparing Rice in a Pressure Cooker

To make a tad over 4 cups of long-grain or basmati rice, add 1½ cups of rice, 2½ cups of broth or water, and 1 tablespoon of butter or oil to a pressure cooker. Cook for 3 minutes on high pressure. Remove from the heat and allow the pressure to release naturally for 7 minutes. Quick-release any remaining pressure. Uncover and fluff with a fork.

Appendix

Ingredients and Equipment Sources

Ingredients

Most of the ingredients in this cookbook are readily available at any major supermarket or grocery store. Others, however, take a little more effort to track down, and sometimes you may want to treat yourself by cooking with gourmet ingredients. The resources in this appendix will help you find the materials you need, no matter what your reasons are.

Birds Eye Foods
Frozen vegetable blends
www.birdseyefoods.com

Crown Prince
Boiled baby clams and
other canned seafood
www.crownprince.com

Dik Jaxon Products Company
Cornmeal mush
6195 Webster Street
Dayton, OH 45414
(937) 890-7350

Yoder's
Prepared mashed potatoes,
dips, cheese, and desserts
www.yoderssalad.com

Dole Food Company, Inc.
Salad mix and canned
fruits and vegetables
www.dole.com

Hormel Foods
Prepared food, including Hormel less-sodium chili (canned)
www.hormel.com

Nutty Guys
Dried fruit and nuts
www.nuttyguys.com

MapleLeafInc.com
Freeze-dried green beans
and other specialty foods
www.mapleleafinc.com

Mrs. Dash
Mrs. Dash Salt-Free Seasoning Blends
www.mrsdash.com

Muir Glen Organic

Organic canned tomatoes
www.muirglen.com

Pillsbury

Refrigerated peel-and-unroll pie
crusts, refrigerated pizza crust,
refrigerated biscuits and dinner rolls,
frozen pie crust, frozen biscuits
www.pillsbury.com

American Spoon

Specialty foods, including
cherry peach salsa, fruit butter, and ginger pear butter
www.spoon.com

Wellshire Farms

Nitrate-free bacon, corned
beef, ham, and other meats
www.wellshirefarms.com

Equipment

Your cooking equipment can make a difference in the ease with which you
can prepare foods. Buy the best you can afford. Better pan construction equals
more even heat distribution, which translates to reduced cooking time and more
even cooking. Better doesn't always have to be the newest and most expensive
pan on the market. A well-seasoned cast-iron skillet can go from the stovetop
to the oven. Other considerations, like glass lids for saucepans and skillets, can
cut the cooking time because they let you see the food cooking inside the pot.
You don't have to remove the lid as much, so less heat escapes.

Chicken Rocket

Used as a more efficient way to
make "beer can chicken," the
Chicken Rocket is a 4-pound cast-
iron pan insert that holds the
seasoning liquid and onto which
you mount the chicken during
the baking process; it can also be
set directly on an outdoor grill.
www.chickenrocket.com

Mr. Bar-B-Q

This company produces the Chicken
Roaster, a nonstick "beer can
chicken" pan insert that holds the
seasoning liquid and onto which
you mount the chicken during
the baking process; it can also be
set directly on an outdoor grill.
www.mrbarbq.com

Chicago Metallic

This company sells Chicago Metallic custom baking pans and other products.
www.cmbakeware.com

Cuisinart

Probably best known for their innovative food processors, Cuisinart also has a wide selection of countertop appliances and cookware, including toaster ovens, rotisseries, fondue pots, microwave ovens, pressure cookers, food processors, and slow cookers.
www.cuisinart.com

Hearth Kitchen

Hearth Kitchen Hearth-kit Brick Oven Insert
www.hearthkitchen.com

Le Creuset

This company sells high-quality enameled cast iron Dutch ovens, roasters, soup pots, and other pans.
www.lecreuset.com

Kaiser Bakeware

This company sells springform pans and other quality bakeware.
www.kaiserbakeware.com

Pleasant Hill Grain

A full-service distributor for a wide variety of helpful cooking appliances, which includes stick blenders, water purifiers, pressure cookers, and pressure frying pans.
www.pleasanthillgrain.com

Taylor Precision Products

This company sells a digital oven thermometer/timer.
www.taylorusa.com

Index

Note: Page numbers in **bold** indicate recipe category lists.